The Decades of Life

Also from Donald Capps by Westminster John Knox Press:

Jesus the Village Psychiatrist
Losers, Loners, and Rebels: The Spiritual Struggles of Boys (with Robert C.
    Dykstra and Allan Hugh Cole Jr.)
The Poet's Gift: Toward the Renewal of Pastoral Care
The Child's Song: The Religious Abuse of Children

THE DECADES OF LIFE

A Guide to Human Development

Donald Capps

Westminster John Knox Press
LOUISVILLE • LONDON

Scripture quotations, unless otherwise indicated, are from the New Revised Standard Version of the Bible, copyright © 1989 by the Division of Christian Education of the National Council of the Churches of Christ in the U.S.A., and used by permission. Scripture quotations marked RSV are from the Revised Standard Version of the Bible, copyright © 1946, 1952, 1971, and 1973 by the Division of Christian Education of the National Council of the Churches of Christ in the U.S.A., and are used by permission.

"Bess" copyright © 1970, 1988, "A Farewell, Age Ten" copyright © 1993, 1998, "Old Blue" copyright © 1991, 1998, and "Waiting in Line" copyright 1987, 1998 by the estate of William Stafford. Reprinted from *The Way It Is: New & Selected Poems* with the permission of Graywolf Press, Saint Paul, Minnesota. "By Tens" © 1987 by William Stafford from *An Oregon Message* (Harper & Row). Reprinted by permission of The Estate of William Stafford. "Chart 2 Psychosocial Crises," from *The Life Cycle Completed: A Review* by Erik H. Erikson. Copyright © 1982 by Rikan Enterprises, Ltd. Used by permission of W. W. Norton & Company, Inc. "Christmas Sparrow" from *Nine Horses* by Billy Collins, copyright © 2002 by Billy Collins. Used by permission of Random House, Inc., and reprinted by permission of SLL/Sterling Lord Literistic, Inc. "The Death of the Hat," from *Picnic, Lightning* by Billy Collins copyright © 1998 by Billy Collins. Reprinted by permission of SLL/Sterling Lord Literistic, Inc. "Fiftieth Birthday Eve" and "On Turning Ten" from *The Art of Drowning*, by Billy Collins, © 1995. Reprinted by permission of the University of Pittsburgh Press. "Flash Cards," from *Grace Notes* by Rita Dove. Copyright © 1989 by Rita Dove. Used by permission of the author and W. W. Norton & Company, Inc. "The Last Hours" and "Sixty," from *Different Hours* by Stephen Dunn. Copyright © 2000 by Stephen Dunn. Used by permission of W. W. Norton & Company, Inc. "The Life of Riley: A Definitive Biography" from *Questions About Angels*, by Billy Collins, © 1991. Reprinted by permission of the University of Pittsburgh Press, and by permission of SLL/Sterling Lord Literistic, Inc. "The Order of the Day," from *The Trouble with Poetry* by Billy Collins, copyright © 2005 by Billy Collins. Used by permission of Random House, Inc. "The Span of Life" from *The Poetry of Robert Frost* edited by Edward Connery Lathem. Copyright © 1969 by Henry Holt and Company. Copyright ©1936 by Robert Frost, copyright © 1964 by Lesley Frost Ballantine. Reprinted by permission of Henry Holt and Company, LLC. "Touch Me." Copyright © 1995 by Stanley Kunitz from *The Collected Poems* by Stanley Kunitz. Used by permission of W. W. Norton & Company, Inc. "Turning Fifty." Copyright © 1991 by Stephen Dunn from *New and Selected Poems 1974–1994* by Stephen Dunn. Used by permission of W. W. Norton & Company, Inc.

Book design by Sharon Adams
Cover design by Eric Walljasper, Minneapolis, MN

First edition
Published by Westminster John Knox Press
Louisville, Kentucky

This book is printed on acid-free paper that meets the American National Standards Institute Z39.48 standard. ∞

PRINTED IN THE UNITED STATES OF AMERICA

08 09 10 11 12 13 14 15 16 17 — 10 9 8 7 6 5 4 3 2 1

Library of Congress Cataloging-in-Publication Data

Capps, Donald.
　　The decades of life : a guide to human development / Donald Capps. — 1st ed.
　　　　p. cm.
　　Includes bibliographical references and index.
　　ISBN 978-0-664-23241-2 (alk. paper)
　　1. Developmental psychology. I. Title.

BF713.C3557 2008
155—dc22

2008002521

To Karen

"The lines have fallen for us in pleasant places"

(Ps. 16:6 RSV)

Contents

Acknowledgments

I want to express my appreciation to Jon Berquist, executive editor at Westminster John Knox Press, for encouraging my writing of this book, and to everyone at the Press who have contributed to its production and distribution. I dedicated my first Westminster John Knox Press book, *The Poet's Gift*, to my wife, Karen, noting in the acknowledgments that the book was "a small token of gratitude to my wife, Karen, for her friendship throughout the years. I cannot imagine life without her." On the dedication page, I wrote "to Karen, who worries for us." Fifteen years have elapsed since I wrote these words, and I can now report that the friendship, the inability to imagine life without her, and the worrying are as true today as they were then.

I dedicated the book to her because, when we were dating, I had the rather romantic idea that the best way to win a woman's heart was to write poetry to her. It seemed like a good strategy at the time. Now, some forty-odd years later, she will occasionally recite the lines from one of these poems—"Hand in hand what better way / to say the things I want to say"—knowing that the recitation will cause us both to laugh and evoke my rather defensive response, "But you fell for it, didn't you?" I know better, of course. What won her over was the fact that I didn't own a car. I think she was curious to see if I could make good on my declaration that I would take good care of her.

Donald Capps

Introduction

When I think about my own life, I think in terms of decades: what I did when I was in my twenties, thirties, forties, or fifties. This is also how I think about the lives of other persons I have known: I typically think, "When he was in his forties . . . ," or "When they were in their eighties. . . ." Using decade language enables me to "place" myself or another in life-span terms but to avoid having to be too precise. I occasionally use my exact age when I mention a life experience—"I got married when I was twenty-five years old"—but most of the time identifying the decade in which something happened is close enough. The same is true with my recollection of the lives of other persons whom I have known. Off the cuff, I couldn't tell you my grandfather's exact age when he died—I'd have to look it up—but I know for certain that he was in his nineties.

I assume that this is how it is with you too. You, too, are able to place events or experiences in your life in terms of decades—"When I was in my twenties . . ." or "In my thirties . . . ," and you may want to add "my *early* twenties" or "my *late* thirties." But if someone were to say to you, "Can you be more precise? Were you 22 or 23? 37, 38, or 39?" you might suspect that this person was a mathematician or works for the Internal Revenue Service.

There is a great precedent for thinking in terms of decades. The Bible uses decades to talk about our expected longevity. Genesis 6:3 reports, "Then the LORD said, 'My spirit shall not abide in mortals forever, for they are flesh; their days shall be one hundred twenty years." That's twelve decades. Although Ps. 90:10 (RSV) is not nearly so generous, it, too, speaks of our expected longevity in terms of decades: "The very years of our life are threescore and ten, / or even by reason of strength fourscore." That's seven or possibly eight decades. The psalm adds, "Their span is but toil and trouble; / they are soon gone, and we fly away," but, for the moment at least, this is beside the point.

Decades language also permeates our society's ways of thinking. In the 1960s, we heard that you cannot trust anyone over thirty. That's a lot of untrustworthy people. In the 1990s, we began hearing about "twentysomethings," or "thirtysomethings," the "somethings" supporting my point that decades language is considered close enough. Also, many of us prefer this way of identifying a whole group of persons over, say, the "baby boomers," because the "baby boomers" are much harder to identify. Because the first baby boomers were born around 1945 and the last were born around 1963, we have to do some calculation in our minds to figure out how old the "boomers" are at any given time.

One of my favorite examples of how decades language permeates our society's ways of thinking are "milestone" birthday cards. You can go into any card shop and find a section of birthday cards for persons who are turning 30, 40, 50, 60, 70, 80, 90, and 100. The only adult age that is typically missing is 20, but that's because the cards make a big issue of turning 21, the legal age for buying and ordering alcoholic beverages. Nor are there any cards for persons turning 110, apparently because these cards would be a commercial loss.

Given this tendency to think in terms of decades, one would assume that developmental theories would reflect this way of thinking. But that is not the case. The best-known developmental theory, Erik H. Erikson's life-cycle model with its eight developmental stages, is not structured according to decades. I wanted to write this book because I believe Erikson's developmental stages can be structured in this way, and can thus be related to our tendency to think in terms of decades.

I was in my mid-twenties when I was introduced to Erikson's life-cycle model through Christian education and pastoral care courses at Yale Divinity School. I immediately embraced it because it helped me gain an understanding of life as a whole, not just individual parts or slices of it. Also, it brought back memories of when I read John Bunyan's *The Pilgrim's Progress* (1957) when I was in my early teens. Published in 1678 as "a dumpy and badly printed little pocket pamphlet" and read "chiefly by the poorer classes of England" (v), this book captured my youthful imagination as no other book did: it told the story of a man named Christian who set out from the City of Destruction and made his way to the Celestial City. I understood that this was a book about the whole journey of life, and because the hero of the story was named Christian, I felt that it was my story too. So, Erikson's life-cycle model seemed like a contemporary version of Bunyan's *The Pilgrim's Progress,* and I began to view my own life through the lens his model provided me.

I will have much more to say about Erikson's life-cycle model in the chapters that follow. For now, I simply want to make the observation that his eight stages of life do not conform to the decades of life. Four of the stages occur between birth and the onset of adolescence; one stage occurs in the adolescent years; and three of the stages occur in the adult years. So five of the eight stages occur in the preadult years. Thus, the model implies that we go through more stages in our early years, and then, in our later years, each stage lasts much longer.

It was when I was in my early sixties that this thought occurred to me: What if the eight stages were "relocated" according to the decades of life? If Ps. 90:10 says that we can expect to live seven or even eight decades, this relocation of Erikson's eight stages would conform to the life span envisioned by the psalm. Because some persons have even more strength than the psalm considers possible and live as many as fivescore years, and sometimes even longer, I realized that Erikson's model would need to be augmented in some way. I will, of course, have more to say about my efforts to do this.

This book reflects an idea that came to me in my early sixties. I doubt that this idea *could* have come to me any earlier in my life because, before this, I hadn't lived long enough for it to be a matter of existential importance for me personally. But I also had become so used to thinking of Erikson's stages in the way that he intended that I would not have trusted this deviation from the norms that he established. Even now, I would certainly not be so presumptuous as to suggest that his "location" of the stages was wrong. After all, many parents, married couples, educators, psychologists, psychotherapists, and historians have found Erikson's model enormously helpful for understanding their own lives and the lives of others (their children, their spouses, their students, their counselees, as well as famous political figures, religious leaders, writers, and artists).

At the same time, I think that we gain some important new insights into our own lives and the lives of others when we relocate the stages according to decades. This relocation does not require any alteration of the chronological order of the stages, and it actually reinforces the idea that each stage involves a psychodynamic conflict between a positive and negative tendency. Erikson lamented the fact that some readers minimized the negative tendencies (some human development texts eliminate them altogether). By locating the stages according to decades, the experiences that give rise to the negative tendencies are more difficult to ignore.

Erikson's life-cycle model is not the only model available for understanding the human life span. Courses on human development in psychology and education curricula typically include a variety of models, and the deficiencies in Erikson's model are often pointed out. But because his was the first to cover the whole span of life, it continues to hold an honored place in the study of human development. Furthermore, he was very interested in the implications of his model for the study of religion and, conversely, the significance of religion for the model.

Such is not necessarily the case for other life-span models. It thus makes sense for us to focus on his model in a book intended for readers who are not only concerned with issues of coping with life's changes as one grows older but also with changing understandings of the Christian life as we pilgrims progress along the journey.

INFLUENTIAL PRECURSORS: FREUD AND SHAKESPEARE

Before discussing the life-cycle model and its stages, I would like to comment briefly on Erikson's indebtedness to Sigmund Freud and William Shakespeare. For the idea that the model would consist of identifiable stages, Erikson was indebted to Freud. For the idea that the model should cover the whole life span, Erikson owed a debt to Shakespeare.

Freud and the Concept of Stages

Freud proposed three stages of psychosexual development in infancy and early childhood, a fourth stage in late childhood, and a fifth stage in adolescence. The three early stages are popularly known as the oral, anal, and genital stages, terms that refer to the primary focus of the child's psychosexual development. In the oral stage, the focus is the infant's act of sucking at the maternal provider's breast. In the anal stage, the focus is the child's act of defecating, together with parental efforts to help the child gain control over this process. In the genital stage, the somewhat older child becomes aware of and takes considerable interest in his or her genitalia.

The fourth stage is the latency period of later childhood. The word *latency* expresses Freud's view that in this period the child's psychosexual development levels off, and the psychosexual preoccupations of infancy and early childhood are largely forgotten. These preoccupations, especially those relating to the genital stage, return with enormous vigor in the fifth stage of puberty (Kahn 2002, 33–54).

Erikson's life-cycle model, especially its first five stages, reflects his adoption of Freud's theory of psychosexual development. But because he wanted to place greater emphasis on the psycho*social* (or relational meanings) of the psychosexual stages, he suggested that each of the psychosexual "organ zones" that Freud identified have a corresponding "psychosocial mode." For example, the oral stage involves an incorporative mode, the anal stage involves an eliminative mode, and the genital stage involves an intrusive mode of approach to others (Erikson 1950, 67–92; 1963, 72–95).

Once established, these modes are not limited to the organ zone with which they originated and may, in fact, become independent of them. Erikson notes, for example, that the intrusive mode may include "the intrusion into other bodies by physical attack; the intrusion into other people's ears and minds by aggressive talking; the intrusion into space by vigorous locomotion; the intrusion into the unknown by consuming curiosity" (Erikson 1959, 76).

Although the first five stages of Erikson's life-cycle model correspond to Freud's five stages of psychosexual development, they involve many unique features and innovations that cannot be attributed to Freud in any direct way. Some of these reflect the influence of other members of the psychoanalytic profession. For example, Erikson was well aware of Else Frenkel-Brunswik's work on the "course of the life span" because they were colleagues at the University of California at Berkeley when he was developing his life-cycle model (Friedman 1999, 221). But none of these influences were as fundamental as those of Freud.

Shakespeare and the Life Span

William Shakespeare's *As You Like It* (2000, 44–45), also played an important role in the formation of Erikson's life-cycle model. At the beginning of scene 7, act 2, the banished Duke Senior and his attending lords enter. The speech by Jacques, one of the attending lords begins:

> All the world's a stage,
> And all the men and women merely players;
> They have their exits and their entrances,
> And one man in his time plays many parts,
> His acts being seven ages. (44)

Jacques' declaration that "man's acts [are] seven ages" is evident in the chapter title "The Eight Ages of Man" in Erikson's *Childhood and Society* (1963, 147). Moreover, the idea of the world being a stage informed the original chapter title, "Eight Stages of Man," in the first edition of *Childhood and Society* (1950, 219).

Erikson was certainly familiar with Freud's use of Shakespeare to illustrate his own concepts and theories, but the impetus for giving attention to Shakespeare may well have come from his wife, Joan, who, according to Erikson's biographer, Lawrence J. Friedman, "emphasized that Shakespeare was richer than Freud on developmental matters because he had moved beyond the early years in his cast of characters" (1999, 218). Although Erikson is unlikely to have shared his wife's judgment that Shakespeare was richer than Freud, he seems to have been won over by her enthusiasm for Shakespeare: "Not only was Shakespeare discussing epigenetic development from infancy to death, he seemed to be characterizing his seven developmental stages in social and ethical far more than in sexual terms" (218). Years later, they "recalled how exciting it was to reframe Erik's early outlines on the developmental stages and his checkerboard chart by referring to Jacques' speech" (218).

Friedman implies an opposition between Freud's sexual emphasis and Shakespeare's social and ethical emphasis, an opposition that Erikson would not have supported because he saw the two as interrelated (as did Freud himself). Also, there is a fundamental difference between Jacques' rather cynical view (due, perhaps, to the fact that he was then living in exile) and Erikson's cautiously hopeful view of the human life span. But the speech would have provided valuable support for Erikson's emphasis on the importance of social roles in an individual's psychosocial development. For Jacques, these roles include the infant ("mewling and puking in the nurse's arms"), the whining schoolboy ("with his satchel and shining morning face, creeping like snail unwillingly to school"), the lover ("sighing like furnace, with a woeful ballad made to his mistress' eyebrow"), the soldier ("full of strange oaths and bearded like the [leo]pard, jealous in honor, sudden and quick in quarrel, seeking the bubble reputation even in the cannon's mouth"), the justice ("in fair round belly with good capon lined, with eyes severe and beard of formal cut, full of wise saws and modern instances"), the ridiculous old man ("with spectacles on nose and pouch on side, his youthful hose, well saved, a world too wide for his shrunk shank, and his big manly voice, turning again toward childish treble, pipes and whistles in his sound"), and finally second childhood ("last scene of all, that ends this strange eventful history, second childishness and mere oblivion, sans teeth, sans eyes, sans taste, sans everything") (Shakespeare 2000, 44–45).

In her introduction to the play, Frances E. Dolan points out that the speech "does not describe how lives really unfolded," but it does "reveal cultural expectations" (xliii). If the speech reflects cultural expectations, the man's life builds to stage five (the justice), suffers decline in stage six (the ridiculous old man), and oblivion in stage seven (the second childhood). Yet in the play itself, Adam, an old servant and therefore a representative of the final stages, demonstrates that "moral fortitude can grow even as physical strength diminishes" and that a person who is both physically and socially dependent can, nonetheless, be "an ethical guide" to others (xliv). In other words, there is at least one character in the play whose life belies the speech's unflattering portrayal of the older man.

Dolan also points out that Jacques has nothing to say about the life cycle of women: "In its generic focus on man, the speech fails to account for the rather different stages of a woman's life, which might be expected to build toward marriage and motherhood (despite the fact that many women never married)" (xliii). On the other hand, because he refers at the beginning of his speech to "all the men and women," we may assume that if a woman had been among these exiles, she could have made a parallel speech about women's roles, one equally cynical.

But despite its cynicism and neglect of the life cycle of women, Jacques' speech and Erikson's model have much in common. Both emphasize the whole span of life, both emphasize that there are identifiable "ages" over the course of a lifetime, and both suggest that an individual's life is cyclical—that the final stage marks a return, in some sense, to the initial stage.

But Erikson's model consists of eight stages. Why the difference? Part of the explanation is that Erikson was building his life-cycle model on Freud's earlier construction. Thus, whereas Jacques had only two ages (infant and schoolboy) for childhood and youth, Erikson had five. For a seven-stages model, this left only two ages for adulthood. In her preface to the extended version of *The Life Cycle*

Completed (Erikson & Erikson 1997), Joan Erikson notes that her husband's original model did consist of seven stages, the two adult stages being intimacy vs. isolation and integrity vs. despair and disgust.

She relates the story of how it was expanded to eight: They were living in Berkeley, California, at the time. In the late 1940s, they were invited to present a paper on the stages of life at the Mid-century White House Conference on Children and Youth. This paper, "Growth and Crises of the Healthy Personality," was subsequently published in an expanded version in *Identity and the Life Cycle* (Erikson 1959, 50–100). Shortly before the White House Conference, Erik had been asked to present the model, which consisted of seven stages, to a group of psychologists and psychiatrists in Los Angeles. Joan drove him to the train station in South San Francisco. On the way, they discussed the fact that Shakespeare's model also had seven stages. But as they talked, it occurred to Joan that even though Shakespeare wrote many plays, he did not have anything comparable to the "play age," which was the third stage in the Erikson model. This suggested that he had left out a stage that was crucial to his own life.

If Shakespeare left something out of his model, was it possible that something had been omitted from theirs? Joan writes, "In a shocking moment of clarity I saw what was wrong: 'We' were missing, and so were the children" (3). The seven-stage model jumped from the intimacy vs. isolation conflict to the integrity vs. despair and disgust conflict and omitted a vital aspect of adult life, that of parents with teenage children: "We surely needed another stage between the sixth and seventh" (3). So, in the short time available to them, they sketched out a new seventh stage, and the original seventh stage was "promoted" to the eighth stage.

In retrospect, we may wonder how Erikson, who was in his late forties at the time, could possibly have left out the middle adult years. But when we consider the fact that the model was so strongly oriented toward infancy, childhood, and youth, and that there were few if any developmental theories at the time that focused on adulthood, this omission seems more understandable. In any event, somewhere between the family home in Berkeley and the train station in South San Francisco, the model no longer conformed to Shakespeare's seven ages.[1]

Having identified these two important influences in the formulation of the model, let's turn to the model itself.

---

1. In *The Seven Ages of Man's Best Friend* (2005), Jan Fennell uses Jacques' speech to structure her model of a dog's life: puppy (0–8 weeks), pioneer (8–12 weeks), playboy (3–9 months), protégé (9–18 months), pretender (18–28 months), protector (28 months to 7 years), and pensioner (7 years to death). Her playboy (stage 3) corresponds to Erikson's play age, her protégé to his school age, and some would argue that her pretender (stage 4) corresponds to his adolescence stage. Like his model, the first five stages cover a much shorter time span (first 28 months). Because the average life span for dogs ranges from 6.7 years (the bulldog) to 14.4 years (the miniature dachshund), Fennell might want to consider adding an eighth age between the protector and pensioner ages. My faculty colleagues at Princeton Theological Seminary may be counted on to suggest the *presbyter* age, but other possibilities would be the panhandler, paramour, party pooper, potentate, and patriarch, all of which reflect features of the middle adulthood of man's best friend.

THE EIGHT STAGES OF LIFE

Erikson proposes that the life span consists of eight stages of unequal duration and that each of the stages involves a dynamic interaction or conflict between a positive tendency and a negative tendency or tendencies. I use the word *tendency* because it refers to "an inclination or disposition to move in a particular direction or act in a certain way, especially as a result of some inherent quality or habit" (Agnes 2001, 1474). This suggests that it is not merely behavioral, but neither is it merely emotional or mental. As an inclination or disposition, it is an integral aspect of the process of life. This process is a dynamic one, with both tendencies playing an essential role.

Some of the names given to these tendencies changed slightly over the years, but the following is the final version presented in *The Life Cycle Completed* (1981):

Infancy: Basic Trust vs. Basic Mistrust

Early Childhood: Autonomy vs. Shame and Doubt

Play Age: Initiative vs. Guilt

School Age: Industry vs. Inferiority

Adolescence: Identity vs. Identity Confusion

Young Adulthood: Intimacy vs. Isolation

Maturity: Generativity vs. Stagnation

Old Age: Integrity vs. Despair and Disgust

Erikson did not assign specific ages to every stage, but the periods in which the first five stages occur is rather easy to discern. The first three stages occur in the first five years of life, and his writings on these stages indicate that the first stage is roughly from birth to age 1, the second is from age 1 to 3½, and the third is from age 3½ to 5, or concluding with the shift from "nursery school" to "grammar school" (1959, 60, 75, 83–85). The fourth stage continues to the stage of adolescence, which marks the end of childhood and the beginning of youth (88–89).

Erikson was probably thinking that youth begins around the ages of 12 or 13. Developmental theorists today typically divide adolescence into early and late adolescence and assign ages 11–14 to early and 14–18 to late adolescence. Erikson's writings suggest he would have agreed that the shift from adolescence to young adulthood occurs in the late teens; thus the first five stages occur in the first two decades of life. On the other hand, the duration of the identity vs. identity confusion conflict is somewhat indeterminable because the process of discovering one's identity is often a difficult and protracted one. It is not unusual, therefore, for this stage to continue well into one's mid-twenties, sometimes even longer. Thus, there is often a period of overlap between the end of the fifth stage and the beginning of the sixth stage of young adulthood.

The age at which the sixth stage of young adulthood ends and the seventh stage of maturity begins is unspecified, but a reasonable assumption is that the seventh stage is well under way in one's forties, if not a few years earlier. The Eriksons were in their mid-forties when they made the discovery that their own "age" had been omitted from the model. The age of transition from the seventh stage to the eighth stage is also unspecified, but in an autobiographical essay Erikson suggested that his own old age began in 1975, when he was seventy-three years old (Friedman 1999, 428).

The flexibility of the stages is one of the real strengths of the model because it recognizes that we are individuals, and each individual life has its own unique form and structure. On the other hand, the ambiguity of when these adult transitions occur and the fact that the model is so heavily weighted toward the early years are reasons that the relocation of the stages according to decades can be enormously useful. This assumes, of course, that the positive and negative tendencies assigned to each of the stages are an accurate reflection of what actually transpires in these ten-year periods. But this assumption is precisely what I want to show to be the case.

Each stage involves a dynamic interaction between a positive and one or more negative tendencies. Erikson believed that both are integral to healthy development. For example, it would not be healthy for an infant to have no mistrust whatsoever. Such an infant would be especially prone to accidents and more vulnerable to traumatic experiences. Because Erikson believed that an infant's trust should not be assumed, that it needs to be cultivated, it is actually more likely that an infant may not develop the positive tendency.

Erikson spoke of a "ratio" between the two poles but didn't say what this ratio should be. Because he considered the negative pole essential, he certainly did not assume that the ideal ratio would be 100 percent to 0 percent. I think it would be something like 70 percent to 30 percent. In *Vital Involvement in Old Age*, Erikson, Erikson, and Kivnick (1986) underscored the importance of this "ratio" in a chart suggesting that too much of the positive tendency may be maladaptive while too much of the negative tendency may be malignant (45). Identifying terms were given to each. For example, in the third stage of initiative vs. guilt, initiative that is not counterbalanced by guilt may cause ruthlessness, while excessive guilt may result in inhibition.

The importance Erikson attached to the "ratio" idea can hardly be overstated. It greatly concerned him that in some representations of his model the negative tendencies were omitted altogether. In a footnote added to the revised edition of *Childhood and Society* (1963) Erikson alluded to "certain misuses of the whole conception" of the life cycle, noting that among them "is the assumption that the sense of trust (and all the other 'positive' senses postulated) is an *achievement*, secured once and for all at a given state" (273). In fact, "some writers are so intent on making an *achievement scale* out of these stages that they blithely omit all the 'negative' senses (basic mistrust, etc.) which are and remain the dynamic counterpart of the 'positive' ones throughout life" (273–74).

This discounting of the negative senses falsifies the actual state of affairs, for "the personality is engaged with the hazards of existence continuously, even as the body's metabolism copes with decay. As we come to diagnose a state of relative strength and the symptoms of an impaired one, we face only more clearly the paradoxes and tragic potentials of human life" (274).

Erikson acknowledges that he may have invited these misinterpretations by employing words that have acquired in the past "certain connotations of superficial goodness, affected niceness, and all too strenuous virtue" (274). But we are not compelled to accept these particular understandings of these venerable words, and "despite passing vicissitudes certain basic words retain essential meanings" (274). In the discussion of the stages in the following chapters, I will give particular attention to the meanings of these words, including their official dictionary definition and Erikson's own sense of their meaning in the context of his life-cycle model.

In addition to the "ratio" of positive and negative tendencies, there are other important principles or assumptions: (1) that we carry earlier stage dynamics with us as we move to subsequent stages and that earlier dynamics therefore interact with later ones; (2) that we may experience in rudimentary fashion later-stage dynamics before we reach the appropriate chronological age, largely because we are a future-oriented species with eyes in the front of our heads; (3) that earlier-stage dynamics may be reworked in later stages; (4) that physiological development (or decline) plays a major role in the movement from one stage to another because new physiological capacities make for new psychosocial experiences and challenges; (5) that there may be differences as to when individuals enter or exit a stage, and that some of these differences are due to cultural traditions; and (6) that having a more optimal ratio of the positive over the negative tendencies becomes cumulative, even as the greater ratio of the negative over the positive tendencies also becomes cumulative.

Erikson often uses the word *crisis* to express the conflict that the individual experiences between the positive and negative tendency of a stage, but *crisis* is not itself a negative word. It means that a significant change is occurring in one's psychosocial development and that there are new possibilities as well as potential vulnerabilities as the stability of the previous stage is being disrupted.

THE SCHEDULE OF VIRTUES

Erikson made two important additions to his life-cycle model. One was a "schedule of virtues" related to the life stages (Erikson 1964a). The other addition proposed correlations between the psychosocial conflicts of a given stage and the habits and routines ("ritualizations") of everyday life (Erikson 1977). Because the schedule of virtues figured much more prominently in his own discussions of the life stages, and also because it is more germane to my proposed relocation of the life stages according to decades, this book will focus primarily on the first of these two additions.

Erikson proposed his schedule of virtues in an address presented to the Psychoanalytic Institute and the Mt. Zion Medical Center in San Francisco in 1960. This address was expanded into a chapter in *Insight and Responsibility* titled "Human Strength and the Cycle of Generations" (Erikson 1964a, 109–57). The basic idea behind it was that over the last half-century, psychoanalysts "have developed an 'unofficial' image of the strengths inherent in the individual life cycle and in the sequence of generations" (111). He was thinking here of those occasions when a therapist can agree that a patient "has really improved—not, as the questionnaires try to make us say, markedly improved, or partially improved—but essentially so" (111–12). It's not simply a matter of the reduction or even disappearance of the patient's symptoms but the fact that there has been a very significant and self-evident "increase in the strength and staying power of the patient's concentration on pursuits which are somehow right, whether it is in love or in work, in home life, friendship, or citizenship" (112).

He thought that there should be as many of these strengths as there are stages of the life cycle, and that it should be possible to identify them by reflecting on the optimum personal development at each of the life stages. So he proposed these eight strengths to correspond to the eight stages: hope, will, purpose, competence, fidelity, love, care, and wisdom. He used the word *virtue* for these strengths, emphasizing that he was not using this word in a narrowly moral or even ethical sense, but in the sense that it had before these narrower connotations came about. He noted that in old English *virtue* is defined as an inherent strength or active quality, and it was therefore applied, for example, to "the undiminished potency of well preserved medicines and liquors" (113). In other words, it captures the idea that these eight strengths are matters of spirit, but not in the vague sense in which the word "spirituality" is often used. Rather, he means that the person who is in possession of them has a genuine sense of being alive and well (112).

Erikson discusses each virtue in relation to the developmental stage to which it has been assigned, and within these discussions he offers a one-sentence formulation of each of the virtues. These formulations or working definitions reflect the dynamic interaction of the positive and negative tendencies of each stage, and necessarily emphasize that the positive tendency is the stronger of the two. Rather than present these formulations here, I will incorporate them into my discussion of the individual life stages. This will enable us to view them within the context of the dynamic interaction of the positive and negative tendencies of each stage.

As noted, Erikson thinks of these virtues as matters of spirit. When each is viewed in association with a decade of life, it also makes sense to think of them as integral to the development of the *self,* which *Webster's New World College Dictionary* (Agnes, ed, 2001; hereafter referred to as *Webster's*) defines as a person's "identity, character, or essential qualities" (1300). In *Identity: Youth and Crisis* (1968), Erikson points out that we have "various selves which make up our composite Self," and suggests that these selves reflect the fact that we have a body, a personality, and social roles to which we are "attached for life" (217). He adds that it takes a healthy personality to be able to hold these various selves together in "a reasonably coherent Self" (217). He also notes that our composite Self is recognized and validated by the One who responded to Moses who asked who should he say had called him, "I AM WHO I AM" (Exod. 3:14)(220).

The chapter headings of this book reflect my proposal that we consider the virtues to be the various selves which comprise the composite Self. Viewed as a whole, they provide us with the model of a Self that is reasonably coherent and generally healthy. The decade to which each self is assigned is the one in which the development of this particular self is especially vital if the composite Self is to be coherent and healthy. As with the psychosocial dynamics of each stage, however, these selves undergo further development in later stages and appear in rudimentary form in earlier stages.

CHARTING THE STAGES OF LIFE

In my earlier discussion of Shakespeare's influence on Erikson, I quoted Lawrence J. Friedman's comment on Erikson's "checkerboard chart." The chart, which in Erikson's later writings always included the virtues assigned to each stage, has been a popular means of making the basic outline of the stages readily accessible and understandable (see fig. 1). But as many charts do, it has also made the theory seem much simpler than it actually is. In the revised edition of *Childhood and Society* (Erikson 1963), Erikson added a section to his chapter on the eight stages explaining what the chart is intended to represent and communicate:

> The underlying assumptions for such charting are (1) that the human personality in principle develops according to steps predetermined in the growing person's readiness to be driven toward, to be aware of, and to interact with, a widening social radius; and (2) that society, in principle, tends to be so constituted as to meet and invite this succession of potentialities for interaction and attempts to safeguard and to encourage the proper rate and the proper sequence of their enfolding. (270)

His essay "The Human Life Cycle" (1987f) has a chart identifying the social relations that comprise what he calls the "widening social radius," for which he also uses the image of ever-widening concentric circles, like the circles produced by throwing a stone in a lake (see fig. 2). This radius begins with the mother-infant relationship and concludes with the older person's relations with the human species, which may also include an identification with some segment of the species. Although he recognized the importance of being able to locate oneself as a member of a subspecies of the whole species, he was also critical of what he called "pseudo-speciation," the tendency of race, nation, creed, or gender to "defend the illusion of having been chosen to dominate" (Erikson 1987a).

Figure 1
Psychosocial Crises

	1	2	3	4	5	6	7	8
Old Age								Integrity vs. Despair, Disgust. WISDOM
Adulthood							Generativity vs. Stagnation. CARE	
Young Adulthood						Intimacy vs. Isolation. LOVE		
Adolescence					Identity vs. Identity Confusion. FIDELITY			
School Age				Industry vs. Inferiority. COMPETENCE				
Play Age			Initiative vs. Guilt. PURPOSE					
Early Childhood		Autonomy vs Shame, Doubt. WILL						
Infancy	Basic Trust vs. Basic Mistrust. HOPE							

Figure 2

	Psychosocial Crises	Virtues	Radius of Significant Relations
I	Trust vs. Mistrust	HOPE	Maternal Person
II	Autonomy vs. Shame, Doubt	WILL	Parental Persons
III	Initiative vs. Guilt	PURPOSE	Basic Family
IV	Industry vs. Inferiority	COMPETENCE	Neighborhood, School
V	Identity vs. Identity Confusion	FIDELITY	Peer Groups and Outgroups; Models of Leadership
VI	Intimacy vs. Isolation	LOVE	Partners in Friendshp, Sex, Competition, Cooperation
VII	Generativity vs. Stagnation	CARE	Divided Labor and Shared Household
VIII	Integrity vs. Despair, Disgust	WISDOM	"Humankind" "My Kind"

Having argued in the revised edition of *Childhood and Society* (1963) for the chart's usefulness, he noted that "a chart is only a tool to think with, and cannot aspire to be a prescription to abide by, whether in the practice of child-training, in psychotherapy, or in the methodology of child study" (270). Furthermore, any one chart applies to only one aspect of human development, and it should not therefore be assumed that his "outline of the psychosocial schedule is intended to imply obscure generalities concerning other aspects of development—or, indeed, of existence" (270). Also, if the chart "lists a series of conflicts or crises, we do not consider all development a series of crises: we claim only that psychosocial development proceeds by critical steps—'critical' being a characteristic of turning points, of moments of decision between progress and regression, integration and retardation" (270–71).

Other ways of representing Erikson's life-cycle model have been proposed. In her book *Wisdom and the Senses* (1988), Joan Erikson presents it as a weaving. She notes that this way of representing it emphasizes the integrity of the stages themselves because their interrelatedness—their interwovenness—is clearly depicted through a weaving. Also, she chooses colors that seem to fit the strengths or virtues for each stage: dark blue for hope, orange for will, dark green for purpose, yellow for competence, light blue for fidelity, rosy red for love, light green for care, and purple for wisdom. Grey is used for the negative tendencies (78).

But what the weaving, like the chart, could not do was to depict the cyclical nature of the whole of life. This feature is effectively portrayed in a video created by John and Faith Hubley titled "Everybody Rides the Carousel" (Hubley Studio, 1975). The carousel, of course, goes around and returns to the place where it began. The carousel, however, has another, perhaps unexpected dividend as far as the conceptualization of human life is concerned, namely, that not everyone enters or disembarks at the same time. Thus, it conveys the *intergenerational* nature of the human life cycle. Erikson thought of this as the *cogwheeling* of the generations, an image suggesting that there are times when the generations in a family or other social grouping may experience greater interaction than at other times.

Finally, Erikson regularly used Ingmar Bergman's film *Wild Strawberries* in his undergraduate course on "The Human Life Cycle" when he was a professor at Harvard University. He also wrote about the film in "Reflections on Dr. Borg's Life Cycle" (Erikson 1978). Unlike "Everybody Rides the Carousel," this film makes use of real human actors and focuses on the social roles of father, mother, son, daughter-in-law, uncle, nieces, housekeeper, and strangers that the central character—Dr. Isak Borg—encounters along the journey of life. As such, it has certain affinities with Jacques' portrayal of the roles that a man plays during his lifetime. But there is also a dramatic difference: Dr. Borg is continually interacting with others, and even in his moments alone, he is in touch through reveries with persons who are no longer among the living.

HOW THIS BOOK IS STRUCTURED

The book contains four parts: the first part focuses on preadulthood (birth through nineteen); the second, on younger adulthood (twenty through thirty-nine); the third on middle adulthood (forty through sixty-nine); and the fourth on older adulthood (seventy through ninety-nine). Individual chapters center on a single decade.

The first eight chapters follow Erikson's life-cycle model, thus covering the life span from birth through age seventy-nine. But many individuals live into their eighties; some of these live into their nineties; and quite a few of these live one hundred years and more. For these decades, some ingenuity, improvisation, or a bit of both is needed. Do we say that the integrity vs. despair and disgust conflict is unique in the sense that it is central for these later decades as well? Do we suggest that the life cycle starts over again at age eighty, with the eighty-year-old returning to the basic trust vs. basic mistrust stage, and the ninety-year-old moving from there to the autonomy vs. shame and doubt stage? Or do we prefer to say that life goes on—that even the old pilgrim continues to progress and therefore involves a couple more stages?

This dilemma was anticipated by Joan Erikson. After her husband died at the age of ninety-two in 1994, she set to work on the extended version of his earlier book *The Life Cycle Completed* (1982). A ninety-year-old herself, she added a chapter titled "The Ninth Stage" (Erikson & Erikson 1997, 105–14), in which she suggested that in the eighties and nineties the negative tendencies of all the previous stages tend to take the "more dominant position" (106). Thus, she proposed a ninth stage in which the eight previous stages play a vital role, but with the positive (systonic) and negative (dystonic) tendencies reversed. She made this proposal not to suggest that the final years of life are to be dreaded but to make the point that "if elders can come to terms with the *dystonic* elements of their life experiences in the ninth stage, they may successfully make headway on the path leading to *gerotranscendence*" (114). *Gerotranscendence,* a word coined by a Swedish gerontologist, Lars Tornstam, describes "the peace of mind" with which some older persons anticipate their approaching death (124).

Following the decades approach employed for the earlier years of life, I propose a different way of construing the ninth and tenth decades. It involves the creation of two new psychosocial conflicts: release vs. control and the virtue of gracefulness for the ninth decade, and desire vs. struggle and the virtue of endurance for the tenth. A "ratio" that favors the positive over the negative tendency in these two conflicts would also be conducive to gerotranscendence.

The epilogue contains a brief discussion of the eleventh decade of life (persons one hundred or more). Instead of giving this decade a name, I borrow the term that my denominational magazine employs when it announces the birthdays of members one hundred or over: *The 100 Club. Webster's* (Agnes 2001) defines *club* as "a group of people associated for a common purpose or mutual advantage, usually in an organization that meets regularly" (278). Because the members of the 100 Club are geographically dispersed and may have physical mobility issues, there isn't much likelihood that the magazine will announce an annual meeting. But, as someone who wearies a bit of organizations that meet regularly for a common purpose or mutual advantage, I can't think of a club that I would rather belong to. Or so I would like to believe.

Finally, the matter of gender-inclusive language: Erikson's writings from the 1950s through the 1960s use traditional language—"man" for "humankind," and "he" when he refers to all persons, both female and male. He made an effort in the 1970s to employ gender-inclusive language. For example, paragraphs from his 1966 essay on "The Ontogeny of Ritualization in Man" (Erikson 1987, 575–94) were totally rewritten for gender inclusiveness in his chapter on "Ritualization in Everyday Life" in *Toys and Reasons* (1977).

Because Erikson's major writings on the life cycle were written in the fifties and early sixties, this presents a problem for a book written in 2007 in which his work is extensively quoted. I decided that it was pointless either to try to rewrite what he wrote or to use a device to alert the reader to the fact that a gender-inclusive violation had been committed and that I was aware of this fact. At times, for the sake of coherence, I felt that I needed occasionally to use male-gender wording when commenting on what Erikson had just said, but I avoided this wherever possible. The same decisions were made with respect to quotations from Paul Tillich's *Dynamics of Faith* (1957).

By Tens

In my twenties, the days came with a war wind
buffeting buildings and signs. Whole forests learned
their primitive gestures all over again and whined
for help. Finally the storm overwhelmed mankind.

In my thirties a lake of wisdom began
its years of expansion. To promises it answered, "When?"
And it grew by tributaries that would run
whenever my blunders brought rebukes from anyone.

In my forties a smog began to cover
the world. At first it stayed down on the level,
then it climbed. It sought out leaders wherever
a leader was. It changed the world forever.

In my fifties people began to move
away from each other. Roads we traveled were of
divergent claims. A sunset, even, would arrive
differently on successive nights of our lives.

In my sixties all that the years have brought
begins to shine—friends, the lake of wisdom,
the kindly curtain of smog where leaders are hidden,
and this path of knowing that leads us all toward heaven.

William Stafford (1987, 110)

PART ONE
THE PREADULT DECADES

Chapter 1

The First Decade:
The Hopeful Self

Almost everyone in the United States agrees that persons who have lived fewer than twenty years are not yet adults. Before the late nineteenth century, all of these persons would have been called children. Now, the younger ones are called children, and the older ones are called adolescents or youths. The two exceptions are those in the first year of this period (infants) or in the last year or two of this period. The latter are not exactly adolescents, but neither are they are young adults, so we don't really know what to call them.

The concept of adolescence was developed by G. Stanley Hall, whose two-volume book on *Adolescence* (Hall 1904) was published when he was sixty years old. Views on when childhood ends and adolescence begins are constantly changing, but the current theory is that early adolescence begins at age eleven and continues to age fourteen, and late adolescence begins at age fourteen and ends at eighteen.

For my purposes here, however, deciding when childhood ends and adolescence begins or when adolescence ends and young adulthood begins are somewhat beside the point. My concern is to show that the first decade (from birth through age nine) is one in which the dynamic conflict of basic trust vs. basic mistrust is central, and that the second decade (from age ten through age nineteen) is one in which the dynamic conflict of autonomy vs. shame and doubt is central.

In my view, these two decades, which comprise the preadult decades, have a vitally important relationship to one another. We may think of them, perhaps, as a two-act play, the second act being the culmination of the first, and the second rather impossible to know the meaning of without knowing what happened in the first.

A general overview of Erikson's life-cycle model was provided in the introduction. But as we focus on individual life stages, we need a much clearer sense of the meanings of the words that Erikson assigned to each stage. In some cases, their meanings might seem rather self-evident. In other cases, their meanings seem more obscure. Fortunately, he made a concerted effort to clarify all of the words he used. Because English was not his native tongue (he grew up in Germany), he seems to have had his own personal need to clarify their meanings. In his discussion of the word *integrity*, the positive tendency of the eighth stage, he specifically noted that he found it useful to consult the English dictionary (Erikson 1950, 233). So, in the following chapters, I will begin with dictionary definitions of these words, then move to Erikson's reflections on their meanings in relation to our psychosocial development. I will follow the same procedure with respect to the human strengths or virtues assigned to each stage.

THE TRUST VS. MISTRUST CONFLICT

For Erikson, the trust versus mistrust conflict occurs between birth and age one. *Webster's* has several definitions of the word *trust*, but the central ones are these: (1) "a firm belief or confidence in the honesty, integrity, reliability, justice, etc. of another person or thing; faith; reliance"; (2) "confident expectation, anticipation, or hope (to have *trust* in the future)"; and (3) "something entrusted," for example, to a person, institution, and so forth (1537). *Mistrust* means the "lack of trust or confidence; suspicion; doubt" (923).

Thus, the first definition emphasizes that trust involves relations with another person. It may also involve an institution, such as a bank, or a thing, such as an automobile, but because we are concerned here with psychosocial development, the interpersonal relationship is primary. The second definition suggests that trust is forward looking, and that trust and hope have much in common. This has relevance to the fact that hope is the human strength or virtue that Erikson assigns to this stage. The third definition suggests the transfer of something of value to the care of another. This might be one's possessions, but it may also be an individual, as when parents entrust their child to other adults, such as nannies or preschool teachers. This meaning of trust has relevance to the belief that a newborn baby is a child of God, and that God has entrusted this baby to the care of human parents or other adults.

The definition of *mistrust* relates to the first two definitions of *trust*, and especially to the first one. Instead of descriptive words like *confidence, faith*, and *reliance*, it employs words like *lack of confidence, doubt*, and *suspicion*. Much has been written in theological works about faith and doubt (for example, Tillich 1957).

In his reflections in *Childhood and Society* on the basic trust vs. basic mistrust conflict, Erikson (1950) points out that the word *trust* is more naïve and has more mutuality in it than the word *confidence*, so that "an infant can be said to be trusting where it would go too far to say that he has confidence" (220). Thus, Erikson would have had some difficulty with the dictionary definitions emphasizing that trust involves confidence, at least with regard to the infant. "Firm belief" also makes the infant's emerging sense of trust seem more cognitive than it actually is.

Erikson also notes that the general state of trust implies that the infant "has learned to rely on the sameness and continuity of the outer providers," and has also gained a certain amount of self-trust, which is reflected in the infant's ability to "cope with urges" so that "the providers will not need to be on guard" (220). Thus, trust involves the emerging sense or impression that one can trust another and that one is also becoming trustworthy.

Erikson makes much the same point in *Identity and the Life Cycle* (1959, chap. 2). Here, he suggests that basic trust "is an attitude toward oneself and the world derived from the experiences of the first year of life" (55–56). This suggests that the first year of life is decisive for the basic trust on which one relies throughout life. By trust he means "what is commonly implied in reasonable trustfulness as far as others are concerned and a simple sense of trustworthiness as far as oneself is concerned" (56). When he refers to this trust as basic, he means "that neither this component nor any of those that follow are either in childhood or in adulthood, especially conscious" (56).

What are the experiences in the first year of life that suggest that such trust is developing? In *Childhood and Society*, Erikson (1950) indicates that the "first demonstration of social trust in the baby is the ease of his feeding, the depth of his sleep, and the relaxation of his bowels" (219). He adds, "The experience of mutual regulation of his increasingly receptive capacities with the maternal techniques of provision gradually helps him to balance the discomfort caused by the immaturity of homeostasis with which he was born" (219). Homeostasis is the maintenance of the internal stability of an organism by coordinated responses of the organ systems that automatically compensate for environmental changes (Agnes 2001, 682). Thus, the maternal techniques together with the infant's increasingly receptive capacities work together to enable the infant to acquire this internal stability.

Erikson notes that as the infant experiences a gradually increasing number of waking hours, "he finds that more and more of the senses arouse a feeling of familiarity" (219). This feeling—especially recognition of the mother and sense of her presence—enables the infant, in time, "to let the mother out of sight without undue anxiety and rage, because she has become an inner certainty as well as an outer predictability" (219). In effect, the infant trusts her as much when she is absent as when she is present. Erikson calls this the infant's "first social achievement" (219).

The infant's second social achievement is to become trustworthy. Here, the infant needs to learn to exercise some restraint, to control certain urges, so that he does not do things that cause his mother to withdraw. Erikson is thinking here especially of the infant's tendency to bite, causing his mother to be on her guard and perhaps even making her incapable of providing the nurturance that he wants and needs. Thus, the infant's experience of basic mistrust may be due to maternal failure, which may or may not be avoidable, but it can also be due to his own urges and inability to control them.

These two achievements—trust and trustworthiness—are equally important components of basic trust. In effect, the first achievement entails the ability to entrust oneself to the other, and the second achievement entails the ability to trust oneself. As Erikson emphasizes, these two achievements are relatively rudimentary in the first year of life. They tend to center around a single relationship, that of infant and mother or primary caregiver, and they have mainly to do with the realization of physiological homeostasis. The full development of these achievements will take a lifetime.

In the revised edition of *Childhood and Society*, Erikson (1963) notes, "Each successive stage and crisis has a special relation to one of the basic elements of society, and this for the simple reason that the human life cycle and man's institutions have evolved together" (250). For the first stage of life, this basic element is religion: "The parental faith which supports the trust emerging in the newborn, has throughout history sought its institutional safeguard (and, on occasion, found its greatest enemy) in organized religion. Trust, born of care is, in fact, the touchstone of the actuality of a given religion," for all religions have in common "the periodic childlike surrender to a Provider or providers who dispense earthly fortune as well as spiritual health" (250). This childlike surrender is "the most primitive layer in all religions, and the religious layer in each individual" (250).

Based on Erikson's own writings about this stage of the life cycle, there are several reasons why it makes sense to propose that the trust vs. mistrust dynamic is centrally important throughout the first decade of life. These are two of the most obvious ones: First, as Erikson himself notes, we can only expect a very rudimentary achievement of trust and mistrust in the first year of life. But the next several years of a child's life are directly continuous with the first year of infancy, so we have every reason to assume that the child will continue to be concerned with these two achievements. During the next several years, the child will become increasingly aware of the importance of trust and trustworthiness in relationships with others, and develop these basic achievements in ways that would be completely unimaginable in the first year of life. The child will also become increasingly aware of situations that warrant mistrust and develop strategies for coping with them. Thus, it makes sense to propose that the trust vs. mistrust conflict will play a central role during the first decade of life.

Second, Erikson suggests that religion is the institutional safeguard of basic trust. In the first year of life, the infant is unaware of the very existence of institutionalized religion, but as the first decade unfolds, children tend either to become involved in an expression of institutionalized religion or to be conscious of the fact that other children are. A major emphasis of these institutions is the further development of the trust and trustworthiness initiated in the first year of life.

THE VIRTUE OF HOPE

Erikson assigns the human strength or virtue of hope to the basic trust vs. basic mistrust life-cycle stage. *Webster's* defines *hope* as "a feeling that what is wanted is likely to happen; desire accompanied by expectation" and *hopeless* as "having no expectation of, or showing no sign of, a favorable outcome" (Agnes 2001, 687). Thus, hope is an expectation of a favorable outcome. One has a "feeling" that the expected outcome will happen, but it is not a passive feeling, for hope is fueled by desire.

In "Human Strength and the Cycle of Generations," Erikson (1964a) defines *hope* somewhat differently, largely because he wants to relate it to the first stage of life: "Hope is the enduring belief in the attainability of fervent wishes, in spite of the dark urges and rages which mark the beginning of existence" (118). This understanding of hope implies that one may believe that what is wanted is likely to happen even if one acts toward one's benefactor in ways that *could* cause the other person to withdraw from the relationship or withhold what one desires.

On the other hand, Erikson admits that it is not at all easy to identify the characteristics of hope in an infant: "If we ascribe to the healthy infant the rudiments of *Hope*, it would, indeed, be hard to specify the criteria for this state, and harder to measure it; yet he who has seen a hopeless child, knows what is *not* there" (115). But despite the difficulties we may have in identifying what makes a healthy baby hopeful, hope "is both the earliest and the most indispensable virtue inherent in the state of being alive. Others have called this deepest quality *confidence*, and I have referred to *trust* as the earliest positive psychosocial attitude, but if life is to be sustained hope must remain, even where confidence is wounded, trust impaired" (115). On the one hand, clinicians know that an adult who has lost all hope "regresses into as lifeless a state as a living organism can sustain," and on the other hand, "there is something in the anatomy even of mature hope" that suggests it is "the most childlike" of all the virtues (115–16).

A central dynamic of hope is mutuality: "The infant's smile inspires hope in the adult and, in making him smile, makes him wish to give hope" (116). But smiling is only one of the many ways that an infant awakens in the giver a strength that the giver "is ready and needful to have awakened and to have consolidated by the experience of mutuality" (116). Thus, the infant is not simply a passive recipient of the adult's attentions and ministrations. In fact, the adult's own hopefulness, possibly dormant for years, may be reawakened by the infant's own need for hope.

Once established as a basic quality of experience, hope becomes an enduring acquisition and is therefore not dependent on each and every desire being met. Hope "remains independent of the verifiability of 'hopes,' for it is in the nature of man's maturation that concrete hopes will, at a time when a hoped-for event or state comes to pass, prove to have been quietly superseded by a more advanced set of hopes" (117). In effect, Erikson is making an argument here for having more than one hope at any given time and for not putting all of our hopeful eggs in one basket. Thus, over time, a "gradual widening of the infant's horizon of active experience provides, at each step, verifications so rewarding that they inspire new hopefulness. At the same time, the infant develops a greater capacity for renunciation, together with the ability to transfer disappointed hopes to better prospects" (117). He "learns to dream what is imaginable and to train his expectations on what promises to prove possible," and in this way "maturing hope not only maintains itself in the face of changed facts—it proves itself able to change facts, even as faith is said to move mountains" (117).

Consistent with his view that religion is the institutional safeguard of the personal acquisition of trust and trustworthiness, Erikson relates hope to the "religious sentiment," noting that it "induces adults to restore their hopefulness in periodic petitionary prayer" (116). Given his definition of hope as "the enduring belief in the attainability of fervent wishes, in spite of the dark urges and rages which mark the beginning of existence," we can see why hopefulness would be restorable through petitionary prayer. For the religious sentiment is one in which we believe in the attainability of our fervent wishes despite the fact that we may consider ourselves unworthy of divine favor.

Erikson concludes his reflections on the virtue of hope by noting that "an exclusive condition of hopefulness" would not be desirable, for this would mean "a maladaptive optimism" (118). That is, one would simply assume that one's desires will be met regardless of environmental circumstances and irrespective of one's own contributions to their realization. Hope, then, is not synonymous with optimism, and, in fact, one could argue that persons who are overwhelmingly optimistic do not need hope, because they believe that everything will turn out as they expect that it will. If the optimist says the glass is half full, the pessimist says the glass is half empty, and the rationalist says the glass is too large, the hopeful person says, "Let's pray that there will always be water, and let's also do what is in our own power to assure that this will be the case."

SAM: A NEUROLOGICAL CRISIS IN A SMALL BOY

Having presented Erikson's commentaries on basic trust vs. basic mistrust and the virtue of hope, I now want to turn to my proposal that this dynamic and virtue are central to the development of the child throughout the first decade of life. To provide concrete evidence in support of this proposal, I will focus on the life experiences of children who are between the ages of three and nine.

Several of Erikson's own case studies in *Childhood and Society* lend themselves to this proposal. I will discuss one of them, a case he calls "A Neurological Crisis in a Small Boy" (Erikson 1950, 21–34).

Erikson was a faculty member of the Department of Psychiatry at the University of California in Berkeley when he encountered Sam. He became Sam's therapist when the boy was five years old. Sam's difficulties had begun two years earlier, and he had had two therapists prior to Erikson. At the time, Erikson was using a lot of play therapy in his work with children.

When he was three years old, Sam began to suffer convulsions shortly after the death of his grandmother. His first attack occurred five days after her death, the second occurred a month later when he found a dead mole in the back yard, and a third happened two months after that, following his accidental crushing of a butterfly in his hand. After the second attack, the hospital staff diagnosed the affliction as idiopathic epilepsy (idiopathic meaning that the cause was unknown or uncertain), possibly due to a brain lesion in the left hemisphere. EEG tests following the third attack, however, were inconclusive. They only indicated that "epilepsy could not be excluded" (22).

As he became acquainted with the case, Erikson learned that Sam's mother had been extremely nervous about her husband's mother's visit shortly after they had settled into their new home in a new town: "The visit had the connotation of an examination to her: had she done well by her husband and by her child?" (22). Aware that Sam enjoyed teasing people, she warned him that his grandmother's heart was not very strong. He promised not to tease her, and at first everything went well. Still, his mother seldom left the two of them alone together, especially because the enforced restraint seemed to be hard on the vigorous little boy, causing him to appear pale and tense.

When she slipped away for a while one day, leaving Sam in her mother-in-law's care, she returned to find the older woman lying on the floor. She had suffered a heart attack. Sam's mother was later informed by her mother-in-law that Sam had climbed up on a chair and had fallen: "There was every reason to suspect that he had teased her and had deliberately done something which she had warned against" (22). Sam's grandmother was ill for several months, during which she remained at her son's and daughter-in-law's home. But she failed to recover and eventually died. Five days later, Sam suffered his first attack.

For some inexplicable reason, Sam's parents did not disclose to him that his grandmother had died. Instead, the following morning, his mother told him that his grandmother had gone on a long trip north to Seattle. He cried and asked, "Why didn't she say goodbye to me?" Then, when her body was removed from the house in a casket, his mother compounded the deception by telling him that his grandmother's books were in the big box. But Sam had not seen his grandmother bring so many books with her and could not understand why the relatives who had gathered in their home would have shed so many tears over a box full of books.

When he heard the story from Sam's mother, Erikson "doubted that the boy really believed the story" (23). This doubt was confirmed by other remarks by "the little teaser" (23). Once when his mother had wanted him to find something that he did not want to look for, he had said, mockingly, "It has gone on a lo-ong trip, all the way to Se-attle" (23). Also, in the play group that he later joined as part of the treatment plan, he would build innumerable variations of oblong boxes, the openings of which he would carefully barricade: "His questions at the time justified the suspicion that he was experimenting with the idea of how it was to be locked up in an oblong box" (23).

Belatedly, his mother decided to tell him the truth, informing him that his grandmother had, in fact, died. But he refused to accept it. Instead, he responded, "You're lying. She's in Seattle. I'm going to see her again" (23). So, if he questioned his mother's earlier story, he also refused to believe her retraction of the earlier story and substitution of the true story. It was as if he wanted his mother to know that he didn't know what he could believe anymore.

Erikson also learned through conversations with Sam's mother that he had lost his good-natured mischief and sense of humor at about the time of his grandmother's arrival, and had become uncharacteristically aggressive. He had hit another child, hard enough to draw blood, and his punishment was that he would have to remain at home with his grandmother and not go outside and play. He had also thrown a doll at his mother, and the impact loosened one of her teeth. In reaction, she had struck him back, displaying "a rage which neither she nor he had known was in her" (26).

One day, in play therapy, Erikson arranged for Sam to lose consistently at a game of dominoes "in order to test his threshold" (25). As Sam's losses mounted, his face grew very pale. Suddenly, he stood up, grabbed a rubber doll, and hit Erikson in the face with it. At that very moment, his eyes took on an aimless stare, he gagged as if about to vomit, and he swooned slightly, thus suffering "one of his minor spells" (25). After regaining consciousness, he rearranged the dominoes into an oblong, rectangular configuration, a miniature version of his grandmother's casket. Erikson said to him, "This must mean that you are afraid you may have to die because you hit me." Sam replied, "Must I?" Erikson reassured him, "Of course not. But you must have thought that you did make your grandmother die and therefore had to die yourself. That's why you built those big boxes in your school, just as you built this little one today. In fact, you must have thought you were going to die every time you had one of those attacks." He simply replied, "Yes" (26).

Erikson presented this case in the first chapter of *Childhood and Society* (1950) to illustrate the relationships that he would be exploring throughout the book between the somatic process (reflected in Sam's seizures and convulsions), the ego process (reflected in Sam's effort to protect his individuality by adopting the role of the little teaser in reaction to anxieties arising from his family's change of residence and the visit of his grandmother), and the larger social process (reflected in the fact that his parents had chosen to live in a town in which they were the only Jewish family) (30–33).

This case interests me, however, because it illustrates the basic trust vs. basic mistrust conflict in a five-year-old child, and reflects the fact that this dynamic conflict may remain central several years after the infancy period. Specifically, his mother's deceptions challenged his trust in her at a time when he could ill afford to lose this trust, and his reactive aggressive behavior (lashing out) challenged his fundamental trust in himself. Previously, his penchant for teasing had held his darker urges in check, but now his aggressive behavior meant that he had lost control over these urges, that they threatened to take control of him. Thus, mistrust—of others and of himself—was becoming stronger than his earlier acquired sense of trust.

His preoccupation with death and his belief that he was destined to die also indicate that he was teetering on the edge of hopelessness. He may not yet have become the "hopeless child" who manifests the very absence of the criteria for the state of hope (Erikson 1964a, 115). But his attacks, symbolic of the heart attack suffered by his grandmother, and his play with oblong boxes indicate that his former confidence was wounded and his *trust* impaired. His mother's response to his aggressive act of throwing a doll in her face (was the fact that it was a doll significant?) also indicates that her own ability to disregard his dark urges and rages was not unlimited. Her own sense of hope seems to have become precarious on that occasion, and by hitting him back, she jeopardized the trust that had been so essential to their relationship since his infancy.

It *could* be argued that the very fact Sam was struggling with the trust vs. mistrust conflict was because he had suffered a traumatic experience that caused him to regress to the earliest stage of life, and that if he had not suffered this trauma he would have been well on his way to a later conflict. But although Sam's trust vs. mistrust conflict had been exacerbated by a trauma, one for which he held himself to blame, this does not mean that it would not otherwise have been a struggle for him. In fact, there is much evidence that his "little teaser" role was formed out of this very struggle, and well before his grandmother set foot in the house.

I think that Erikson gave this case such a prominent place in his book because he had had a very similar experience when he was a young boy. His mother, a Danish Jew, had been married several years before he was born, but she and her husband had split up just a few days after their wedding took place because she had discovered that he was involved in suspicious financial dealings. When she later became pregnant by another man, she left Copenhagen and settled in Karlsruhe, located in southern Germany. A few months later, Erik was born. His birth certificate indicates that her estranged husband was the father of the child, but this could not have been true because she had not seen the man for several years. She raised Erik by herself for the first three years of his life, then accepted his pediatrician's proposal of marriage. She and Erik moved into the doctor's home, where he also maintained his office. He insisted that her son be told that he was his biological father.

In his autobiographical essay, Erikson (1975a) says that he "played in with" this deception, "and more or less forgot the period before the age of three, when

[his] mother and [he] had lived alone" (27). Whether a child can in fact "forget" the first three years of his life is, of course, rather doubtful. Also, if he believed the story his mother and her new husband told him, he most likely would have wondered why his father had lived in a separate home, and why he saw him only when his mother had taken him to the man's home for medical purposes.

Looking back, he thinks they thought this deception "was not only workable (because children then were not held to know what they had not been told) but also advisable, so that [he] would feel thoroughly at home in their home" (27). But as time went on, the fact that he was "blond, and blue-eyed and grew fla-grantly tall" (27) made it patently obvious that his stepfather, being Jewish, was not his biological father. After all, a Jewish man and woman could not both be the biological parents of a son with such obvious Scandinavian features.

At this time, his mother created another false story, informing him that he was the son of her estranged husband. But because this man, too, had been Jewish, her son found this story as incredible as the first story. Over the years, she con-tinued to give him false information. In his late forties, he made a concerted effort to find out who his father was. Family lore suggested two possible candi-dates, both named Erik, but he never learned the man's identity. It's possible that even his mother did not know. When he was seventy-four-years old, he wrote to a friend, "How many discordant signals she must have given me as to my origins" (Friedman 1999, 39).

In any event, for the early deceptions to have been effective in the long run, young Erik would have had to view his own perceptions and judgments as untrustworthy. But as the counterevidence mounted, it became evident that his mother, at least on this issue, was not to be trusted. As the first definition of *trust* in *Webster's* puts it, he would have had great difficulty sustaining "a firm belief or confidence in the honesty" of his mother, and this difficulty would, in turn, affect his "faith" and "reliance" on her words, testimony, and so forth (Agnes 2001, 1537). Years later, when writing his autobiographical essay, he could view the original deception as intended to make him "feel thoroughly at home in their home" (27), an interesting choice of words for a boy who was moving into his stepfather's home with his mother and not, for example, as the adoptive child of both parents. But, in any case, this was the view of an adult, not that of the young boy himself.

Sam faced a similar difficulty. His own perceptions and judgments, such as the size of the box that was allegedly filled with books his grandmother did not own, would have to be discounted or denied if he were to believe what his mother told him. It was clear that her words were unreliable. But then, when she *did* tell the truth, which Erikson's mother never did, he seemed to need to deny it. Why? Was it because he wanted to give his mother notice that once she had lied to him, he could never trust what she said to him? Or was he so conscience stricken that he wanted to believe that his mother's original story was true? Or both? And why did she lie to him in the first place? Had she wanted to spare her son the guilt he felt for having been responsible for his grandmother's heart attack? Or was she struggling with her own guilt feelings for having slipped out that day, leaving him in the older woman's care? Or both?

One thing seems reasonably clear: his mother's original deception would have made it very difficult for him to work through his feelings of guilt through direct conversation with his mother. He would have to deal with them on his own, in his own way. So we should not be surprised that his guilt feelings took a physiological form, and that he would suffer an attack similar to that of his grandmother. Their similarity was congruent with his mother's later recollection that the evening before his first attack, he had piled up his pillows the way his grandmother had done to avoid congestion and had gone to sleep in the nearly sitting position that his grandmother had adopted following her heart attack. Also, because she lived a few months after her initial attack, he may have viewed his own survival of several attacks as merely a temporary reprieve. In any event, Erikson learned through their play together that Sam believed he would have to die for having brought on his grandmother's heart attack.

Thus, the dynamic conflict of trust vs. mistrust became a much more complex affair than it would have been in infancy. If his mother was still the central figure in this dynamic conflict, the conflict was no longer confined to this single relationship. At the very least, it became a triangular affair, involving son, mother, and grandmother. And where there is one triangular relationship, there is almost certainly another lurking behind the more self-evident one—triangles, I like to say, come in twos—so we should not overlook the fact that his mother had become anxious about her husband's mother's visit, especially about whether the older woman would feel that her son's wife had "done well by her husband and by her child" (22).

But then, there was Erikson himself. He was yet another participant in this dynamic conflict, the third of three therapists called in to help the family by uncovering the psychodynamic roots of Sam's physical seizures. But Erikson did much more than simply diagnose the problem. His therapeutic interventions, especially on the day that he caused Sam to lose at dominoes, played a major role in the boy's recovery of trust. By reassuring Sam that he would not need to pay for what he had done, Erikson became the one person in the conflict in whom the young boy could confide—acknowledging that he knew his grandmother was dead—and thus begin to regain his own sense of trustworthiness, which had been severely damaged when he felt he could not face what he knew to be true.

Furthermore, if Erikson's own capacity to be a person in whom Sam could place his trust was partly due to the fact that he saw himself in this troubled young boy, then there was yet another relationship in this trust vs. mistrust conflict: the relationship between two small boys who share in common the awareness that they cannot take for granted the reliability of their mothers. This could have become grounds for hopelessness. But as Erikson (1964a) says of hope:

> The gradual widening of the infant's horizon of active experience provides, at each step, verifications so rewarding that they inspire new hopefulness. At the same time, the infant develops a greater capacity for renunciation,

together with the ability to transfer disappointed hopes to better prospects; and he learns to dream what is imaginable and to train his expectations on what promises to be possible. (117)

New and different seeds of hope were sown that day when a small boy was unable to control his dark urges and rages and the man he hit on the face with a rubber doll conveyed to him that he fully understood.

In my discussion of this case, I have, of course, attempted to show that the central dynamic was one of trust vs. mistrust, and that the virtue that was most relevant to it was that of hope. This case is also valuable in another sense, for it supports the point that I expressed in the introduction: the decades approach I am advocating does not mean that Erikson's own location of the stages is therefore misguided.

In his own presentation of the case, Erikson made frequent allusions to Sam's guilt, especially his guilt for what he felt he had done to his grandmother, and he also noted that on these occasions Sam would lose his usual energy and vitality, going pale, for example, or beginning to swoon. Given that Sam was three to five years old, Erikson's original formulation would place him in the initiative vs. guilt stage. Thus, Erikson's original schema is certainly relevant.

My proposal, however, would claim that trust vs. mistrust was the central, or underlying, dynamic conflict in this case. It would also take note of the fact that this conflict was more complex—less *basic*—than that experienced by the infant in the first year of life. As I have suggested, this complexity was largely due to the fact that there were multiple relationships involved, not merely the singular relationship—infant and mother—that underlies the basic form of this dynamic conflict.

In addition to the multiple relationships involved, language also played a significant role, adding to the complexity of the conflict. Sam was confronted with the discrepancy between what he intuited to be the case from what his eyes perceived (the long black box and the tears shed by the gathered relatives) and what his mother said to him. This discrepancy presented a trust vs. mistrust dilemma that was difficult to resolve, especially because he wanted to believe that his mother's original story was true. An old joke makes the point: Morty comes home to find his wife and his best friend, Eddie, naked together in bed. Just as Morty is about to open his mouth, Eddie jumps out of the bed and says, "Before you say anything, old pal, what are you going to believe, me or your eyes?"

On the other hand, language also played a decisive role in the resolution of the dilemma. When Sam said, "Must I?" in response to Erikson's observation that Sam must feel he would have to die because he had hit his play partner, Erikson replied, "Of course not. But you must have thought that you did make your grandmother die and therefore had to die yourself." This was language that Sam could trust: it challenged the idea that he would have to suffer an extreme punishment for a lesser wrongful act, and it accurately expressed what Sam had been thinking about his grandmother's death and his complicity in it. With this reassurance, the reason for his physical attacks was dispelled.

In his *Introductory Lectures on Psycho-Analysis,* Sigmund Freud (1966) addressed the skepticism with which he was frequently confronted by the relatives of his patients. They doubted that "anything can be done about the illness by mere talking" (20). But Freud drew attention to the power of words: "Words were originally magic and to this day words have retained much of their ancient magical power. By words one person can make another blissfully happy or drive him to despair" (20). To this I would add that by words a person can create a deep sense of lasting trust and by words a person can cause a mistrust that will never be entirely eradicated, no matter how hard one tries to make amends.

OTHER ILLUSTRATIONS OF THE TRUST VS. MISTRUST DYNAMIC

Sam was only five years old when Erikson became his therapist. Thus, this case focuses on a boy whose trust vs. mistrust conflict occurred in the first half of the first decade of his life. But one could cite many similar examples of the trust vs. mistrust conflict in the second half of this decade. I will mention just a few, beginning with the very first autobiography, the *Confessions* of St. Augustine (1960), which was written when he was in his early forties.

When he was a young schoolboy, Augustine was severely beaten by his teachers at school for being "slow at learning" (51). Though this was bad enough, even worse was the fact that the boys' parents "laughed at the torments [they] suffered from [their] teachers" (52). He realizes that he and his classmates should have worked harder in school than they did, but they liked to play. Their penchant for play, he wrote, "was punished in us by men who did the same things themselves," but the adults got away with it, because "the trivial concerns of adults are called business, while such things in children are punished by adults" (52).

He associates his first recourse to prayer with these beatings, for it was at this time that he began to pray to God: "While still a boy, I began to pray to you, my help and my refuge, and in praying to you I broke the knots that tied my tongue. A little one, but with no little feeling, I prayed to you that I would not be beaten at school, but you did not hear me" (52).

Clearly, he had become mistrustful of adults because they imposed a standard on children that they themselves did not meet. There was also the fact that he received no sympathy from his parents when they saw the physical effects of the beatings. Most troubling of all was the fact that when he prayed to God that he would be spared the beatings, God did not hear or listen either. Thus, there was no one to whom he could turn. As a result, he began to mistrust himself, a mistrust reflected later in an incident when he was sixteen years old and some other boys suggested that they steal some pears from a nearby garden. He describes his distress by saying, "I stole a thing of which I had plenty of my own and of much better quality. Nor did I wish to enjoy that thing which I desired to gain by theft, but rather to enjoy the actual theft and the sin of the theft" (70). Thus, he could no longer trust himself to do what he himself knew was right. The beatings by his teachers, therefore, undermined the two major achievements of infancy: trust and trustworthiness.

In *The Long Loneliness* Dorothy Day (1952), founder of the Catholic Worker Movement, tells about her experiences during the San Francisco earthquake that occurred on April 18, 1906. She was eight years old at the time, and her family was living in Oakland, across the bay from San Francisco. She recalls that the earthquake "started with a deep rumbling and the convulsions of the earth started afterward, so that the earth became a sea which rocked [their] house in a most tumultuous manner" (21). Her father took her two older brothers from their beds and rushed to the front door, where her mother stood with her baby sister: "She had snatched [her] from beside me. I was left in a big brass bed, which rolled back and forth on a polished floor" (21).

She is unsure whether she realized what was happening: "But I do know that the whole event was confused in my mind with something which might have occurred a few nights earlier, my mother fainting on the floor of my room on her way to the bathroom, and my father carrying her back to bed. The illness of my usually strong and cheerful mother and the earthquake were both part of the world's tragedy to me" (21).

She suspects that her nightmares began after the earthquake, not before: "[In these nightmares] God became in my ears a great noise that became louder and louder, and approached nearer and nearer to me until I woke up sweating with fear and shrieking for my mother" (20). Within a week after the earthquake, the family moved to Chicago, because her "father's newspaper job [as a sports editor] was gone when the plant went up in flames" (20).

Day's is another story of mistrust, this one created by a natural disaster but exacerbated by her mother's earlier fainting spell. While she does not speculate on why she was the only one of the children who was left in the house, we can assume that having to experience the earthquake all by herself was deeply distressing to her. Having to leave Oakland within a week also meant leaving familiar surroundings and pleasant routines—she especially mentions having enjoyed working in the garden, sitting and listening to a brook, and going to Sunday school and church with Birdie, a neighbor woman.

Yet, on the positive side, Day recalls that "all the neighbors joined [her] mother in serving the homeless" refugees from San Francisco which, unlike Oakland, had been ravaged by fire. "Another thing I remember about California" she writes, "was the joy of doing good, of sharing whatever we had with others after the earthquake, an event which threw us out of our complacent happiness into a world of catastrophe" (21). Thus, out of an experience of mistrust, new seeds of trust were sown, and she herself began to become a person who in her adult life sought to be someone in whom others could place *their* trust. Founder of the Catholic Worker Movement, she devoted her life to the care and welfare of the homeless. Thus, she became the very personification of hope for others.[1]

In *Prairie Reunion* Barbara J. Scot (1995) recounts the story of her father's death by suicide in 1950 when she was eight years old. He had left Scotch Grove, Iowa, for Colorado in 1943, leaving behind his wife and their two small children—Barbara, age one, and her brother Bobbie, age three. He returned for several weeks a few months later, left again, and never returned. Sometime later, he married another woman and had three more daughters. They lived in Luzerne, Iowa, some sixty miles west of Scotch Grove. He was thirty-seven years old when he died.

When informed of his death, her mother said to Barbara and her brother, "Your father is dead. He died last night. God wanted it that way because he was not a happy man. He will be happier with God" (13). She went on to say that there was no reason why they should not go to school: "Because you never knew him. If anything is said, say you never knew him. Do you understand?" (13). On the school bus that morning, Barbara conceived this poem in her mind: "My mother said / my daddy's dead / I want to cry / I don't know why / I didn't know him anyway / They said that he had run away" (15). She hurried to write the poem in her notebook because, unlike her second-grade teacher, who had put her poems on the blackboard for everyone to see, her third-grade teacher had scolded her for writing poems during arithmetic class.

Trust and mistrust issues abound in this account of the death of her father, her mother's admonition to her children to tell anyone who asked that they had not known him, the very different responses of the two teachers to her writing of poems, and the poem itself with the concluding line "They said that he had run away." *Prairie Reunion* centers on her attempt, when she was in her early fifties, to find out the truth behind her father's decision to "run away."

THE LESS-DRAMATIC STORIES OF MANY OF US

The stories that I have presented here—stories that could be multiplied by reference to other personal autobiographies—are dramatic ones. But what about those of us who had rather normal, uneventful childhoods? Does the argument that this was the decade in which the trust vs. mistrust conflict was central apply to us as well? I am convinced that it does. If personally disposed or encouraged to do so, all readers of this book could produce an account of a personal trust vs. mistrust experience, even several, in the first decade of their lives.

---

1. William James was a visiting professor at Stanford University when the earthquake occurred, and its effects were felt in Palo Alto, thirty-five miles south of San Francisco. He was able to get a train to San Francisco the following day and spent four hours there, then returned to the city eight days later. In his account of these visits in "On Some Mental Effects of the Earthquake" (James 1987, 1215–22), originally published in *Youth's Companion* (June 7, 1906), he wrote about the resiliency of those who endured the earthquake's most devastating effects and the fact that, despite their own losses, there were so many who volunteered to help others.

I myself think of the time when our family had gone to the train station to meet a relative. I was four years old. As usual, the train was late, so my father, my older brothers, and I went out onto the walkway between the two train stations maintained by the two companies that provided train service in our city. The walkway overlooked the train tracks some thirty-five feet below. As we watched, my father apparently thought I would like a better vantage point from which to see the trains below, so he picked me up and held me out over the three-foot wall of the walkway. I begged him to put me down, and he eventually responded to my pleas, but it seemed an eternity before I was back on solid footing again.

A trivial story, perhaps, but the fact that I recall the incident suggests it had an enduring psychological effect. It also symbolizes, for me, the dynamic conflict of trust vs. mistrust. On the one hand, I had no doubt that my father was strong enough to hold me out over the edge of the bridge and the thought that he might deliberately let go of me would never have crossed my mind. Thus, in an odd sort of way, the incident would have supported the feeling of trust. On the other hand, being held out over a bridge some thirty-five feet above the ground can be a rather terrifying experience, and I can now think of all sorts of circumstances that might have led to my falling to the train tracks below. Foremost among these would be that my own fear or fright would cause *me* to do something that would cause *him* to lose his hold on me. Which is to say that *I* could have proven *untrustworthy* in the situation given my inexperience in situations of this kind. I cannot help but wonder why an adult would have done what he did. I know that I would not have done it to a child of mine, or anyone else's child for that matter.

Was there a momentary lapse in judgment because he was under some sort of stress? Was he motivated by a genuine desire to enable me to see more easily what my older and taller brothers could see unaided? Was it meant to teach me the benefits that may accrue from risk taking? If the latter, my fright made it impossible for me to look at the trains below. The very fact that I do not know the answers to these questions—years later—makes it difficult to set these mistrustful thoughts aside or to lay them to rest, and they make the maintenance of trust and of hope all the more essential.

Then there's the story of what occurred when I was nine years old. This story illustrates the fact that the trust vs. mistrust conflict often involves multiple relationships. My younger brother, then four, had been unusually difficult that day. When my father came home from work, my mother told him about my little brother, how he was becoming more than she could handle. At dinner that evening my brothers and I could feel the tension. No one was speaking. A sense of doom was in the air. After dinner my parents told all of us to stay close. We were not to go running off. Then my father pulled the car out of the garage, and my mother came out of the house. They directed us to get into the car, my younger brother between my parents in the front seat and my two older brothers and I in the back. My father pulled out of the driveway and started up the street. "Where are we going?" one of us had the courage to ask. No answer. My father drove on. Dusk was approaching.

Then, on our right, we recognized the building and began to realize what was going on. We felt dread in the pits of our stomachs. It was the orphanage, and our parents were about to send my little brother away. My father stopped the car and turned to my brother and said, "This is the end of the line." My mother opened the door and began to get out so that my brother could follow. The three of us in the back seat were stunned. I somehow found my voice and, amid sobs, pleaded, "Don't send him away. He'll be good. Just give him a second chance."

What I did not know, of course, is that they had no intention of leaving him at the orphanage that night. He—and the others of us—were being taught a lesson. Years later he told me that he suspected it was a ruse because he noticed that no lights were burning on the first floor of the orphanage, suggesting to him that the offices were closed for the evening. But I took them at their word, first believing that they were going to abandon him, next assuming that my pleading in his behalf may have had some effect in making them change their minds.

My brother and I have joked about the fact that he grew up to be a lawyer and I grew up to be a clergyman. Were our vocations in life established for us that evening when one of us saw through the charade while the other petitioned those who held our common destiny in their ordinarily trustworthy hands to give the sinner a "second chance"? If so, his lawyerly ways throughout the years are captured in the old joke about the lawyer who asked the judge to show mercy on a young man who had murdered his parents on the grounds that he was an orphan.

But if humor can ease the pain of this experience, it cannot erase the fact that it was an experience in which the weeds of mistrust threatened to overtake the wheat of trust (Matt. 13:24–29). Like my previous experience at age four, it, too, illustrates the vital importance of maintaining a sense of trust, the strength of hope, and the intelligence to outwit the enemy who sowed the weeds among the wheat. By the end of the first decade of life, we have met the enemy many times, and hopefully we have learned that we have the ways and means to keep him in his proper place.[2]

THE HOPEFUL SELF

Where children are permitted and encouraged to express their inner disposition to hope, they possess the foundation for a reasonably coherent and generally healthy Self. The greatest threat to the formation of a hopeful self is despair, the feeling that our future is closed, that what we desire will not occur. This despair

2. This story also appears in my *The Child's Song* (1995, 169–70). In *Caring Through the Funeral*, Gene Fowler (2004) tells of a pastor who cited this story and quoted some reflections not included here in a funeral sermon which emphasized that the healing that had eluded the deceased before death may be completed in heaven (157).

may, in turn, give way to apathy, the very absence of desire, a state of not really caring what the future holds (see Capps, 2001).

Erikson, however, notes that "Hope is the ontogenetic basis of faith" (Erikson 1964a, 118) and the author of *Hebrews* says that "faith is the assurance of things hoped for" (11:1). Thus, to say that the hopeful self is formed in the first decade of life is to claim that these are the years when we also develop the capacity for faith. Admittedly, this is a great deal to ascribe to the first decade of life, but it was Jesus himself who said, "Let the little children come to me, and do not stop them; for it is to such as these that the kingdom of heaven belongs" (Matt. 19:14). He also said, "Take care that you do not despise one of these little ones," adding that they have angels who "continually see the face of my Father in heaven" (Matt. 18:10). Thus, they have every reason to be hopeful selves. It helps, though, if they also have angels on earth—adults who are worthy of their trust and who nurture their capacity to trust themselves.

Chapter 2

The Second Decade:
The Willing Self

When we use the term "the teenage years," we naturally and appropriately think of that period of life that begins at age thirteen and continues through age nineteen. When we use the word "decade," as I do here, we think instead of the period of life from age ten through age nineteen. Thus, in the decades perspective, the three years at the beginning of this decade are not overlooked and are not considered to be a mere extension of the years that preceded them. In a sense, the decades perspective enables us to take the child's own perspective, because, for most children, the transition from nine to ten is a momentous occasion.

Birthday cards for children turning ten can be somewhat deceptive in this regard, because for children, every birthday is important. But one card in particular caught my attention because it offers ten reasons why "it's great to be ten." The main reasons that it's great to be ten are that only kids who've been around a whole decade know what's going on; that you're starting to pass up those shrimps who aren't tall enough; that being a teenager's only three short years away; that you are now perfectly balanced (ten toes, ten fingers, ten years); that single digits are *so* last year; and the best reason of all: you can't get any more perfect than a perfect 10! From this perspective, turning ten is a great event. In fact, it doesn't get any better than this!

Poets, however, have a more circumspect view of being a ten-year-old. When she was ten, Rita Dove (Harper and Walton, eds., 1994, 283) felt a great deal of pressure:

Flash Cards

In math I was the whiz kid, keeper
of oranges and apples. *What you don't understand,*
master, my father said; the faster
I answered, the faster they came.

I could see one bud on the teacher's geranium,
one clear bee sputtering at the wet pane.
The tulip trees always dragged after heavy rain
so I tucked my head as my boots slapped home.

My father put up his feet after work
and relaxed with a highball and *The Life of Lincoln.*
After supper we drilled and I climbed the dark

before sleep, before a thin voice hissed
numbers as I spun on a wheel. I had to guess.
Ten, I kept saying, *I'm only ten.*

She is being drilled on her numbers when the number of her age—*only ten*—raises the question of whether it's a bit early in life for a girl to be going to bed worrying about numbers. After all, her father comes home after work and relaxes while she comes home from school knowing that her work day is just beginning.

Billy Collins (1995, 48–49) is also troubled by the progression from nine to ten:

On Turning Ten

The whole idea of it makes me feel
like I'm coming down with something,
something worse than any stomach ache
or the headaches I get from reading in bad light—
a kind of measles of the spirit,
a mumps of the psyche,
a disfiguring chicken pox of the soul.
You tell me it is too early to be looking back
but that is because you have forgotten
the perfect simplicity of being one
and the beautiful complexity introduced by two.
But I can lie on my bed and remember every digit.
At four I was an Arabian wizard.
I could make myself invisible
by drinking a glass of milk in a certain way.
At seven I was a soldier, at nine a prince.

But now I am mostly at the window
watching the late afternoon light.
Back then it never fell so solemnly
against the side of my tree house,
and my bicycle never leaned against the garage
as it does today,
all the dark blue speed drained out of it.

This is the beginning of sadness, I say to myself,
as I walk through the universe in my sneakers.
It is time to say good-bye to my imaginary friends,
time to turn the first big number.
It seems only yesterday I used to believe
there was nothing under my skin but light.
But now when I fall upon the sidewalks of life,
I skin my knees. I bleed.

Turning "the first big number" is no less a momentous occasion here than in the birthday cards, but there's a solemnity, and a sense of sadness, loss, and vulnerability that the birthday cards do not express.

A poem by William Stafford (1996, 21) suggests a similar sense of loss as one enters the second decade of life:

A Farewell, Age Ten

While its owner looks away I touch the rabbit,
its long soft ears fold back under my hand.
Miles of yellow wheat bend; their leaves
rustle away and wait for the sun and wind.

This day belongs to my uncle. This is his farm.
We have stopped on our journey; when my father says to
we will go on, leaving this paradise, leaving
the family place. We have my father's job.

Like him, I will be strong all my life.
We are men. If we squint our eyes in the sun
we will see far. I'm ready. It's good, this resolve.
But I will never pet the rabbit again.

This poem emphasizes a ten-year-old boy's strength and ability to look far ahead. Yet there is a sense of sadness, both in the tenderness he expresses toward the rabbit and in the awareness that such tenderness is to be left behind as he continues the journey of life.

The new decade promises and portends many things. Among them, I suggest, is the dynamic conflict of autonomy vs. shame and doubt. Autonomous strivings will play a dominant role in this decade, but so will experiences and feelings of shame and of doubt. But what do these words mean? What is implied in the suggestion that autonomy, shame, and doubt will have a central role to play throughout the decade? To answer these questions, I will first note what the dictionary says about these words, then present Erikson's own understanding of what they mean in the context of the cycle of life. For him, they are integral to the psychosocial crisis experienced by the one to three-and-a-half-year-old child.

THE AUTONOMY VS. SHAME AND DOUBT CONFLICT

Webster's defines *autonomy* as "the fact or condition of being autonomous; self-government; independence" (Agnes 2001, 96). This definition reflects the two basic meanings of *autonomous*: "having self-government" and "functioning independently without control by others" (96). The first of these two meanings—"self-government"—reflects the distinction between autonomy and heteronomy. *Heteronomy* means "subject to another's laws or rule" (669). Thus when the United States declared that it would no longer be subject to England's laws or rule, it was declaring its autonomy. The first definition is therefore more restrictive than the second definition of *autonomous* as "functioning independently without control by others." This is because the word independent can mean two different things. It can mean "self-governing," but it can also mean "relying only on oneself or one's abilities, judgment, etc." (725).

Some readers of Erikson's writings have assumed that when he used the word *autonomy*, he basically meant independence in the sense of relying only or primarily on oneself. They associated this with the "individualism" that they considered to be rampant in American society (Capps 1993, 101–25). Other readers have suggested that by using the word *autonomy*, Erikson revealed his male bias, because the male child is oriented toward independence while the female child is oriented toward relationships with others (Gilligan 1982, 11–12). Both inferences are based on the assumption that, in effect, Erikson had the second meaning of independence in mind when he used the word *autonomy*.

I believe, though, that Erikson actually had the other meaning in mind, that of self-governance, and that his readers fail to recognize this because the meaning itself is not used very much today. After all, autonomy follows trust in his developmental schema, and as we have seen, he understands trust as relating not only to the infant's trust in another but also to the infant's own sense of trustworthiness—of being able to control certain urges so that the other will not withdraw or withhold what the infant needs. Thus, the self-governance of the second stage builds on and greatly expands the scope of the trustworthiness of the first stage.

Of course, the growing child is also trying to become more self-reliant, learning to do things that were previously done for the child. But Erikson is not suggesting that the child is becoming less relational. This would conflict with his view that with each successive stage of the life cycle, the circle of social interaction widens: "Personality can be said to develop according to steps predetermined in the human organism's readiness to be driven toward, to be aware of, and to interact with, a widening social radius" (Erikson 1959, 52). Rather, the child's ways of relating are changing.

The negative tendencies of this stage are shame and doubt. *Webster's* (Agnes 2001) has several definitions of *shame,* but the most relevant is "a painful feeling of having lost the respect of others because of the improper behavior, incompetence, etc. of oneself or someone that one is close to or associated with" (1317). In the case of the very young child, shame is unlikely to be felt because of something that someone else did. The shame is due to the child's own improper behavior or incompetence.

Also, the definition emphasizes the loss of the respect of others, but the loss of one's own self-respect may create even greater painful feelings. Nonetheless, the sense that one has damaged or lost one's own self-respect would require a well-developed sense of self, an achievement that we would not expect in a very young child. For Erikson, the occasions for experiencing shame in early childhood involve the development of muscles, especially those that enable the child to walk, handling objects with relative ease, and, perhaps most important of all, exercising control over the bowels. After all, this is Freud's anal stage.

Webster's has several definitions of *doubt,* most of which view doubt in terms of "opinion or belief" (429). As this gives the word a cognitive aspect that is a bit advanced for a very small child, I think the more relevant definitions are those that focus on the person's general mental and/or emotional state, such as "a condition of uncertainty," or "to hesitate," or "apprehension or fear" (429). In this stage of life, uncertainty, hesitation, and apprehension are due not only to uncertain relations with others but also to one's own capacities or the lack thereof. Thus, many of the experiences in which doubt plays a significant role involve self-doubt, which the dictionary defines as "lack of confidence or faith in oneself" (1301).

Erikson's most extensive discussion of autonomy vs. shame and doubt occurs in *Identity and the Life Cycle* (1959, 65–74). It begins with a summary of some of the items discussed by Dr. Benjamin Spock in his popular book on baby and child care (Spock 1946). The purpose of this summary is to "enable those of us who, at this time, do not have such inquisitive creatures in our homes to remember our skirmishes, our victories, and our defeats" (Erikson 1959, 65). They include such things as children's feeling their oats, having the passion to explore, and being more dependent and independent at the same time; parents' arranging the house for a wandering baby, avoiding accidents, putting poisons out of reach, and making them leave certain things alone; children's dropping and throwing things; attempting to control their own aggressive feelings, and biting; and parents' keeping bedtime happy and dealing with the small child who won't stay in bed at night (65–66). (This list is taken from Spock's chapters "The One Year Old" and "Managing Young Children").

Erikson intended his selection of these items from Spock's book to convey "the range of problems" that are likely to emerge at this stage of life. He also applauded the doctor's "excellent advice" and his "good balance" in depicting "the remarkable ease and matter-of-factness with which the nursery may be governed." Most importantly, these items provide "an indication of the sinister forces which are leashed and unleashed, especially in the guerilla warfare of unequal wills; for the child is often unequal to his own violent drives, and parent and child unequal to each other" (66). But the overall significance of this stage lies in the maturation of the muscle system, and "the consequent ability (and doubly felt inability) to coordinate a number of highly conflicting action patterns such as 'holding on' and 'letting go,' and the enormous value with which the still highly dependent child begins to endow his autonomous will" (66).[1]

Thus, in this stage, the child struggles with the tensions between "cooperation and willfulness," and between "the freedom of self-expression and its suppression" (66). The resolution of these tensions in a healthy way results in "a sense of self-control without loss of self-esteem" (66). From this sense of self-control without loss of self-esteem "comes a lasting sense of autonomy" (66). Conversely, from a sense of impotence, loss of self-control, and parental overcontrol "comes a lasting sense of doubt and shame" (68).

Erikson notes the connection between the basic trust acquired in the first stage and the autonomy of the second stage. For autonomy to develop, the child needs "a firmly developed and a convincingly continued stage of early trust" (68). The child needs to feel that the basic trust in himself and the world that he acquired in the first stage of life will not be jeopardized by his newly emergent desire to have a choice, to make demands, and to refuse to comply with the requests and demands of others. Adults need to help him preserve this basic trust. They do this through firmness that protects the child against "the potential anarchy of his as yet untrained sense of discrimination" and support that backs him up in "his wish to 'stand on his own feet' lest he be overcome by that sense of having exposed himself prematurely and foolishly which we call shame, or that secondary mistrust, that 'double-take,' which we call doubt" (68).

These two responses by caring adults—firmness and support—are very much in keeping with the "good balance" that Erikson recognized in Dr. Spock's book. As Erikson puts it, the "practical and benevolent advice of the children's doctor" adds up to this injunction: "Be firm and tolerant with the child at this stage, and he will be firm and tolerant with himself. He will feel pride in being an autonomous person; he will grant autonomy to others; and now and again he will even let himself get away with something" (70). He added the caveat about a child allowing himself to get away with something because he wanted to address the danger that the child may overcompensate and become overly self-restrained, imposing on himself more exacting restrictions than what his parents expect or consider healthy.

1. Erikson's use of Spock's book on baby and child care raises the interesting question of its influence on the development of his life-cycle model. Erikson's dynamic interplay of two contrary tendencies at each stage of development is congruent with Spock's "good balance," and Spock's admonition to parents to "trust yourself" in the chapter "Preparing for the Baby" (Spock 1946, 3–9) is consistent with Erikson's emphasis on mutual trust in the infancy stage. Of course, the influence of Freud and Shakespeare are much more evident in the overall design of the life-cycle model.

Erikson discusses the negative tendency of shame in considerable detail, in part because shame "is an infantile emotion insufficiently studied" (68). In *Childhood and Society* he noted that the main reason for this neglect of shame is that "in our civilization it is so early and easily absorbed by guilt" (1950, 223). What is shame? If the dictionary definition indicates that shame involves the loss of respect, Erikson emphasizes that it is the sense of being exposed. Thus, shame "supposes that one is completely exposed and conscious of being looked at—in a word, self-conscious. One is visible and not ready to be visible" (1959, 68–69). Thus, in our dreams, shame expresses itself in situations in which "we are stared at in a condition of incomplete dress, in night attire, 'with one's pants down'" (69), and shame "is early expressed in an impulse to bury one's face, or to sink, right then and there, into the ground" (69). More recent literature on the psychology of shame supports Erikson's emphasis on exposure (for example, Lewis 1992).

Erikson is especially concerned about adults' use of shame to effect obedience and compliance. The shaming that adults inflict on the child at this stage "exploits an increasing sense of being small, which paradoxically develops as the child stands up and as his awareness permits him to note the relative measures of size and power" (69). Furthermore, "too much shaming does not result in a sense of propriety but in a secret determination to try to get away with things when unseen, if indeed, it does not result in deliberate *shamelessness*" (69). For "many a small child, when shamed beyond endurance, may be in a mood (although not in possession of either the courage or the words) to express defiance" (69).

After all, there is a limit to a child's endurance "in the face of demands which force him to consider himself, his body, his needs, and his wishes as evil and dirty, and to believe in the infallibility of those who pass such judgment" (69). When this limit is reached, he "may be apt to turn things around, to become secretly oblivious to the opinion of others, and to consider as evil only the fact that they exist: his chance will come when they are gone, or when he can leave them" (69).

Erikson does not discuss doubt in any explicit way in *Identity and the Life Cycle* and devotes only a brief paragraph to doubt in *Childhood and Society*. But what he does say supports my earlier point that doubt in the young child is largely a sense of self-doubt. Whereas shame is the experience of being exposed and expresses itself in the desire to hide or bury one's face, doubt arises from the fact that one has a "back side" or "behind." It is related, therefore, to "this reverse area of the body, with its aggressive and libidinal focus in the sphincters and in the buttocks" (224). This area "cannot be seen by the child, and yet it can be dominated by the will of others" (224).

Thus, the "behind" is the child's "dark continent, an area of the body which can be magically dominated and effectively invaded by those who would attack one's power of autonomy and who would designate as evil those products of the bowels which were felt to be all right when they were being passed" (224). The "basic sense of doubt" created by the experience of being dominated from behind, and having one's eliminative products defined as dirty or objects of disgust, "forms a substratum for later and more verbal forms of compulsive doubting" (224). Thus, later on, the definitions of doubt that concern belief become relevant.

In his concluding reflections on autonomy vs. shame and doubt in *Identity and the Life Cycle,* Erikson (1959) comments on the role that parents play in helping their child develop a genuine sense of autonomy. He suggests that the "kind and degree of a sense of autonomy which parents are able to grant their small children depends on the dignity and the sense of personal independence which they derive from their own lives. Just as the sense of trust is a reflection of the parents' sturdy and realistic faith, so is the sense of autonomy a reflection of the parents' dignity as individuals" (72).

In the revised edition of *Childhood and Society,* Erikson (1963) suggests that the institutional safeguard of autonomy is "the principle of law and order" (254). From everyday interactions to high courts of law, "this principle apportions to each his privileges and his limitations, his obligations and his rights" (254). Parents' own sense of rightful dignity and lawful independence gives the child "the confident expectation that the kind of autonomy fostered in childhood will not lead to undue doubt or shame in later life" (254). Thus, for autonomy to flourish, one must be able to believe that one's social world is based on justice.

THE VIRTUE OF WILL

Erikson assigns the human strength or virtue of will to the second life stage. *Webster's* (Agnes 2001) has several definitions of *will,* which tend to fall into two identifiable groups: one emphasizing the power of choice, decision, or of being able to control one's own actions; the other, the strength and determination expended in securing a desired outcome (1637). It distinguishes between *will* as the ability to control one's own actions and *willfulness* as "doing what one pleases; self-willed" (1638).

Both definitions of *will* are discernible in Erikson's discussion of the virtue of will in "Human Strength and the Cycle of Generations" (Erikson 1964a). His understanding of will reflects his view that it originates in early childhood: "Will is the unbroken determination to exercise free choice as well as self-restraint, in spite of the unavoidable experience of shame and doubt in infancy" (119). This dual emphasis on free choice and self-restraint implies a distinction between will and willfulness. Thus, he notes that "as the infant's senses and his muscles grasp at opportunities for more active experience, he faces the double demand for self-control and for the acceptance of control from others. To *will* does not mean to be willful, but rather to gain gradually the power of increased judgment and decision in the application of drive" (118). Thus, the small child is beginning to learn, albeit in very rudimentary form, what the healthy adult must make a practice of: "To will what can be, to renounce as not worth willing what cannot be, and to believe he willed what is inevitable" (118).

In this stage, parent-child interactions are often experienced by both as scenes of combat. It is vitally important, therefore, that the child experiences some victories and some defeats. Through defeat, the child can learn "to accept the existential paradox of making decisions which he knows 'deep down' will be predetermined by events, because making decisions is part of the evaluative quality inherent in being alive" (119). But too many defeats can produce a sense of defeat that leads to "deep *shame* and a compulsive *doubt* whether one ever really willed what one did, or really did what one willed" (119).

Yet even as a sense of hope endures despite the failure of a given hope to materialize, so, too, does a sense of will. Often, for the child, there are things willed that "do not really seem worth despairing over when the moment of testing arrives, provided only that growth and development have enough leeway to present new issues, and that, all in all, expectable reality proves more satisfactory and more interesting than fantasy" (119).

The very idea that will is a virtue means that the child is developing a will that is fundamentally good. Thus, Erikson notes that the maintenance of goodwill between the parents and the child "depends on a mutual limitation of wills" (119). Judicious parenthood will "gradually grant a measure of self-control to the child who learns to control willfulness, to offer willingness, and to exchange good will" (119).

Yet Erikson concludes his discussion of the virtue of will with the observation that this development of a goodwill has not been without cost. From this time forward, the child will experience a split self-image due to the sense that one is, to some degree at least, self-contradictory, and this is "truly a fall from grace" (120). Given the child's own sense of this internal split, "only judicious parenthood, feeling itself part of a reasonably just civic and world order, can convey a healing sense of justice" (120).

There are several grounds for locating the autonomy vs. shame and doubt conflict in the second decade of life. I will mention three. The first is that this is the decade in which one is experiencing dramatic physiological changes that, like the physiological changes in the second stage of life but on a much larger scale, are changing the ways in which one relates to others, both one's peers and those in authority. For the first time in one's life, one can, if one is so inclined, pose a serious physical threat to one's parents and other adults.

These physical changes are also accompanied by emotional changes due especially to sexual development, and these lead inevitably to the desire to function independently of the control of others and to the need to exercise self-governance. The combat between parents and their offspring that occurs in the second stage of life is rather miniscule in comparison to the potential combat that occurs in the second decade of life. At least some of this combat is due to parents' reasonable doubt that their sons and daughters are, in fact, capable of governing themselves. The sons and daughters often claim that they *are* capable of governing themselves, and thus complain that their parents do not trust them to do what is right and prudent, but they are also unsure of themselves as they now confront occasions for self-doubt that are new and potentially catastrophic.

The second is that this is the decade in which shame moves from the adult-child arena and enters the arena of peer-group relationships. Shame experiences, especially those involving sexual encounters, with their inevitable consequences of feeling exposed instead of revealed for who one truly is, may produce more self-doubt than one can handle. When shamed beyond one's endurance, one may retaliate by becoming shameless, and such shamelessness may take the form of open defiance.

The third is that the institutional safeguard of autonomy—the principle of law and order—is of special concern to the adolescent who has a heightened sensitivity to how privileges, limitations, obligations, and rights are apportioned. Some will actually experience the courts of law firsthand. Others will have work experiences that enable them to witness how privileges and rewards are apportioned in the workplace. But virtually all will experience the quality of their society's commitment to justice in the educational setting. Thus, the safeguarding of autonomy falls largely to their teachers, whose task it is to represent the society's commitment to equality, fairness, and genuine lawfulness.

STEVE: "I CAN'T REALLY WIN"

A good illustration of the prominence of the autonomy vs. shame and doubt conflict in the second decade of life is the case of a teenager named Steve in *Real Boys' Voices* by William Pollack (2000). All cases in this book are based on interviews, but none of the questions or comments of the interviewer are included. The intention is that the boys' own voices will be heard without the interpretive comments of adults. Because my concern is to show how this case illustrates the centrality of the autonomy vs. shame and doubt conflict in the second decade of life, I will necessarily need to offer my own interpretation of Steve's reflections.

Steve is a seventeen-year-old boy who lives in a suburb in New England. No other personal facts are provided. He begins his story with the observation that his relationship with his parents is "really good." "We talk a lot about everything: politics, books, whatever," he says. "But there are certain things that fall into the 'don't talk about it' category, like anything to do with parties" (332). He explains: "My mom will say, 'So, you went to a party. What happens at these parties?' And I say, 'It's a party.' It feels like she knows what happens at parties and thinks that I don't. She'll say, 'We should really be honest about this'" (332).

Steve agrees that they should talk about it, but he has reservations: "I know it's a mistake because we've tried to talk about it before. She'll say, 'It's good you're being honest with us. I'd much rather have an open dialogue and I don't condone what's going on, but if you are going to do it, it's much better that you can be open about it.' But then she wants to restrict the parties I go to" (332). As a result, he says, "We just don't talk about the things that make my parents uncomfortable. They say they want to hear it, because they want to know what I'm doing. But they don't really want to hear it. If they hear, then I end up in trouble" (332).

Steve admits that he is doing "stuff" on the weekends that his parents would not approve of. He cites the example of a party where the kid's parents were not at home. So there was a lot of drinking and drugs. Some of his friends' parents wouldn't ask if the kid's parents were going to be home. Not his parents. They always ask whether the parents will be home, when he is planning to get home, and who's going to be there. He thinks his parents "are a bit anal about it, particularly [his] mother, because she never did any of that in high school and doesn't get it" (332).

He tells about a recent "confrontation" between his mother and himself. He was personally "upset" because he went to a kid's party a couple of weeks ago and the kid's parents *were* there but deliberately chose to "look the other way." So the kids were "running around outside and getting drunk and that kind of thing." The kid himself is not supposed to do this stuff, "but it's reached the point where it's so blatantly obvious—they're not stupid people, they can't just have missed it—they just chose to look the other way," which Steve feels is "pretty irresponsible" (332).

It turns out that this very kid had had another party awhile back to which Steve did not go, but his mother had heard about it. So when this more recent party invitation came up, Steve told his mother that he was going to go and that the kid's [Brian's] parents would be there. His mother replied, "Yeah, right. As if that means anything." Steve says he didn't try to deny it or cover it up, but simply answered, "Yeah, pretty much." And his mother said, "All right. Whatever." In effect, he said, "She didn't say yes or no. So I went. She knew that I went. I stayed the night and came back and we didn't talk about it" (333).

But then at dinnertime, his mother said she had heard about the party, and then she "did the raised-eyebrow thing." Irritated, Steve said, "What's your implication? If you're implying something, get it out on the table. Don't do this raised-eyebrow crap." She replied, "I just heard it was a pretty racy party." Steve answered, "Oh, for God's sake. That's such a ridiculous statement." She said, "Why is that a ridiculous statement?" He answered, "First of all, that you used the word 'racy.' And second of all, you knew this was going to happen." She responded that she really doesn't feel that she "entirely knew what was going on," adding, "I'm upset because I don't think you should be over there. I know his parents don't care and they're irresponsible."

Steve found this response a bit disingenuous. He thought to himself that she really knows what goes on at parties like this, but he assumed she "trusted [him] to handle [him]self and not do dumb stuff." But now it had come out that "she really didn't trust [him], and that she really had no idea what was going on." He "felt troubled by this" because they had had conversations previously where he had "basically" revealed what goes on at these parties. So this time he said, "Wow, you really just don't understand." And she responded, "What don't I understand? Tell me what I don't understand." And he replied, "I'm not going to tell you that because the last time I told you I got in trouble." This effectively ended the conversation. But Steve added, "I would like it if we could talk about these things. I really don't like lying to my parents" (333).

He compared his situation to that of his best friend, whose parents, in his view, "do the freedom thing pretty well" (333). This friend is a very good student, and as long as he does his schoolwork "and doesn't screw up the rest of his life, he has a lot of freedom." His parents tell him that he can have a party at home and drink and smoke pot, but they have made it clear that if he ever "got into serious trouble" (got arrested or compromised himself academically) they "would kill him" (334).

Once, his friend's mother said to Steve, "I don't entirely understand your mom's thinking on this. We feel that if Keith wants to have a couple of kids over whom we know, who are close friends, and you guys want to smoke pot or something, that's okay" (334). What they *do* object to is doing it "stupidly," such as "running off to someone's party or going to Motel 6 and partying" (334). Steve says, "There's real honesty there, which I feel I don't have with my parents, and which I kind of envy" (334). He feels that his own mother says, in effect, that he isn't really allowed to do this stuff anywhere.

He concludes by saying that he thinks that he is "more logical" than his mother and that she's "more emotional," but he still has "a big chunk of emotion," and "that's part of the problem because [his] logic is generally beaten by her emotion" (334). An argument typically ends with his saying to her, "I've completely beaten you, you don't have a leg to stand on" to which she replies, "I don't care. I'm your mother, you still lost." So, he concludes, "I can't really win" (334).

Steve's conclusion—"I can't really win"—recalls Erikson's emphasis on the skirmishes, victories, and defeats that occur between parent and child (1959, 65) and the need for a child to experience some victories (1964a, 119). Thus, it invites us to consider Steve's account of the "confrontations" he experiences with his parents, especially his mother, in terms of the autonomy vs. shame and doubt conflict.

As we have seen, the two basic meanings of autonomy are self-governance and functioning independently without control by others. Steve discusses self-governance under the topic of his trustworthiness. He says that he had thought that his mother knew what goes on at the parties he attends, and that her willingness to allow him to go to parties, though with some obvious reluctance, was based on the fact that she "trusted [him] to handle [him]self and not do dumb stuff." The discussion at the table has led him to a different conclusion: "But then it came out that she really didn't trust me, and that she really had no idea what was going on" (333). He believes that he is capable of self-governance but suspects that his mother does not think that he is.

But why does he assume that she doesn't know what goes on at parties? One reason for assuming this is that his mother is inexperienced in these matters: she "never did any of that in high school and doesn't get it" (332). For him, her use of the rather archaic-sounding word "racy" is confirmation of this. He has a point: *racy* means "somewhat indecent; suggestive; risqué (a *racy* novel)" (Agnes 2001, 1181). On the other hand, he also seems to believe that she is being a bit disingenuous—seeming to know less than she really does—because he had informed his parents once before about the things that go on at parties, and because he did, he "got into trouble" (333). Then he adds, "I would like it if we could talk about these things. I really don't like lying to my parents" (333).

In other words, he believes that he is capable of self-governance at a party, knowing the difference between "o.k. stuff" and "dumb stuff," and that he can handle himself so that even if others do "dumb stuff," he doesn't join in. Kids don't all do the same things at a party. But his mother seems to feel that he cannot help but be affected by everything that goes on at these parties, and whether he himself engages in the "dumb stuff" or not, he is there, and he witnesses it, and this itself concerns her. For her, this is a different issue from the issue of whether he can be trusted to handle himself.

From his report of the conversation, it appears that she is genuinely ambivalent about the second issue and what she should do about it. She finally says, point blank, that she "does not think that [he] should be over there" (meaning the house where the parents ignore what is going on at the party in their home). But this statement was preceded by a great deal of innuendo and ambiguity, leading the reader to wonder if she herself is uncertain whether they should forbid him to attend any party, knowing that every party is likely to have some "dumb stuff" going on, or should they set this knowledge aside and rely on Steve's ability to govern himself?

Her rather caustic response to Steve's assurance that Brian's parents would be home—"Yeah, right. As if that means anything"—and what Steve calls the "raised-eyebrow crap" are rather indirect ways of saying that she would rather that Steve not go to these parties but is reluctant to forbid him to go.

This second issue relates to the second meaning of autonomy as "functioning independently without control by others." Steve experiences his mother's comments—"So I heard about Brian's party"—and her raised eyebrows as controlling, and especially reacts to the fact that they are indirect. He asks, "What's your implication? If you're implying something, get it out on the table." This leads to her "pretty racy party" comment, which Steve, knowing what goes on at these parties, finds "ridiculous" because, from his own perspective, there *are* things that go on at these parties that are completely out of line, and the word "racy" hardly describes how far out of line they really are. So we are now confronted with a paradox: they both have difficulties with what "goes on" at these parties, but her difficulties are based on a seeming ignorance of what actually goes on whereas his are based on firsthand knowledge. So now he wonders, Is she really that naïve?

This, it seems to me, raises a related issue, which is that if she thinks the parties are merely "racy," does she gain a certain voyeuristic pleasure from thinking about the parties and imagining what goes on, especially if she "never did any of that in high school"? If so, this would suggest that she is, in some sense, reliving her high school days through her son, and experiencing the same ambivalent feelings she probably had at the time—one part of her congratulating herself on her moral rectitude, the other part longing to be with the other kids and maybe allowing herself to get away with something her other self would frown on, if not condemn.

In the final analysis, however, the independence vs. control issue comes down to what Erikson calls "the guerilla warfare of unequal wills" (1959, 66) or, to change the metaphor, to his mother's ability to play the trump card in any dispute between them: "I don't care. I'm your mother, you still lost." So Steve is right: he can't win in any verbal debate with her because she has the power to declare who wins and who loses. And this is what he finds frustrating in "talking about these things" with her. The very discussion is about control, and this is probably the last remaining context in which she *can* exercise her control. After all, he goes to the parties and his parents are powerless—reluctant—to stop him. Having relinquished power over his behaviors, probably because she does trust him to avoid doing "dumb things," she still has a hold on him through verbal discourse.

Thus, the major change that occurs when we relocate the autonomy vs. shame and doubt conflict to the second decade of life is that language becomes a much more prominent locus of the conflict between independence seeking and control. Of course, the child in early childhood has begun to acquire language, and verbal refusal to comply with a parent's demand is certainly common. But Steve believes that there are appropriate ways to engage in an argument, that one should attempt to advance logical reasons for one's position, and that logic should prevail over mere emotion. On the other hand, Steve admits that his own arguments are not always impeccably logical, for he is also prone to emotion.

In effect, therefore, these verbal confrontations reflect what Erikson says about the internal split that the child begins to experience in the second stage of life. In the final paragraph of his discussion of the virtue of will, Erikson notes that whereas in the first stage of life, "the ideal ('pre-ambivalent,' as we say) image of the loving mother brought with it the child's self-image as reflecting that mother's true recognition of the child as hers and as good," the second stage introduces "the ambivalently loved image of the controlling parent," which corresponds "to an ambivalently loved self, or rather selves" (1964a, 120). From here on, "the able and the impotent, the loving and the angry, the unified and the self-contradictory selves will be part of man's equipment" (120). Steve can claim that he has logic on his side, but his logical self and his emotional self are at odds, and his confrontations with his mother are a reflection of this deeper split within himself.

However, because his overt conflicts are focused in this case around the mother-son relationship, the fact that the autonomy vs. shame and doubt conflict may involve multiple relationships does not come out as clearly as it might if, for example, Steve and his mother were talking about dating rather than going to parties. For example, another boy in Pollack's *Real Boys' Voices* tells about the girl who was "there to support [him]" when he was "going through some rough times with [his] mom" (263). But what does come out in Steve's story is the role of the other parents in relation to parties, and this brings us to the issue of shame.

Steve's opening sentence in the story of his "confrontation" with his mother mentions the parents of the kid who was hosting the party he attended. They were home, "but they are the type of parents who will deliberately look the other way," so much so that Steve feels that what they are doing is "pretty irresponsible" (332). Thus, he has no reason to challenge his mother's subsequent statement that the kid's parents "don't care and they're irresponsible" (333). On the matter of their irresponsibility, Steve and his mother are in complete agreement. Where their differences seem to lie is in what sorts of behaviors parents who *are* responsible should allow at a party in their home.

Here, Steve endorses the approach taken by the parents of his best friend Keith, noting that they "do the freedom thing pretty well," for as long as his friend "does his schoolwork and doesn't screw up the rest of his life" they give him "a lot of freedom" (333). In fact, Keith's mother told Steve that she is not as restrictive (what Steve calls being "anal") as his mother is on the issue. As she puts it, "I don't entirely understand your mom's thinking on this." She says that if her son wants to have a couple of kids over that his parents know, and they want to smoke pot together, that's fine with her. This is much better than if they were to "go running off to someone's party or go to Motel 6" (334).

But how different is this, in fact, from what Steve's mother is saying? Keith's mother seems to have the same objections as Steve's mother to parties where there is no parental supervision. If she had not prefaced her comments with "I don't entirely understand your mom's thinking on this," the reader might well have assumed that there was little difference between the two mothers, apart, perhaps, from the matter of smoking pot. (We assume that Steve's mother would object to smoking pot, but, if so, we don't know if Steve would agree with her or not, because he does not tell us what he himself thinks of it.)

Nonetheless, Steve uses the same word—"understand"—in his confrontation with his mother that Keith's mother uses in her comment about his mother: "Wow, you really just don't understand," to which she responded, "What don't I understand? Tell me what I don't understand!" Steve does not use the word *shame* in reference to his mother, and perhaps *shame* is too extreme of a word to invoke here, but I believe that he experiences shame because she is his mother. This, then, is not shame over his own improper behavior, incompetence, and so forth, but over what his mother says and does. As the previously quoted dictionary definition of shame suggests, one may feel a loss of the respect of others because of the improper behavior or incompetence of "someone that one is close to." Or, as Helen Merrell Lynd (1958) points out in her classic study of shame, "The impact of shame for others may reach even deeper than shame for ourselves" (56).

The shame has partly to do with the fact that Steve's mother appears to have her own ways of finding out what happens at parties: "So I heard about Brian's party." This would naturally cause Steve to wonder what his mother is up to, and is she saying or doing things that make her an embarrassment in the eyes of his friends. That Keith's mother knows, or thinks she knows, what Steve's mother thinks about parties suggests that his mother is not keeping her concerns about these parties to herself.

The shame also has to do with Steve's sense that his mother is something of an anachronism. She didn't go to parties when she was in high school; she uses words like "racy" to describe the parties that he goes to; and so on. His word "ridiculous" in reference to her "racy" statement suggests that she makes herself vulnerable to ridicule, and this, too, makes him feel shame because of her. His shame is not only due to what the other kids (or their parents) may think of her; it is also due to the shame he feels for her. He suspects, rightly or wrongly, that she really doesn't know what goes on at parties. Keith's mother comes across as a parent who knows what kids today are like and do. Steve's mother seems out of touch, and because she does, Steve feels shame—for her and for himself.

This, though, raises the related issue of doubt. Here, again, Steve does not experience doubt in the sense of self-doubt (at least, insofar as the issue of going to parties is concerned). He knows that he can be trusted not to do the "dumb things" that the other kids did at the party two weeks ago ("running around outside and getting drunk and that kind of thing"). In fact, he thinks his parents should trust him because he knows that he can trust himself.

Rather, his doubts have to do with his mother and what she thinks and feels. There is sufficient ambiguity or ambivalence in what she says to him—even in this brief vignette—that he cannot be certain about this. He would like for her to give him clear signals, to "get it out on the table," so they can talk about it rationally or "logically." Instead, she relies on implication ("raised eyebrows") and exaggeration ("If it's in my house, I'll kill you" and "If you do it anywhere else, then I'll kill you"). He compares Keith's mother's statement with his own mother's way of communicating and says that there is "real honesty there, which I feel I don't have with my parents, and which I kind of envy" (334).

But it is relatively easy to see that his mother's use of implication, innuendo, ambiguity, and so forth is a means of control, especially, as he himself discerns, of emotional control, which is all the more powerful because she is "ambivalently loved." As already noted, he realizes that his claim to be the logical one while she is emotional is a bit overdrawn, as he, too, has "a big chunk of emotion," but his observation that in battles with his mother logic is no match for emotion seems entirely right. As a result, he seems to regret being drawn into these controversies and to feel that he sabotages himself because he has "a big chunk of emotion" that will not allow him to disregard the raised eyebrows and hyperbole ("I'll kill you").

Are Erikson's words of advice about how parents can help their child develop a genuine sense of autonomy relevant to this case? He suggests that the child's sense of autonomy depends on "the dignity and the sense of personal independence" that the parents derive from their own lives. There is insufficient evidence from this brief vignette to enable us to decide whether his mother, especially, possesses such dignity and sense of personal independence. But what *does* seem clear is that Steve wishes this for her because, apart from the issue of partying, his "relationship with [his] parents is really good" (332). If she were to know that he believes this about their relationship, and if she were to believe that he is right about it, she might not feel that confrontations like the one that Steve describes are necessary at all.

In the final analysis, the relationship between a parent and a son (or daughter) should not be a matter of winners and losers. The very fact that Steve shares his mother's belief that the parents of the kid who hosted the party two weeks ago "don't care" and are "pretty irresponsible" indicates how much the two of them are in agreement. Steve's mother should not ignore or thoughtlessly squander this agreement by placing her son in the position of having to defend what he himself believes is indefensible. On the other hand, this very agreement may well be grounds for Steve to make a voluntary decision to forgo the parties at Brian's house, thus demonstrating to his mother that he is a person of goodwill—that he is able to exercise both free choice and self-restraint and to recognize that maintaining a "really good" relationship with his parents "depends on a mutual limitation of wills" (1964a, 119).

This discussion of Steve's lament—"I really can't win"—shows, I believe, that the autonomy vs. shame and doubt conflict is operative even in cases that do not seem, on the face of it, to have a great deal to do with this conflict. The only overt tip-off is Steve's use of the word "freedom" to describe what his friend Keith's parents afford their son, and even the word "freedom" fails to convey the full meaning of autonomy.

MARGARET: "EVEN A HARD LOOK MADE ME BOW MY HEAD IN SHAME"

Steve's autonomy vs. shame and doubt conflicts centered around parties. In the following case, the issue is an unwanted pregnancy. There is no need for us to make invidious comparisons between the two by suggesting that struggles over parties seem rather insignificant when pitted against pregnancies, for this would detract attention from the fact that virtually all individuals in the second decade of life experience the autonomy vs. shame and doubt conflict.

In *Waiting to Forget* Margaret Moorman (1996), who grew up in Arlington, Virginia, tells the story of how she became pregnant at age fifteen and gave up her son for adoption. She wrote her story when she was forty years old, shortly after the birth of her daughter, for she realized that she was excessively anxious about her daughter's safety as a result of the fact that she had given her first child away. Her pregnancy at age fifteen occurred a few months after her older sister had returned from an eighteen-month stay in a mental hospital and her father had died of a sudden heart attack on New Year's Eve. Despite the fact that her mother and sister were home when her father suffered his heart attack, Margaret was the one who called an ambulance and covered her father's body until the ambulance arrived, and that night she told herself that she must be "the strong one."

When she was thirteen, and in eighth grade, her mother had encouraged her involvement with a college boy they had met on vacation in southern Virginia.

Decades later, when Judy Blume's books for preteens were becoming popular, her mother suggested that she write a book of her own "about a mother who flirts with a college boy and keeps him around by encouraging her young daughter to go out with him" (25).

As she entered ninth grade, she found another boy her own age, and although they kissed at parties, he had none of the "needs" that her previous boyfriend had expressed, and she was "relieved to be rid of sexual pressures" (26). But before long this boy also broke up with her. She felt bereft, and one chilly, lonely night she picked up a razor from her dresser and made a shallow, exploratory slice across her left wrist. She told her parents what she had done, was rushed to an emergency room far from their neighborhood so that no one they knew would learn about it, and her mother asked her if she wanted to talk to her sister's psychiatrist. She gave this some thought, then decided no, and concluded that she had two choices: be like her sister or pull herself together.

She began dating Dan, a boy from her church, and in the wake of her father's death, she felt that the best way to keep her grief "in its place" was to keep herself busy, "to be physically involved in some activity that took [her] mind off the troubles of [her] heart" (29). Necking for countless hours with Dan in the back seat of his family's car was effective in this regard, and in April they decided to try sexual intercourse, making elaborate plans for the evening in which they would consummate their relationship. She calculated her menstrual period and decided that it would be perfectly safe that evening, but later learned to her enormous regret that she should have counted from the first day of her last period rather than the last. For his part, Dan had thought that he could drop into a restaurant they knew of on the way to the woods and purchase a condom from the machine in the men's room. But when he returned to the car, he said, "No machine."

By July she was certain that she was pregnant, and she knew that she would have to stop going to church because she sang in the choir. She had spent her childhood and teenage years in Sunday School, Methodist Youth Fellowship, and the choir. But now that she was pregnant, it was embarrassing to sit down in the middle of a hymn in front of the congregation: "And besides, I was by now beginning to lose even that minimal faith that had made church service possible for me" (39).

Sometime in July Margaret and Dan informed her mother, announcing that they were going to get married and were going to have a baby. Her mother's reaction was explosive: "How could you do this to me? How could you?" (39). Finally, her mother calmed down and asked how far along she was. When informed she had gotten pregnant in April, her mother replied, "Jesus Christ. It's too late for an abortion. Why the *hell* didn't you tell me before this?" The following days were filled with humiliation, as her mother and Dan's father alternately derided and harangued them. The only support she received was from Dan's mother: "Alone of our three parents, she never directed a single wounding remark my way. I was in the sort of emotional state where even a hard look made me bow my head in shame. She not only never looked at me that way, but when her husband asked us such contemptuous questions as 'What makes you think you could raise a child?' it was she, my silent, helpless ally, whose eyes turned down" (40).

The subsequent events were orchestrated by her mother and Dan's father. Dan left for basic training in the Army and anticipated that they would marry after she graduated from high school, which was two years away. But "subconsciously, [she] was making other plans" (60). She decided to give her baby up for adoption, knowing that this was what her mother and Dan's father wanted, and spent the rest of her pregnancy in a private home for young women who came from southern colleges to student teach in the highly rated Arlington school district. Her son was born and was placed with an adoption agency, and she returned to school in midyear.

Back in school, she said she "was cut off from [her] friends": "I had been altered, first by my father's death and then by my pregnancy, and I could not seem to re-enter the world of classes and church choirs and weekend dates, much as I wanted to. I was nothing like the 'good' girls who studied and joined clubs that performed community service. Nor was I like the girls who in those days were called 'fast,' who seemed to be enjoying themselves and hoping their luck would hold. I was brokenhearted" (81). Some of her teachers "could not bring themselves to look at" her, but there was one, Mr. Shelton, her English teacher, who shook her hand and told her he was delighted to have her in his class. But as if her return to school were not difficult enough, the first book studied in the second semester of junior English was Nathaniel Hawthorne's *The Scarlet Letter*. Mr. Shelton smiled encouragingly in her direction several times a day and did not call on her until the class had moved on to another text.

By spring she must have been feeling better, because she joined a new friend who wanted to try out for cheerleading. Week after week Margaret practiced, and several of the cheerleader coaches predicted that she would be chosen. On the afternoon of the tryouts, with five teachers—the judges—seated at a long table at one end of the gymnasium, her name was called, and she "began to do [her] stuff" (81). In practice, she had smiled and even laughed as the girls went through the "ridiculous motions together," but now the muscles of her face refused to form a smile: "The teacher-judges, looking as uncomfortable as I felt, saw a trim, strong teenager leaping and yelling with all her might, but with a grim expression on her knowing face" (81). It was then she realized that as a happy-looking girl she was a fraud: "An infinitesimal part of me also knew that I was too smart for this nonsense. In my reduced state, that inkling led not to self-respect, as it might well have, but to the simple certainty that I just did not belong" (82).

Eventually, Margaret, now in her forties, was able to find out the whereabouts of her son. She wrote him, and he responded with a letter that informed her that his life had turned out well, but he suggested that it would not be good for them to meet, for now, because "it might cause his mother to worry" (214). Enormously relieved, for several days, she would hold the letter, touch it, quote it, and as she looked for the right safe place to put it, her husband said, "Just don't try to bronze it" (214). She returned to college, which had been interrupted because she found she could not concentrate on her courses, and devoted herself to the cause of mental illness, her sister having been diagnosed with bipolar disorder (Moorman, 1992). Her memoir ends on a grateful note: "I close my eyes and say the prayer of thanks that I have wanted to say for years. Thank you, God, for all your blessings. Thank you for the daughter, thank you for the son" (214).

This is a story of shame and doubt, but it is also a story of how a new sense of autonomy emerges from this very shame and doubt. Margaret's shame and loss of self-respect dramatically altered her interpersonal relationships, as old friends were lost and most teachers avoided her; even more importantly, she herself realized that she could no longer fit herself into the high school ethos. Similarly, religious doubt, following on the heels of shame, led to her decision to leave the church, the very community in which she had grown up and she and Dan had met.

But deeper than her doubts about the faith in which she had been raised were her doubts about herself. These doubts reflected her loss of confidence in the sense of autonomy that she formed around her self-perception as "the strong one." Based on what happened the night her father died, she had felt that she, despite the fact that her mother and sister were older, needed to be the strong one, the one who was capable of governing her emotions at a critical time and doing what needed to be done. When she became involved with Dan, she had again believed that she was capable of maintaining control over the situation, that she and Dan could engage in sexual intercourse in an intelligent and prudent manner that would preclude an unwanted pregnancy. But this time, her capacity to exercise self-control was insufficient, for what she also needed was accurate knowledge about when it is safe to engage in sexual intercourse. This mistake unleashed a series of events in which she came to doubt herself.

Yet out of the pain and struggle that followed a new and different sense of autonomy emerged, one based on the awareness that our own autonomy is circumscribed by events and forces that are outside and beyond our control. This is not heteronomy, for heteronomy involves a sense of being subject to foreign control, a situation in which the claim to personal autonomy is so much whistling in the dark. Rather, it is a form of autonomy that recognizes that we are not the masters of our fate, but that this does not mean that we should relinquish our freedom to act, to decide, to make things happen.

This is the autonomy that Erikson identifies in his observation that despite the fact that one is often defeated, one "nevertheless learns to accept the existential paradox of making decisions which he knows 'deep down' will be predetermined by events, because making decisions is part of the evaluative quality inherent in being alive" (1964a, 199). This chastened yet vital sense of autonomy enables Margaret to conclude her memoir with a deeply felt expression of gratitude to God for her life: "I close my eyes and say the prayer of thanks that I have wanted to say for years."

THE WILLING SELF

When the virtue of will is located in early childhood, it is inevitable that discussion will center on the conflict of wills between the adult and the child. This very conflict is the focus of Carl E. Pickhardt's (2005) book for parents on "the strong-willed child." He believes, however, that this conflict of wills can be transformed into a spirit of willingness but observes that "many parents seem most aware of willingness when they don't get it, taking it for granted when they do" (60).

The cases of Steve and Margaret indicate that the development of the disposition of willingness, of doing what is expected of oneself in a cheerful and voluntary spirit, is neither easy nor assured, but these cases also suggest that the predisposition for such willingness exists, and that oftentimes all that is needed to bring it out into the open is the kindly attention of a Mr. Shelton, the English teacher who shook Margaret's hand and told her how delighted he was to have her in his class.

PART TWO
THE YOUNGER-ADULT
DECADES

Chapter 3

The Third Decade:
The Purposeful Self

Finding a "milestone" birthday card for a person turning twenty is more difficult than finding one for a person turning one hundred. The reason for this is not that the birthday card manufacturers think more persons will be turning one hundred than twenty. Rather, it's that in American culture turning *twenty-one* is a bigger milestone than turning twenty. Twenty-one is the age when one may legally buy liquor and order an alcoholic drink in a restaurant or bar; thus a birthday card for a twenty-one-year-old says, "A lot of people stay home on their 21st birthday. They're called losers. Go out and have a good one!"

Another card for a twenty-one-year-old says, "Everyone's eagerly anticipating your 21st birthday—your friends, your family, your coworkers, the bartender, the bouncer, the police, the judge." This one has an implicit cautionary note, but it's the same basic message: now you can drink legally in any bar in the country. Another one suggests that the recipient of the card has had to wait an awful long time for this day. It says, "Here's a joke for you on your 21st birthday: A guy goes into a bar. . . . Finally."

No doubt, in years past, when the legal voting age was also twenty-one, turning twenty-one meant that the right to vote and the right to purchase alcohol went hand in hand, and together they signaled that society believed that you were now responsible for your actions and your parents were no longer responsible for your debts. You are now on your own and capable of making a life for yourself. With the legal voting age changed to eighteen and turning twenty-one now viewed as the event when you can drink, the notion that turning twenty-one equals being a responsible adult has been, as it were, watered down.

Because this book emphasizes decades, this change in the significance of turning twenty-one is somewhat irrelevant. In fact, it goes against the conventional wisdom reflected in the birthday cards that twenty-one marks a big turning point. It suggests that it is much more significant that in turning twenty you have left the teen years behind. In this sense, turning twenty-one is a rather insignificant event in comparison to the experience of entering one's twenties.

Following the sequence of Erikson's life stages, I assign the initiative vs. guilt conflict to the third decade of life. In his original schema this conflict occurs in the play age (ages three-and-a-half to five) that precedes the school age. When Erikson was working out his life-cycle model in the 1940s, there were few preschools, and a minority of children attended nursery schools. I doubt, however, that he would have changed his model to reflect this widespread societal change. Instead, he may well have emphasized even more strongly that despite the fact that these children are in a school environment, the emphasis should continue to be on play. In one sense, this issue is irrelevant when we relocate the initiative vs. guilt conflict to the third decade of life. But we should keep in mind that its original locus was the play age, so perhaps in this rather limited sense, the birthday cards get it right when they advise those who are turning twenty-one not to stay at home alone but to go out and play with their friends.

THE INITIATIVE VS. GUILT CONFLICT

Webster's defines *initiative* as "the action of taking the first step or move; responsibility for beginning or originating," and the "ability to think and act without being urged" (Agnes 2001, 735). It defines *guilt* as "the state of having done a wrong or committed an offense" and "a painful feeling of self-reproach resulting from a belief that one has done something wrong" (632). What constitutes a *wrong*? Essentially, something that is "not in accordance with an established standard, previous arrangement, given intention, etc." (1653). Thus, the initiative vs. guilt conflict centers to a great extent on being active, or being an actor and not a passive observer. It also concerns responsibility, both for beginning or originating something, and for being held personally accountable for what one has done. Because one acts on one's own accord and does not simply wait for instructions or demands issuing from others, one is liable to make mistakes or errors of judgment, and to fail to achieve the intended outcome. When these things happen, one cannot simply shift the blame onto others. Thus, if one is honest with oneself, self-reproach is virtually inevitable.

In the first paragraph of his discussion of initiative vs. guilt in *Childhood and Society*, Erikson (1963) notes that initiative builds on the autonomy of the preceding stage: "Initiative adds to autonomy the quality of undertaking, planning and 'attacking' a task for the sake of being active and on the move" (255). In *Identity and the Life Cycle* (1959), he suggests that there are three strong capacities involved in the development of initiative: (1) the child learns to move around more freely and more violently and therefore establishes a wider radius of goals; (2) the child's sense of language becomes perfected to the point where he understands and can ask about many things just enough to misunderstand them thoroughly; and (3) both language and locomotion permit the child to expand his imagination over so many things that he cannot avoid frightening himself with what he himself has dreamed and thought up (75). Thus, movement, language, and imagination are central to the child's capacity for initiative.

The most important evidence that a sense of initiative is developing is that the child seems to be "self-activated": "He is in free possession of a certain surplus of energy which permits him to forget failures quickly and to approach what seems desirable (even if it also seems dangerous) with undiminished and better aimed effort" (75). Erikson places particular emphasis on the ability of the child to move around. A child can walk long before the end of the third year, but "from the point of view of personality development he cannot really walk as long as he is only able to accomplish the feat more or less well, with more or fewer props, for short spans of time" (75). As the fourth year gets underway, the child makes "walking and running an item in his sphere of mastery when gravity is felt to be *within*, when he can forget that he is doing the walking and instead can find out what he can do *with* it" (75).

If the child in the second stage became adept at piling things up and throwing them away with a bang, the child in the third stage becomes intrusive, including intrusion into other bodies by physical attack, into other people's ears and minds by aggressive talking, into space by vigorous locomotion, and into the unknown by consuming curiosity, some of which is sexual in a rudimentary sort of way. If "holding on" and "letting go" were basic social modalities in the second stage, the basic social modality in the third stage is "being on the make," which suggests enjoyment of competition, insistence on goals, and pleasure of conquest.

If the struggle for autonomy was concentrated on keeping younger rivals (a baby sister or brother) out, the struggle for initiative "brings with it *anticipatory rivalry* with those who were there first and who may therefore occupy with their superior equipment the field toward which one's initiative is directed" (79). Thus, rivalry with an older sibling is its most obvious form, but there may also be a rivalry with one parent for a favored position with the other parent.

This sense of rivalry and jealousy introduces the issue of guilt, the negative tendency of this life stage. Erikson emphasizes that not all of the child's initiative is necessarily well-intentioned. Some of it may be destructive. Yet he also believes that there is little in the child's development "which cannot be harnessed to constructive and peaceful initiative" if the adults with whom the child interacts can "learn to understand the conflicts and anxieties of childhood" (79). The child's own development of a conscience during this stage, which begins with the internalization of the parental voice, also plays an important role.

In *Childhood and Society*, Erikson (1950) notes that the development of a conscience means that the child's psyche is split between "an infantile set which perpetuates the exuberance of growth potentials, and a parental set which supports and increases self-observation, self-guidance, and self-punishment" (225). In *Identity and the Life Cycle* (1959), he notes that conscience is "the cornerstone of morality in the individual sense" (80). He recognizes that there are children whose conscience is too lax and permissive, but he is especially concerned for the child whose "conscience is primitive, cruel, and uncompromising," which is observable in instances where children "learn to constrict themselves to the point of overall inhibition; where they develop an obedience more literal than the one the parent wishes to exact; or where they develop deep regression and lasting resentments because the parents themselves do not seem to live up to the new conscience which they have fostered in the child" (80).

Erikson suggests that the effects of a largely punitive conscience in childhood may continue to reverberate in adulthood. For example, the self-restriction in childhood may inhibit the adult "from living up to his inner capacities or to the powers of his imagination and feeling" (81). This may, in turn, lead to overcompensation, expressed in "a great show of tireless initiative, in a quality of 'go-at-itiveness' at all cost" (81). Many adults, he notes, feel that their worth as people consists entirely in what they are doing, or rather in what they are going to do next, and not in what they are as individuals. The strain that this causes in their bodies, "which are always 'on the go,' with the engine racing, even at moments of rest, is a powerful contribution to the much-discussed psychosomatic diseases of our time" (81). Here, Erikson anticipates by some forty to fifty years the emphasis on stress and its mental and physiological effects that we hear so much about today.

In the concluding paragraph of the revised edition of *Childhood and Society,* Erikson (1963) ends his discussion of initiative vs. guilt on a decidedly positive note. He points out that there is no other stage of the life cycle in which the child is "more ready to learn quickly and avidly" and to "become bigger in the sense of sharing obligation and performance" (258). The child "is eager and able to make things cooperatively, to combine with other children for the purpose of constructing and planning," and is willing "to profit from teachers and to emulate ideal prototypes" (258). In *Identity and the Life Cycle* (1959), he identifies these ideal prototypes as people who represent "occupations which the child can grasp: firemen and policemen, gardeners and plumbers" (81–82). Preschools emphasize sharing and working cooperatively through play and encourage children to enter imaginatively into the work roles of productive adults through the use of toys, augmented by stories that are read to them by their teachers.

In his last sustained discussion of children's play in *Toys and Reasons*, Erikson

(1977) declared that the best—also the briefest—formulation of play is to be found in Plato's *Laws*. Plato, he noted, "sees the model of true playfulness in the need of all young creatures, animal and human, to leap. To truly leap, you must learn how to use the ground as a springboard, and how to land resiliently and safely" (17). It also means testing "the leeway allowed by given limits, to outdo and yet not escape gravity," and this implies that "wherever playfulness prevails, there is always a surprising element, surpassing mere repetition or habituation, and at its best suggesting some virgin chance conquered, some divine leeway shared" (17).

Thus, against the inhibition that an overly severe conscience may produce in a child—and an adult—playfulness recognizes the inherent flexibility of laws of nature and of society and takes advantage of the leeway given. Plato's image of leaping implies physical movement, but as the child grows and eventually reaches young adulthood, language and imagination are even more likely to afford occasions for testing the leeway allowed by the given limits we confront in all forms of human social life.

In the revised edition of *Childhood and Society*, Erikson (1963) proposes that the institutional form related to the initiative vs. guilt stage is a society's "economic ethos" (258). This proposal is consistent with his acknowledgement that although initiative "is a necessary part of every act, and man needs a sense of initiative for whatever he learns and does," the word *initiative* has an "industrial connotation" (255). In *Toys and Reasons* (1977), he added the idea that, because the play age is also the dramatic age, this age is also reflected in the theatre (98–103). Both proposals are implied in his observation in *Childhood and Society* that the economic ethos appears to young children in "the form of ideal adults recognizable by their uniforms and their functions, and fascinating enough to replace the heroes of picture book and fairy tale" (258). Thus, the economic ethos is reflected in ideal adults recognizable by their uniforms and social functions, while the dramatic ethos is manifested in heroes and heroines who capture the child's imagination and encourage the child to aspire to the heroic life.

THE VIRTUE OF PURPOSE

In his essay on "Human Strength and the Cycle of Generations" (1964a), Erikson assigns the virtue of purpose to the third stage of the life cycle. *Webster's* defines *purpose* as (1) "something one intends to get or do"; (2) "resolution [or] determination"; and (3) "the object for which something exists or is done; end in view." *Purposeful* means "resolutely aiming at a specific goal" or "directed toward a specific end"; thus the action or activity is "not meaningless," whereas *purposeless* implies action or activity that is aimless (Agnes 2001, 1165). Thus, if *initiative* connotes action or agency as opposed to inaction or passivity, *purpose* adds that the action is goal directed and has a reason behind it. Put another way, the purpose of the action is not merely for the sake of being active.

Reflecting his view that the virtue of purpose originates in the initiative vs. guilt stage, Erikson (1964a) sees purpose as "the courage to envisage and pursue valued goals uninhibited by the defeat of infantile fantasies, by guilt and by the foiling fear of punishment" (122). Elaborating on this definition, he says that purpose is "the strength of aim-direction fed by fantasy yet not fantastic, limited by guilt yet not inhibited, morally restrained yet ethically active" (122). This means, of course, that the purpose expressed by the small child is rather rudimentary in comparison to that of the adult. On the other hand, because the adult's sense of purpose has its origins in child's play, there is "a residue of play-acting and role-acting even in what he considers his highest purposes" (122).

Erikson emphasizes that purpose is based on the previous virtue of will. Will needs to be trained to set its sights on certain goals, for otherwise it will degenerate into mere willfulness. This is where purpose comes in. For the child, play is the context in which the rudiments of purpose are formed: "Play is to the child what thinking, planning, and blue-printing are to the adult, a trial universe in which conditions are simplified and methods exploratory, so that past failures can be thought through, expectations tested" (1964a, 120).

In the toy world, the child "plays out" the past and "begins to master the future by anticipating it in countless variations of repetitive themes" (120). (In chapter 1, we saw how Erikson used the tendency of the child to play out the past in his therapeutic work with the five-year-old boy named Sam.) Moreover, by taking the various role images of his elders "into his sphere of make-believe, he can find out how it feels to be like them before fate forces him to become, indeed, like some of them" (120–21).

Some adults think that the child at this age "spends on his play a sincere purposefulness out of proportion to what he soon must learn, namely, what things are 'really for,' what their 'real purpose' is" (121). Parents who think this way may push the child's preschool teachers to include "more serious" and "more useful" material in the curriculum. But, in Erikson's view, they underestimate "the evolutionary necessity for representational play in an animal who must learn to bind together an inner and an outer world, a remembered past and an anticipated future, before he can learn to master the tools used in co-operation, the roles distributed in a community, and the purposes pursued in a given technology" (121).

I propose locating the initiative vs. guilt conflict in the third decade of life for several reasons. First, it is the decade in American culture when one is expected to become an adult who is no longer dependent primarily or exclusively on one's parents for the basic necessities of life. This means that one needs to settle on an occupation or profession (which may, of course, include the profession of homemaker). In other words, it is the decade in which one's life focuses on initiative, on taking responsibility for becoming a worker and making important decisions for one's life without having to be urged by others—parents, siblings, friends, and other interested adults. The fact that Erikson identifies the economic ethos as the institutional safeguard of this stage supports this relocation of the initiative vs. guilt conflict to the third decade of life.

Second, the third decade is also the time when one is especially prone to guilt if one is floundering as far as establishing oneself is concerned. Some twenty-year-olds have considerable difficulty figuring out what they want to do with their lives, and this seems especially problematic when it involves vocational indecision. The longer it takes twenty-year-olds to make this decision, the guiltier they are likely to become. As we have seen, a wrong is something that is not in accordance with an established standard, previous arrangement, or given intention. The failure to settle on an occupation or profession in one's early to mid-twenties is not in accordance with established standards, and because this is so, one is very likely to feel inwardly guilty even when others are tolerant or even sympathetic. In *Identity and the Life Cycle* and *Identity: Youth and Crisis*, Erikson (1959, 91; 1968, 131) cites the moment in Arthur Miller's *Death of a Salesman* when Biff, the son of Willy Loman, confesses to his mother, "I just can't take hold, Mom, I can't take hold of some kind of life."[1]

A third reason for locating the initiative vs. guilt conflict in this decade arises from Erikson's suggestion that in the third stage of life one develops a rudimentary sense of life as theatre that takes the form of an identification with the heroes and heroines that one role plays with toy figures (such as firefighters and soldiers) or learns about through inspiring stories of heroes—especially animals who risk their lives to rescue or protect weaker animals from danger and threat.

This sense of theatre is reflected in the third decade of life in what Daniel J. Levinson in *The Seasons of a Man's Life* (1978) identifies as the developmental task of forming and living out one's Dream (91). In its primordial form, it is a vague sense of the self-in-adult world: "It has the quality of a vision, an imagined possibility that generates excitement and vitality" but "is poorly articulated and only tenuously connected to reality" (91). In this nascent stage, it might take "a dramatic form as in the myth of the hero: the great artist, business tycoon, athletic or intellectual superstar performing magnificent feats and receiving special honors" or it might assume "mundane forms that are yet inspiring and sustaining: the excellent craftsman, the husband-father in a certain kind of family, the highly respected member of one's community" (91). Whatever its initial form, the "young man has the developmental task of giving it greater definition and finding ways to live it out" (91). In *The Seasons of a Woman's Life*, Levinson (1997) provides a similar account of the young woman's formation and living out of the dream (231–33).

A fourth reason, one that is often related to the second reason, concerns what we may call the inhibition vs. initiative conflict with which many persons in their

---

1. Biff is thirty-four years old, so he is no longer in the third decade of his life. But he tells his brother Happy that he spent six or seven years of his life after high school trying to work himself up in various jobs in business of one kind or another and hated the idea of having to compete with "the other guy" in order to "build a future." He has recently returned home after realizing that his job working on a horse farm in Texas wasn't the way to "be makin' my future" (Miller 1976, 22). Thus, the third decade of life may be viewed as the decade in which one is, or should be, making a future for oneself.

twenties struggle. The dictionary definition of purposeful is especially relevant in this regard, as it suggests that the individual is resolutely aiming at a specific goal and that this goal is meaningful to the individual. Yet, as Erikson points out, inhibition presents a powerful threat to purposeful initiative. In *Identity and the Life Cycle* (1959), he notes that the child's conscience may not allow him to pursue this goal. An uncompromising conscience may cause certain children to "learn to constrict themselves to the point of overall inhibition," and this self-restriction in early childhood may inhibit the adult "from living up to his inner capacities or to the powers of his imagination and feeling" (80–81).

Because the inhibition is due to one's conscience and not, for example, to one's lack of interest or other limiting factors (physical or mental), the inhibition is due to the sense of guilt that arises when one works toward the realization of a specific goal. Prohibition is an external threat to one's purpose, but inhibition is an internal one. This inhibition derives from the internalization of a "parental set" that "supports and increases self-observation, self-guidance, and self-punishment" against the child's more natural "infantile set," which "perpetuates the exuberance of growth potentials" (1950, 225).

Erikson's own vocational struggles in the third decade of his life illustrate this inhibition, so I will discuss his case before moving to more contemporary examples of the centrality of the initiative vs. guilt conflict in this decade of life.

ERIK: THE INHIBITED ARTIST

During the first three years of his life, when he and his mother were living alone, Erikson's mother's best friends were artists who painted in a folk style popular in the region. In his autobiographical essay (1975), he noted that these artists "provided my first male imprinting" (27). He attended school and synagogue; then, following graduation from *Gymnasium* at age eighteen, he enrolled in art school but also took to wandering. In his case, the traditional year of wandering extended to several years, during which he viewed himself as an aspiring artist.

Looking back, he considered these years "an important part of my training," noting that sketching "can be a fundamental exercise in tracing impressions," and that his work on very large woodprints "conveyed an elemental sense of both art and craft" (28). He traveled to Italy in order to gain a firsthand impression of the scenes that had so captivated Van Gogh. But this is where his problems began. In his biography of Erikson, Lawrence J. Friedman (1999) notes that Erikson "bemoaned the fact that he 'never learned to paint w/ color.' He tried to move beyond 'black and white drawing and woodcuts' and felt that if he wanted a significant career as an artist, he would have to do so. But he could not develop a facility for the use of color and paint; that 'was where the inhibition was,' he recalled" (47). He eventually settled in Florence, but by this time he had pretty much abandoned a career as an artist.

During his sojourn in Italy, he carried around a bound book of large sheets of paper intended for sketching but instead filled its pages with jottings that were abstract, philosophical, and random, lacking any perceptible thematic unity. He returned home to Karlsruhe at the age of twenty-three in a dejected state of mind, and the next couple of years he was, as he put it, "a nonfunctioning artist" suffering from a serious "work disturbance." He added, "There were simply months when I couldn't work at all and didn't feel like putting anything on paper." Often he "did not feel like doing anything at all" (Friedman 1999, 36).

He was considering the possibility of becoming a local arts and crafts teacher when an old friend from their school days, Peter Blos, invited him to come to Vienna to sketch portraits of the children of Dorothy Burlingham. He was not informed as to the motivation behind this invitation. Burlingham had started a school for the children who were either patients, the children of patients, or the children of psychoanalysts practicing in Vienna. The invitation extended to Erikson would enable her to decide whether to accept Blos's recommendation that Erik would join him as a teacher at the newly established school. He later wrote of Blos's recommendation, "Nietzsche once said that a friend is the life saver who holds you above water when your divided selves threaten to drag you to the bottom" (Friedman 1999, 56).

Erik went to Vienna, sketched the portraits, and was offered the teaching position. Thus began his association with Freud's circle. Freud's daughter Anna encouraged him to consider a career as a psychoanalyst, and he was reluctant at first. But he agreed to give it a try, and at the age of twenty-seven began his training analysis with her while continuing to teach in the school.

When Erikson referred to his inability to work with paints and color, he used the word inhibition. *Webster's* defines *inhibition* as a mental or psychological process that restrains or suppresses an action, emotion, or thought (Agnes 2001, 735). Thus, there was more to Erikson's problems with painting than the matter of technical skill. A chart in *Vital Involvement in Old Age* (Erikson, Erikson, & Kivnick 1986) assigns a maladaptive and malignant tendency to each of the life stages, the maladaptive being an excess of the positive dimension and the malignant being an excess of the negative. In this chart, inhibition is the malignant tendency in the initiative vs. guilt stage, and ruthlessness is the maladaptive tendency (45). Thus, "in the third, the play age, an initiative not balanced by a sufficient capacity for guilt may condone an all too guiltless *ruthlessness*," and "an excessive tendency toward guilt and thus an impairment of purpose may result in a malignant *self-inhibition*" (43).

What was behind Erikson's inhibition? In his autobiographical essay, Erikson notes that his stepfather "expected me to become a doctor like himself" (1975, 27). But "like other youths with artistic or literary aspirations, I became intensely alienated from everything my bourgeois family stood for" (28). Thus, the inhibition from which he suffered in the years in which he believed himself to be an artist was prompted by guilt, guilt for what appeared to be a sense of ingratitude for the "legitimacy" his stepfather had bestowed on him when he insisted that little Erik was to be told that his mother's new husband was his biological father. Years later, Erikson applauded his mother and stepfather for "the fortitude to let me find my way unhurriedly," yet he also knew that his stepfather was growing increasingly impatient with the wanderings of "the strange boy he brought up." As Friedman points out, he would have been even more uneasy if he had known that Erikson's mother had assisted her son in this regard by passing to Erik "considerable money through a distant relative who ran a bank" (Friedman 1999, 48).

Erikson did not become a pediatrician. But, as he observes in his autobiographical essay, his "first acquaintance with the psychoanalytic view of childhood coincided with a period of daily contact with children" (1975, 29) as a teacher in Dorothy Burlingham's school. He began his career as a child analyst and emphasized the importance of play therapy. This was not the artist's career that he had desired, and it was not the career in pediatrics that his stepfather envisioned, but it was a workable compromise, and he could invest himself in *this* career path with initiative and a sense of purpose.

Erikson's vocational struggles in his twenties are thus a good example of the initiative vs. guilt conflict. He had some sense of initiative in that he took initial steps toward becoming an artist. But he did not attend art school on a regular basis, and he invested several years in this career choice without a great deal to show for it. Conceivably, if he *had* been able to master the use of paint and color and produce some impressive paintings, his stepfather may have accepted the fact that his son had artistic talent and encouraged him in this direction. But he could not develop these skills precisely because this would have been persuasive evidence that he could become the artist he aspired to be. More than technical inadequacies, which could have been overcome by further training, guilt foreclosed this vocational option.

No doubt, his acceptance of money from his mother and his awareness that she was sending the money secretly so that her husband would not find out added to his sense of guilt. Not only was he *not* following his stepfather's wishes; he was also using his stepfather's money to fund his alternative career choice. Thus a guilty conscience was largely responsible for the fact that he became a "nonfunctioning artist," and when he returned home in defeat, he spent several months in hopeless despair, contemplating a career as an arts and crafts teacher but without taking the initiative to make such a career a reality.

His quotation from Friedrich Nietzsche refers to a person's "divided selves." He was terribly divided, and the career on which he eventually embarked, as a child analyst with particular emphasis on play therapy, healed the split between his two selves by integrating the role that his stepfather wanted him to play—caring for children—and the role that he had wanted to play—the "elemental sense of art and craft" reflected in children's play. In this profession, he could live up "to his inner capacities" and "to the powers of his imagination and feeling" (1959, 81).

SALLY: "SOMEONE TELL ME WHAT TO DO!"

In *The Seasons of a Woman's Life*, Daniel J. Levinson (1996) reports on the findings from a research study based on intensive biographical interviewing of forty-five women born between 1935 and 1945. The interviews were conducted from 1980–82, so these women were between ages thirty-five and forty-five when the interviewing began. The women divided equally into three groups of fifteen: homemakers, women with corporate-financial careers, and women with academic careers. The study confirmed the basic findings of Levinson's earlier study of men, which had led him to propose a life-structure model whose key feature was that human lives follow a rhythmic pattern of several years of stability followed by somewhat fewer years of transition. I will use two of his cases as illustrations of the initiative vs. guilt conflict in the third decade of life.

When Sally Wolford (a pseudonym), one of the career women, was in high school, she wanted to be an accountant like her father: "But he discouraged me. He said there were very few opportunities for women, and they got stuck doing boring work. He thought I should go out and get married and be pretty and have fun. That was what a girl should do in those days. Nobody wanted me to have a career—nobody. I vaguely thought about it but couldn't take it seriously" (209).

She went to college, but when she graduated at twenty-one, she thought, "What am I supposed to do with my life? Someone tell me what to do! It was like looking over the edge of a vast precipice. I didn't know where to start. I felt the world was coming to an end because I wasn't getting married like the other girls" (251). She returned home and lived with her widowed mother: "Age 23 was a really low time in my life. I had been living at home with my widowed mother for the two years since finishing college. I took care of her and did volunteer work as she had done, not getting into any serious paid job. I was dating but nothing much was happening that way either" (280).

Then "this fellow came along" (280). Her friends seemed to like him, and he was "pleasant," and she was bored with her volunteer job. So she said to herself, "I've been too fussy. There isn't anything to do in life except get married anyway; then everything will fall into place, and I'll have children and be busy with family life, and that will be it" (280). So they got engaged. But just at that time a friend got her a job in a bank: "I was so excited about that job!" (280). She was so excited, in fact, that she decided to break off her engagement. But her mother and fiancé "kept charging ahead with the wedding plans." "I kept digging my heels in further," she said, telling them, "I know that I just never seem to want to get married, but this time I *really* don't'" (280). Finally, she broke off the engagement just three weeks before the wedding. Her mother was at her wit's end, and Sally thought to herself, "'What kind of mess am I getting myself into? Here I am breaking off this engagement for a job!'" She admitted, "I felt very guilty, but I really got into my work" (280).

A year later, at twenty-five, she moved out of her mother's house: "I'd never been away from home except for college. It was frightening to leave and hard to break with my mother, but it was clear to me that I wanted to be single for awhile—to work and travel and have fun and be independent" (280). She married at twenty-eight but did not attempt pregnancy for four years, devoting herself instead to work, independence, and leisure. At thirty-two she decided to start a family.

Sally's life during the third decade reflects the initiative vs. guilt conflict. After she graduated from college, there wasn't much sense of initiative. If initiative is "the action of taking the first step, responsibility for beginning or originating" and the "ability to think and act without being urged" (Agnes 2001, 735), it was not what Sally experienced at all. Instead, it was as though the responsibility for beginning or originating something was someone else's. "What am I supposed to do with my life?," she asked. "Someone tell me what to do! . . . I didn't know where to start" (251).

Her father's scenario—go to college and find a husband there—hadn't panned out. Unlike the other girls, she wasn't getting married, and she apparently hadn't figured on needing an alternative plan. So she returned home to live with her mother and did volunteer work as her mother had done—nothing original in that. It isn't very surprising, then, that age twenty-three was "a really low time" (280) in her life. She was dating but "nothing much was happening that way either" (280). The fact that she uses the passive and not the active voice is further evidence of the absence of a *sense of initiative.*

"Then this fellow came along," and she was bored with her volunteer job, so she decided there "isn't anything to do in life except get married anyway," so they got engaged. Like her decision to return home to live with her mother, there is little sense of initiative in this decision to get married. She says that her friends seemed to like him, as though that really mattered in the long run, and that he was "pleasant," which does not seem all that enthusiastic, and she believes that her only real options in life are marriage, having children, and busying herself with family life. It was only a few years ago that she was telling her father that she wanted to be an accountant. If he had affirmed this desire, she may have entered college with this goal in mind and have taken the appropriate courses to enable her to enter that profession when she graduated.

But then a friend came to the rescue and got her a job in a bank. Even this has a note of reliance on others rather than her own initiative. But once she began working, she became enthused about what she was doing. Perhaps Sally was recapturing the initiative that her father had squelched when she was in high school. But there was the inconvenient fact that, in her passivity, she had agreed to get married, and her mother and her fiancé were "charging ahead with the wedding plans." They, not she, were the ones taking the initiative as far as her own wedding was concerned.

But, then, in an uncharacteristic expression of autonomy, Sally began "digging her heels in," saying that she didn't want to get married. At the same time, the doubt that may accompany expressions of autonomy emerged as she wondered what "kind of mess" she was getting herself into. And why reject a chance at marriage "for a job"?

She also felt a strong sense of guilt. In breaking off her engagement, she was doing something wrong as far as established standards, previous arrangements, and given intentions are concerned. Yet for the first time in her adult life, she allowed herself a certain leeway and acted under the conviction that this was the right thing to do in the long run. Although she had every reason to feel guilty, she had at last begun to express and convey to others her capacity for initiative. I would guess that the job in a bank rekindled her initiative as the high school girl who had wanted to become an accountant. In a very real sense, this initiative was based not on what her father said, but what he did.

Her next act of initiative was to move out of her mother's house: "It was frightening to leave and hard to break with my mother, but it was clear to me that I wanted to be single for awhile." As Erikson points out, initiative adds to autonomy the quality of undertaking and planning, and involves learning to move around, thus establishing a wider radius of goals. This could not have happened if she had continued to live in her mother's house.

Sally made this move at age twenty-five. Levinson notes that many of the women in his study made a significant life change at age twenty-five; he calls it "the age 25 shift" (97–99). Though he had not noticed this "shift" in his earlier study of men, he believes it may exist for men as well. The changes are often highly specific: "To get married, to end or stay in a difficult marriage, to have a child, get a job, go back to school, give a markedly higher or lower priority to a particular aspect of living" (98). The specific choices are, however, rooted in more general concerns: "She is taking a firmer position about the kind of life she wants to have" and "seeking a more stable order within which to pursue her aspirations" (98). We will return to Sally's story in the next chapter.

WENDY: "I WAS DETERMINED
TO MAINTAIN MY OWN STRENGTH"

Levinson's case of Wendy Lewis (a pseudonym), one of the fifteen homemakers in the study, is also illustrative of the initiative vs. guilt conflict in the third decade of life. Wendy begins her narrative by noting, "I was a strong achiever in high school. I was going to law school. My parents and I always felt I could do anything" (Levinson 1996, 76). She graduated from high school at seventeen "and went to a first-rate college" (76). She was "a good student and enjoyed college" (76).

When she was eighteen she met her future husband, Hank, "who was four years older. He was an unusual person and impressive: played the piano and had a brand-new Porsche." "Two weeks after we met he asked me to marry him," she said. "I don't think I was passionately in love with him, but he was a good catch. We got engaged right away" (76). Hank was in graduate school in her hometown. He "really fell in love with [her] family, and they were crazy about him" (76). So when they got engaged, he lived with her parents. In her sophomore year she transferred to a local college near home and lived at home with her parents and Hank.

She married at nineteen, the summer between her sophomore and junior years, and her parents paid for her and Hank's tuition. They got a one-bedroom apartment. Hank worked full-time and went to school at night, and she went to school during the day and worked at night: "We were so busy going to school and trying to pay the bills that we sometimes only saw each other in passing" (76). Wendy got pregnant at nineteen and had their daughter Gwen at twenty. She was still planning to go to law school, and although Gwen was not "an accident" (she had stopped taking birth control) she "wanted a baby." "We thought we could do everything. How stupid!" she said (76). She went to school only part-time after that, and her mother took care of Gwen: "The next year the marriage was more difficult. We were both so busy. We had a lot of arguments. I don't even remember my twenty-first birthday at all; it's a blur: going to school, working, taking care of the baby" (76).

In her senior year, when she was twenty-two, she applied to law school and was accepted. But then she got pregnant. Again, she had stopped taking birth control: "It was one of those half-conscious decisions. I knew what I was doing but I didn't. I made the decision before I consciously chose family over law school" (76). "I was half-aware of the contradictions in applying for law school and getting pregnant at the same time," Wendy said. "My parents were really hot for law school. I didn't want to disappoint them, and I couldn't tell them how I felt. I remember pretending that not going to law school was temporary, though I knew it was permanent" (76–77). Wendy's mother had been taking care of Gwen and insisted that she could handle two children. She had never realized her own career dreams and wanted Wendy to go to law school. But Wendy said she "was into having children at that point," adding, "I still think I made the right decision for me" (77).

The second half of the third decade was very tumultuous. Her mother was dying of heart disease. Between age twenty-five and twenty-seven, Wendy took care of her mother "but couldn't deal with [her] own feelings" (129). She was unwilling to give her mother up: "It's like I've kept a room inside myself and not touched it. I still can't look at pictures of her" (129). She believes that she avoided her feelings at the time "by trying to cope with others' problems and hold the family together." She felt "as trapped as any mother does with three children under 6." Gwen, her oldest child, "was an absolutely obstinate child." Wendy found she couldn't handle Gwen and "got nasty with her sometimes." At those times, she felt "like throwing her away and starting all over again."

But her greatest difficulties with Gwen were the father-daughter conflicts between Hank and Gwen. Hank was depressed about the problems of establishing his own computer business and the lack of financial help from his parents: "He couldn't provide adequate discipline or love to Gwen. He would get into rages and sometimes abuse Gwen physically. It was terrible. Looking back, I realize that I devoted myself to taking care of people and mediating the father-daughter struggle, acting as though there wasn't a mother-father and mother-daughter struggle as well" (129).

To make matters worse, after her mother died, Wendy's grandfather got sick. "We decided to take him in," said Wendy. "It was a total disaster. He was absolutely stricken by the loss of my mother and had no will to live. He required constant care. This kept me from helping a husband and kids who were also hurting from my mother's death. I was coping with all this like a real soldier but couldn't deal with the extreme feelings that Hank was beset by" (129).

Then, when she was twenty-eight, Hank had a brain tumor that kept him hospitalized for several months. She "had been coping before, but then it all fell apart. There was no way that [she] could handle having Hank in the hospital, not knowing whether he would live or die, and having three small children and a sick grandpa at home" (130). She phoned her father "and told him he would have to find a home for Grandpa, which he did" (130). Three months later he died.

Hank's recovery was disrupted by worries about his business, so Wendy gradually took on more responsibility. She would call customers, explain what happened to Hank, and place orders: "I really took over his job. If I hadn't, the business would have gone under" (130). Hank got increasingly depressed and angry. The hospital placed him in psychotherapy, and then they entered couples and family therapy: "One big issue was my involvement in the business. He knew I had to do it, but my taking his job made him feel useless, depressed, and angry. And I was angry with him for getting sick and making me perform the husband's role" (130). On the other hand, she said, "I saw that I was capable of handling the whole thing, and everything changed. Before I married I had always thought of myself as independent and competent. Then I had played the housewife for a number of years and lost those feelings. Running the business brought them back to me" (130).

When Hank was able to cope with the business again, he wanted it back but Wendy "wasn't that anxious to hand it back," she explained. "This was the first time we came into direct conflict. He would try to build up his confidence by pushing me down. But this time I wouldn't give in; I was determined to maintain my own strength. It seemed possible for only one of us to be competent" (130).

When their third child was two years old, Wendy felt "it was time to get pregnant again" (130). But this was when Hank was ill. She "really wanted that fourth child," but if Hank were to die she knew that she couldn't raise four kids alone, and if he lived it would be too much strain on him. So, she said, "I decided against it. At 30 my feelings of loss about not having the fourth child got stronger and more conscious. I used to think how it might have been with him, what he'd look like, and all that . . . [but] I "was feeling the weight of so many problems! Every headache of Hank's worried me, and he used that to get me to do what he wanted. I had that *Why me?* feeling. Why did my mother die. Why did my husband get sick. Why wasn't my life going the way I thought it would?" (130).

During the two years after she turned thirty, some significant changes were made: Gwen, who became even more disturbed, was sent to boarding school. The youngest child entered first grade, and Wendy "was bored all by herself," especially because she did not consider herself "a house-wife type person" (131). She "didn't care about things like dusting and cleaning." Hank was home a lot "but he didn't do the housework either. He really felt it was [*her*] *place* to do it," and this "increased [her] desire not to do it" (131). But she didn't take a clear stand until her early thirties, and it wasn't until her late thirties that she freed herself of most household chores (131). Hank urged her to get an outside job so that she could add to the family income, and this time she agreed, realizing that she "had had it with his business." "We couldn't find a way to collaborate," she added, and "I needed a place where I would be free to be competent" (131).

At thirty-two she got a full-time job. Her boss instructed her about the project and then left her totally in charge of carrying it out: "Although I was doing high-quality work in an independent way, there were long periods when the work was routine and I felt like an assembly line worker in a factory. I wanted to do more interesting work but my desire wasn't strong enough to get me to move from a job to a career" (131).

By the age of thirty-three her life became more settled. Gwen was brought home from boarding school, and they bought "a wonderful house in a town with an excellent school system." "Our troubles weren't over," she said "but we were at a new place in our life" (131).

Wendy seems almost the exact opposite of Sally. She had an abundance of initiative, fed by a strong underlying sense of autonomy. As she points out, she especially valued her independence. It appears that she made most of the family decisions, especially with regard to having children. She would make unilateral decisions to stop birth control, and she was the one who knew when it was time to have another baby. She was not reluctant, therefore, to take the "first step or move" or assume "responsibility for beginning or originating" (Agnes 2001, 735).

But what I find somewhat missing in Wendy's story is the virtue of purpose. To be sure, she exhibits considerable "resolution or determination," but what seems rather lacking is "the object or end in view for which something exists or is done" (Agnes 2001, 1165). The relative absence of planning or forethought may have derived from her belief that "she could do anything." The very belief that one can do anything may work against a sense of purposefulness, the ability to focus on a specific goal or end, so that the action or activity is not meaningless (1165). Her "decision" to have a baby was a somewhat unconscious one, and although this was the "right decision" for her, it was not made with much planning or forethought other than the feeling that when her youngest child is two years old, it's "time" to have another one. This was also true of her marriage. Two weeks is not much time for two persons who plan to spend a lifetime together to get to know each other, and her description of Hank as "impressive" because he could play the piano and drove a brand-new Porsche suggests that her knowledge of him was rather superficial.

Because Wendy valued her independence so highly, it would appear that her sense of autonomy was very strong, and that she also had a well-developed sense of will. But, as Erikson points out, will needs to be trained to set its sights on certain goals—to become purposeful—for otherwise it will degenerate into mere willfulness (1964, 120). Various comments in Wendy's narrative suggest such willfulness, especially in relation to her conflicts with her husband over the operation of his computer business. Once she had proven she could run it herself, she was reluctant to give it back to him. One also sees such willfulness in her daughter Gwen, and cannot help but wonder if Gwen had learned to emulate her mother—especially, perhaps, in her relations with her father.

Initiative that is not tempered by purpose may also result in an effort to assume far more responsibility than one is capable of handling. Apparently, Wendy took over the care of her grandfather after her mother's death because her mother had taken care of him and her father was either unable or unwilling to assume that burden. But this means that she had three small children under the age of six, her grandfather, and her ailing husband to cope with. Even so, she seriously contemplated having another child at this time before relinquishing this idea as impractical. Here, again, her belief that she "could do anything" made it difficult for her to be genuinely purposeful—to focus on a concrete set of goals that were meaningful to her—instead of trying to prove to herself that she could, indeed, do anything and everything.

What was behind this conviction that she could do anything and everything? It may have had its roots in her deep conflict over the seemingly incompatible desires to have both a career and children. Her mother had wanted Wendy to fulfill "career dreams" that her mother had not been able to pursue, but Wendy herself "was into having children at that point." At the same time, she may not have fully realized that there is much more to motherhood than "having" them. In fact, for the first years of Gwen's life, she relied heavily on her mother to take care of her daughter. Nor did she see herself as "a housewife-type person." These apparent contradictions between her understanding of herself and her decisions in her twenties suggest that she was conflicted over much the same dilemma as her mother—the desire to be engaged in productive work and the desire to have children. This dilemma was not resolved in the third decade of her life.

In these comments on Wendy Lewis's narrative, I have not had anything to say about guilt. This is mainly because she does not seem to manifest much of it, perhaps because she does not feel that she has done anything wrong—that is, something "not in accordance with an established standard, previous arrangement, given intention, etc." (Agnes 2001, 1653). In a sense, this is not surprising. It is difficult to claim that she *did* anything that did not accord with established standards, previous arrangements, and given intentions, in part because there were few, if any, such arrangements or intentions at the time she and Hank decided to marry. In effect, they made it up as they went along, so at no given time would it have been reasonable for either of them to suggest that the other was guilty of committing a wrong. Also, in saving Hank's business while at the same time coping with the children and his illness, Wendy exhibited a capacity for taking initiative that was truly commendable. One gets the sense that Hank did not express much gratitude to her for what she did under very trying circumstances.

Their conflicts seemed to center around roles, especially relating to traditional husband and wife role expectations, and Hank's assumption that her role was in fact, that of the traditional "housewife-type," her skills in running the business notwithstanding. Had they not have entered so precipitously into their engagement and marriage—an action that seems to have been encouraged and even abetted by her parents—they may have been able to reflect on these expectations before marriage. If conflicts then arose, they could at least acknowledge to one another that they were not acting in accordance with a "previous arrangement" and/or wanted to renegotiate this previous understanding in light of changing conditions, including that of unanticipated self-discoveries.

The cases presented in this chapter do not challenge Erikson's view that the initiative vs. guilt conflict is experienced in rudimentary form in the play age, but they support my claim that the initiative vs. guilt conflict is central to the third decade of life. This is the decade when it is extremely important to develop a sense of initiative if one has been rather passive heretofore, the decade that this sense of initiative becomes tempered by the capacity to acknowledge guilt when one has committed a wrong, and the decade that this sense of initiative is guided by a sense of purpose—"the strength of aim-direction fed by fantasy yet not fantastic, limited by guilt yet not inhibited, morally restrained yet ethically active" (Erikson 1964a, 120).

The lives of Erik, Sally, and Wendy illustrate the difficulties of navigating one's way through the third decade of life. But each, in its own way, also illustrates the importance of viewing this decade as the play age. It the decade in which one especially feels the need of all young creatures, animal and human, to leap. To truly leap, however, you must learn how to use the ground as a springboard and how to land resiliently and safely. You must also learn to test the leeway allowed by given limits, to outdo and yet not escape gravity. One must, above all, anticipate that there will be surprises and that such surprises at their best will afford "some virgin chance conquered, some divine leeway shared" (Erikson 1977, 17).

THE PURPOSEFUL SELF

In Erikson's schema, hope—the belief in the attainability of certain desired outcomes—and will—the determination to exercise free choice as well as self-restraint—are necessary precursors for the development of the spirit and strength of purpose. As we have seen, he defines *purpose* as "the courage to envisage and pursue valued goals uninhibited by the defeat of infantile fantasies, by guilt and by the foiling fear of punishment" (1964a, 122).

His own case, and those of Sally and Wendy, illustrate the disabling role of inhibition in the development of purposefulness in the third decade of life. Inhibiting factors in the third decade of life include the anticipation of failing due to earlier defeats, guilt for wanting to pursue goals that conflict either with the expectations of parents and other influential persons in one's life or with societal expectations and ascribed roles, and the fear of being punished (by other individuals, by societal traditions and processes, by fate or God) for resisting or violating these expectations. In their twenties, Erik, Sally and Wendy responded to the threats to their development of a sense and spirit of purposefulness in their own unique ways, and there was little uniformity in the degree of their success in becoming purposeful selves. However, all three illustrate Erikson's claim that purposefulness requires the realization of an "inner unity" in one's conscience, which, in turn, allows for an "inner freedom" in one's pursuit of one's goals and aims in life (121–22). In other words, one needs to be able to invest oneself in one's objectives with a "good conscience," knowing that what one is about is "right" despite the objections of others.

A major reason why one requires the better part of a full decade in finding one's "purpose" in life is that the realization of such "inner unity" and its concomitant "inner freedom" does not happen overnight. What may therefore be the most helpful words that older adults can offer those who are struggling to find their purpose in life is that they have time on their side. These same adults, however, should also avoid the temptation to advise a set timetable for the younger adult to follow, for the only clock that should really matter is the internal one, and this, too, differs from one individual to another.

Chapter 4

The Fourth Decade:
The Competent Self

According to contemporary birthday cards, the fourth decade (thirty to thirty-nine) seems to usher in a whole new period in life, as it marks the point where one shifts from being a carefree, overaged adolescent and becomes a responsible adult. The fact that one has already assumed significant responsibilities during one's twenties goes unacknowledged, perhaps because these are thought—rightly or wrongly—to have been experimental and not to have involved deep and lasting commitments.

Here are some typical birthday cards for persons turning thirty: "Relax, turning 30 doesn't mean your life is over. Just the young part." Or this: "What is 30? Thirty is not getting carded at bars anymore, knowing that teenagers think you're a dinosaur, hearing people say, 'Well, it's better than turning forty!,' getting a headache at a concert, having furniture that matches. . . ." And this obvious bit of wishful thinking: "If 50 is the new 30, 30 must be the new 10. So . . . up for a game of dodge ball and a juice box?" But a birthday card for the person turning fifty comes the closest to expressing the theme of this chapter: "Five decades of wishes: Age 10, I want a pony; age 20, I want a drink; age 30, I want a raise; age 40, I want a vacation; age 50, I forgot what I want."

I want a raise: This wish reflects the fact that the person in the fourth decade of life is mostly perceived as a worker—engaged in some form of industry—and is in a relatively junior position—viewed as inferior by those who are in senior or superior positions relative to one's own. In some work environments, the best work is being done by those in their thirties, but this is rarely officially recognized or rewarded.

THE INDUSTRY VS. INFERIORITY CONFLICT

Webster's defines *industry* as "earnest, steady effort, constant diligence in or application to work," and "systematic work; habitual employment" (Agnes 2001, 729). *Diligence* suggests "constant, careful effort" and "perseverance" (404). Although the opposite of industry may seem to be laziness or slothfulness, Erikson's choice of the word *inferiority* conveys the sense that the inability to function in an industrious manner may be due to one's sense of one's own inadequacies, which may be due to circumstances over which one has relatively little control. According to the dictionary, *inferiority* means "low or lower in order, status, rank, etc.," "poor in quality," and "below average" (731).

In *Identity and the Life Cycle* Erikson (1959) notes that this stage—the school age—marks the time when children, in all cultures, begin to "receive some systematic instruction" (83). This doesn't necessarily mean that it takes place in a school, but this is where it typically happens. In societies with specialized careers, the child is "given the widest possible basic education for the greatest number of possible careers," and the "greater the specialization, the more indistinct the goal of initiative becomes; and the more complicated the social reality, the vaguer the father's and mother's role in it" (83).

This is also the stage when children actually "like to be mildly but firmly coerced into the adventure of finding out that one can learn to accomplish things which one would never have thought of by oneself, things which owe their attractiveness to the very fact that they are *not* the product of play and fantasy but the product of reality, practicality, and logic" (84). All children need to be left alone in solitary play, and all children need their hours and days of make-believe, but all children also, sooner or later, "become dissatisfied and disgruntled without a sense of being useful, without a sense of being able to make things and make them well and even perfectly: this is what I call the *sense of industry*" (86). At this stage, the child "learns to win recognition by *producing things*. He develops industry, that is, he adjusts himself to the inorganic laws of the tool world. He can become an eager and absorbed unit of a productive situation" and develop "the pleasure of *work completion* by steady attention and persevering diligence" (86).

In *Childhood and Society* Erikson (1950) discusses the primary danger at this stage, "which lies in a sense of inadequacy and inferiority" (227). If the child "despairs of his tools and skills or of his status among his tool partners, his ego boundaries suffer, and he abandons hope for the ability to identify early with others who apply themselves to the same general section of the tool world" (227). He may then consider himself "doomed to mediocrity" (227).

In *Identity and the Life Cycle* Erikson (1959) notes that the selection and training of teachers is vital for the avoidance of the dangers that may befall the child at this stage. One such danger is "the sense of inferiority, the feeling that one will never be any good" (87). Another is the danger of the child "identifying too strenuously with a too virtuous teacher or becoming the teacher's pet," and thus prematurely disposed to being "nothing but a good little worker or a good little helper, which may not be all that he *could be*" (87–88). A third, perhaps the most common of all, is the danger "that throughout the long years of going to school he will never acquire the enjoyment of work and the pride of doing at least one thing well" (88). In identifying these three dangers, Erikson implies that the sense of inferiority may manifest itself in setting one's goals too low in light of what one *could* do and be, or in treating one's work as nothing more than an onerous burden.

In the revised edition of *Childhood and Society*, Erikson (1963) proposes that the institutional safeguard of industry vs. inferiority is the "technological ethos" of a given society. This *ethos* involves the "sense of division of labor and of differential opportunity" (260). These factors become increasingly apparent as one becomes an adult. The effects of "differential opportunity" become apparent as one begins to feel the effects of societal preferences and prejudices and the priority given to these factors over one's ability to do the work itself (260).

But the adult also confronts another, more fundamental danger, the "restriction of himself and constriction of his horizons to include only his work" (260–61). If he "accepts work as his only obligation, and 'what works' as his only criterion of worthwhileness, he may become the conformist and thoughtless slave of his technology and of those who are in a position to exploit it" (261). Thus, the chart in *Vital Involvement in Old Age* (Erikson, Erikson & Kivnick 1986) indicates that the maladaptive tendency of this stage is narrow virtuosity and the malignant tendency is inertia (45).

THE VIRTUE OF COMPETENCE

Erikson assigns the virtue of competence to this stage. *Webster's* defines *competence* as "a condition or quality of being competent" and *competent* as "well qualified; capable; fit (a *competent* doctor)" and "sufficient; adequate (a *competent* understanding of law)" (Agnes 2001, 298).

In "Human Strength and the Cycle of Generations" Erikson (1964a) suggests that a sense of competence "characterizes what eventually becomes *workmanship*" (123). Having acquired the rudiments of hope, will and purpose, which "anticipate a future of only dimly anticipated tasks," the child now needs to be shown "basic methods leading to the identity of a technical way of life" (123). In school, "what 'works' in the fabric of one's thought and in the use of one's physical coordination can be found to 'work' in materials and in cooperative encounters: a self-verification of lasting importance" (123). The child at this stage "is ready for a variety of specializations and will learn most eagerly techniques in line with the *ethos of production* which has already entered his anticipations by way of ideal examples, real or mythical, and which now meets him in the persons of instructive adults and cooperative peers" (124). His "developing capacities permit him to apprehend the basic materials of technology, and the elements of reasoning which make techniques teachable" (124). Thus, "the rudiments of competence and of reasonableness prepare in the child a future sense of workmanship without which there can be no 'strong ego.' Without it man feels inferior in his equipment, and in his ability to match an ever-increasing radius of manageable reality with his capacities" (124). In a word, he feels overwhelmed.

Thus, Erikson understands competence to be "the free exercise of dexterity and intelligence in the completion of tasks, unimpaired by infantile inferiority. It is the basis for cooperative participation in technologies and relies, in turn, on the logic of tools and skills" (124). In effect, competence is the sense that one's industry produces good results and that one is well-qualified to do the job that one is doing. Erikson (1958) anticipated this understanding of competence in his earlier psychoanalytic study of Martin Luther when he noted that

> many individuals should not do the work which they are doing, if they are doing it well at too great inner expense. Good work it may be in terms of efficiency, but it is also bad works. The point is, not how efficiently the work is done, but how good it is for the worker in terms of his lifetime within his ideological world. (220)

He suggested that Luther had a craftsman's point of view, and "considered one craft as good a way to personal perfection as another; but also as bad a potential lifelong prison as another" (220).

Despite the fact that the school age (from five to twelve) is chronologically longer than the previous stages put together, this time frame allows for only the most rudimentary experience of industry. It introduces a lifelong struggle with the fundamental developmental task of learning to do things alongside and together with others.

In my view, the decade in which such learning is centrally important is the fourth decade of life, when one typically settles into "systematic work" and "habitual employment" requiring both "diligence" and "perseverance" (Agnes 2001, 729, 404). These are the years when a person's sense of being a worker— a person of industry—becomes established and forms the bedrock for the years to come. To be sure, almost everyone has been a worker prior to their fourth decade. It simply isn't true, as the birthday cards suggest, that the twenties are carefree years of fun and games. But the thirties introduce the sense of being committed to a particular form of work and of being competent at what one does. Major occupational changes may occur later, but when they happen, one is likely to feel that these changes are atypical and to believe that in making them one is changing the very course of one's life and is taking a major risk.

This sense of risk is a crucial difference between this and the previous decade for, in one's twenties, one is unlikely to have the same sense that a change is a major risk. Instead, the risk is more likely to lie in *not* making a change. A poem by Stephen Dunn (2000, 55–56) illustrates this point. Dunn worked for the National Biscuit Company as a copywriter between the ages of twenty-four and twenty-seven.

The Last Hours

There's some innocence left,
and these are the last hours of an empty afternoon
at the office, and there's the clock
on the wall, and my friend Frank
in the adjacent cubicle selling himself
on the phone.
    I'm twenty-five, on the shaky
ladder up, my father's son, corporate,
clean-shaven, and I know only what I don't want,
which is almost everything I have.
    A meeting ends.
Men in serious suits, intelligent men
who've been thinking hard about marketing snacks,
move back now to their office windows, worried
or proud. The big boss, Horace,
had called them in to approve this, reject that—
the big boss, a first-name, how's-your-family
kind of assassin, who likes me . . .

    . . . Where I sit
It's exactly nineteen minutes to five. My phone rings.
Horace would like me to stop in
before I leave. *Stop in.* Code words,
leisurely words, that mean *now.*
    Would I be willing
to take on this? Would X's office, who by the way
is no longer with us, be satisfactory?
About money, will this be enough?
I smile, I say yes and yes and yes,
but—I don't know from what calm place
this comes—I'm translating
his beneficence into a lifetime, a life
of selling snacks, talking snack strategy,
thinking snack thoughts.
    On the elevator down
it's a small knot, I'd like to say, of joy.
That's how I tell it now, here in the future,
the fear long gone.
By the time I reach the subway it's grown,
it's outsized, an attitude finally come round,
and I say it quietly to myself, *I quit,*
and keep saying it, knowing I will say it, sure
of nothing else but.

In realizing at age twenty-five that he would leave National Biscuit Company in due course, Dunn was confirming Daniel J. Levinson's belief that the "age 25 shift" found in his study of women "may exist for men as well" (Levinson 1996, 98).

But although similar career changes happen in the fourth decade of life or later, these changes are atypical. In his study of forty men, Levinson (1978) found that five changed their career path and for three others the instability of their twenties continued in their thirties. The others remained committed to the same career path, with twenty-two advancing in their careers, seven making no progress, and three taking on new assignments that significantly altered what they had previously been doing. The following illustration is from Levinson's study.

BILL: "I DIDN'T KNOW WHICH WAY I WAS GOING"

Bill Paulsen (a pseudonym) is one of two men in Levinson's *The Seasons of a Man's Life* (1978) whose lives are presented from adolescence through the mid-forties. The sample of forty men was selected in 1969. They were born between 1923 and 1934, so they would have been between the ages of thirty-five and forty-six when they were first interviewed. Paulsen was among the older men interviewed. Levinson places him in the category of men who, in their thirties, were "declining or failing within a stable life structure" (152). Thus, he is an excellent example of a person experiencing difficulties with the industry vs. inferiority conflict, and thus struggling to sustain a sense of competence, in the fourth decade of his life.

Bill was born in 1925 and raised in a Scandinavian and Irish community in the Bay Ridge section of Brooklyn. His grandmother, who came to the United States from Norway as a child, was a central figure in his early years. The whole family revolved around her. There was continual friction between her and her daughter, Bill's mother, leading him to develop the belief that if you put two women under the same roof you are asking for trouble. His grandmother provided the structure and discipline of his life while his mother, a troubled woman, high-strung and nervous, was quite protective and indulgent of him. His grandmother ran a boarding house in upstate New York during the summer months, and Bill, his mother, and his sister would spend the summer there. His mother served as a waitress, while Bill was responsible for many of the chores around the boardinghouse and farm: taking care of the chickens, milking the cows, bringing in the hay. It was "a hard life but a good one" (126).

Bill's father was a good man without ambition, content to settle for a modest place in life. For thirty-eight years he had the same clerical job with a stock brokerage firm on Wall Street. He had a lot of common sense and was generous with his attention and advice. When there was trouble, he and Bill would sit down and talk. According to Bill, he was "more a buddy than a father" (127). He was a kind man who failed to achieve the things Bill wanted, but he was Bill's "best friend" (127).

Bill admired his grandmother's ambition, hard work, toughness, and concern with fairness. Like her, he worked to make a better life for himself. Like his mother, he would have a continuing struggle against the wish to be given what he wanted when he wanted it and the wish to give up and be looked after. Like his father, Bill would strive to make his peace with the world, to settle for a modest place in it, and come to love his pastimes and see them as a major source of pleasure and satisfaction in his adult life (127).

He was drafted shortly after his eighteenth birthday and was in combat for a year and a half in World War II. He was a forward observer, which meant that it was his job to establish forward observation posts locating enemy fire. He was among the troops that moved through France into Germany. Like many other veterans, he had difficulty adjusting to civilian life after the war, but after a few months of doing nothing, he, his best friend, and his friend's brother decided to go to college for a couple of years. They learned that New York State Agricultural College was starting up a technical division, so they applied and were accepted. They decided to take up electrical work, and all three were excellent students.

In the last year of the two-year degree program, he met Ruth, who was two years older. He felt they had a lot in common, and he enjoyed being with her. But his mother was opposed to his marriage because, according to Bill, she felt that Ruth was taking him away from her, and she wanted to hold on to him. There was also the question, which he and Ruth discussed, of whether he was "mature" enough for marriage. In addition, Bill was a Protestant, and Ruth was Catholic, and she wanted him to convert. He defied his mother and received instruction in the Catholic Church, converted, and married Ruth in 1949 when he was twenty-three.

They moved to Long Island, some sixty-five miles from his home in Brooklyn. When they married, Bill was working for IBM and commuting into New York City. Although he liked his job, he found the commute too demanding and wanted to spend more time with Ruth. So he quit after a year and took a job with the Long Island Lighting Company, working there for six years. He began as a "glorified telephone operator," taking emergency calls through the switchboard and directing repair men to the field. He worked up to being "a special service operator" in charge of one of the work shifts. He didn't "get any satisfaction from the type of work [he] was fooling with" but the job offered security, paid well, and met his immediate needs.

On the other hand, it led nowhere. It did not draw on his education in electronics or training at IBM, nor did it prepare him for other positions at Long Island Lighting. So the job proved to be an occupational backwater in which he wallowed for over six years—narrowing his interests, acquiring few new skills, and learning little about capabilities that might enable him to develop a career.

During this time, his wife's mother lived with them, and Bill was extremely fond of her, as she was of him. She would give him advice on problems at work or a decision he and Ruth were facing. Similarly with his father. He would call his father whenever he felt uncertain—when buying his home, for example—and he, too, was always happy to give advice. Bill and Ruth both wanted children but, as Bill put it, "The good Lord didn't see fit to give us one just then" (131). As there was no physical explanation for this, they worried that something was wrong with one or both of them, and tension ensued over the issue for the first several years of their marriage.

At age twenty-nine, a series of events confronted him with losses and responsibilities that he couldn't manage. After an illness of several months, his father died at the age of fifty-three, and Bill was devastated by the loss: "You'd call me a nervous wreck at that time for a year or two" (132). Then his mother moved in with Bill and Ruth. Ruth had, at last, become pregnant and was anxious about her pregnancy and uneasy about living with Bill's mother. His mother was unable to look after herself and demanded a great deal of care—much more than he and Ruth could provide.

Bill suggested that she live in a nursing home, but she was adamantly opposed, and the rest of the family were angry at Bill for even suggesting it. She remained with them, and the situation deteriorated: "It got to the point where my wife was becoming a nervous wreck. My mother would crawl into a shell of sorts and wouldn't talk at all. I just about blew my cork" (132). Ruth, who was also interviewed, said that she tried to commit suicide at that time "because [she] couldn't face it" (132). In the ninth month of her pregnancy, the baby was stillborn.

In their distress and anger, Bill and Ruth insisted that his mother go to live with his sister. She refused at first, saying that he didn't love her, but she eventually went to live with his sister. Bill felt that he had failed in his role as the man of the family. He thought, and so did other family members, that it was up to him to care for his mother for the rest of her days, but he "just couldn't do it" (133). Other family members didn't speak to him for almost ten years.

During this period of turmoil, his wife's mother, who had become ill while she was living with them and was subsequently bedridden for a year, also died. Like his father, she had been a great favorite of Bill's, and he felt her loss sharply. He began to drink heavily, which in turn affected his work. He began to worry about losing his job: "It was like being in the middle of the ocean with no life preserver. I didn't know which way I was going" (133).

Ruth's brother was helpful to Bill during this time. He had come to Long Island from Oregon when his and Ruth's mother was ill, and lived with Bill and Ruth for several months while he separated from his wife. Then he remarried, moved to Florida, and found a job that he liked. Once settled, he encouraged Bill and Ruth to join him, and they decided to make the move. At thirty-one, Bill was ready for a change. Feeling that things had not worked out for him in Long Island, he wanted to go somewhere else and start over, and Florida seemed as good a place as any.

Starting all over again in Florida, though, was difficult for him. He worked six months for a refrigerator dealer as a serviceman, then eight months for "slave wages" with a building company (134). Then, however, Bowles & White, a computer company, opened a new plant in Fort Lauderdale, and he applied for a position. He was hired on the basis of his IBM training and sent to Boston, where he learned to operate the company's new computers. When he returned, he was the first IBM computer operator at the company's research and development center, and he felt greatly encouraged. At thirty-two, he had a position in which he could use his training and skills and was working for a company that offered opportunities for advancement. He was now looking ahead and planning for his future. The new job marked the end of three years of crisis and chaos.

As data processing became more important to the company's operation, Bill began to assume more of a supervisory role. He taught new employees how to operate computers and supervised their work. His role was to take what an experienced programmer had written and make it understandable to the operators, so he saw himself as a link between workers and managers, helping each group understand the other. As he put it, he was chaplain, mediator, and father confessor. His professional goal was now to become the supervisor of the entire data processing section.

When Bill was thirty-three, Ruth became pregnant again, and this time the birth was successful. As Ruth put it, their son Pete's birth "gave [them] a purpose to go on or something to build toward." "I think our lives were never complete before he came" (283), she added. Bill attempted to be both a father and buddy to Pete and, from Ruth's perspective, this led to Pete becoming spoiled because Bill had difficulty saying no to Pete, and Pete took advantage of this "weakness" in her husband (283).

When Bill was thirty-five, they bought a beautiful, comfortable home, and he developed a strong love of fishing. This was a good time in his life. He had a gratifying occupation, a beautiful home, a family, and enjoyable leisure activities. This continued until he turned thirty-eight, when his mother moved to Florida after a long family squabble. Although she lived in a nearby apartment, she made great demands on her son and was enormously trying. Her presence again became a source of conflict between Bill and Ruth. Due to the tension, Ruth developed an ulcer and was hospitalized. Finally, six months after his mother's arrival, Bill realized that her presence placed an intolerable burden on Ruth, so he sent her back to his sister's home in Virginia. The family then decided to place her in a nursing home.

When he turned thirty-nine, he felt he was due for an advancement to a supervisory position. He realized that he did not have experience or training in management, but he felt he had performed well and had earned the respect and affirmation of the company. He wanted to be a more senior member of the organization and to assume greater responsibility and authority. It soon became evident, however, that he was not going to be promoted, that he had gone as far as he could at Bowles & White.

What should he do? Settle for what he had or try to get what he wanted elsewhere? While trying to make this decision, he developed chest pains and became convinced that he had heart disease. But extensive medical tests indicated that his pain was muscular, brought on by "nervousness." He was relieved that he did not have heart disease, yet he was even more aware of the psychological damage of his failure to get promoted to a more senior position. He began to take better care of himself, cutting down on his drinking and trying to stop smoking. At forty, largely on his own initiative, he and Ruth decided to move back north. Having moved to Florida when things were not going well in New York, he was now gambling that a return to New York would have equally favorable consequences. Thus the decade ended with Bill making a risky career move.

The birthday card suggestion that the thirty-year-old wants a raise speaks rather well to Bill Paulsen's situation throughout his thirties, though a promotion would be more accurate in his case because he wanted the recognition and responsibilities that a promotion would provide. Significantly, the issue of advancement had not arisen for him during his twenties. Throughout his twenties, he was content with the fact that his job offered security, paid well, and met his immediate needs. In effect, it was enough that he had carried through on what he had initiated at the beginning of his third decade: completing a two-year college degree, getting married, and finding a secure, well-paying job. As his fourth decade got underway, he felt that this initiative should be leading to something more, something on which he could set his sights and have a reasonable chance of securing.

His first year or so in Florida was largely unproductive. But when he was hired to work at Bowles & White at age thirty-two, he began to envision a career with an upward trajectory. But it simply didn't happen this way. By the end of the decade, he was not much further ahead than where he had begun, and he was eight years older.

Erikson's industry vs. inferiority conflict helps us to understand what had taken place. As noted earlier, inferiority conveys the idea that the inability to function with a genuine sense of industry may be due to one's own inadequacies, and these, in turn, may be due to circumstances over which one has relatively little control. Bill was painfully aware that he lacked managerial training and that without such training it was difficult to gain any managerial experience. At the same time, he felt that his capabilities were far above those of anyone else and that he ought to be promoted on the basis of his technical skills. As the fourth decade of his life continued, Bill felt the weight of being lower in status as others were being promoted and he was being left behind.

We can well imagine that Bill wondered how his father could tolerate the fact that he was in the same job at fifty-three (the year of his death) for which he had been hired at age fifteen. But his father had felt fortunate even to have a job during the Depression years, whereas Bill's thirties (1954–1964) were a time of economic prosperity. Bill had also been made to feel inferior by other members of his family because he had been unable to cope with his mother's presence in his home, thus failing to fulfill the traditional responsibilities of the "man of the family."

Bill's inferiority problem, then, was not that he set his goals too low in light of what he could do or be, but that the opportunity to progress to the next level did not present itself. Levinson hints at personality factors that may have contributed to Bill's failure to gain the recognition that he desired, noting a "thread of self-deception" in his description of his role as supervisor of the computer operators: "He exaggerated his talent for mediating between workers and managers," and because he did not want "to think of his job as clerical, he was overly optimistic about his chances for advancement" (282). Thus, "as he established himself in the job, he was sowing the seeds of future problems" (282). Then, in his late thirties, he came to feel that his "capabilities were far above those of anybody else and that [he] would probably become supervisor of the whole department." "Without realizing it," he said, "I would walk around and give the impression that I was above everybody else" (284). The senior managers probably witnessed this behavior, and it may have been a factor in his not being considered for promotion. In any event, a sense of inferiority was predominant during his fourth decade, and it derived from the fact that he felt he should have a higher status and not from the fact that he felt his work was "poor in quality" or "below average" (Agnes 2001,731).

These feelings of inferiority had a direct impact on his sense of industry. The fact that he was involved in a newly developing industry—computer technology—does not come through in Levinson's portrayal of his work life. Instead, it sounds as dreary and unexciting as his father's clerical job on Wall Street. There is little of the spirit of Erikson's (1959) description of the child becoming "an eager and absorbed unit of a productive situation" and as experiencing "the pleasure of *work completion* by steady attention and persevering diligence" (86). This may, of course, reflect the nature of the work itself, especially the fact that he was in the data-processing end of the business. It may simply have been boring work, and a far cry from the dangerous but exciting work that he did in the Army when he was a forward observer in the field artillery. Thus, *Webster's* definition of *industry* as "earnest, steady effort, constant diligence in or application to work" and "systematic work; habitual employment" (Agnes 2001, 729) characterizes his father's sense of industry (and thus his relative lack of a sense of inferiority as well). Bill, however, was seeking something more akin to Erikson's dynamic understanding of industry as involving a sense of eagerness, absorption, and pleasure, and this had proven elusive.

Contributing to his sense of inferiority was the fact that his relationship with his son was not developing in quite the way he had desired. Ruth emphasized that Pete and Bill both loved one another, noting that after an argument in which Pete would go to his room and close the door, he would reemerge within the hour and the two of them would act as though nothing had happened. But the deep sense that Bill had of his own father—"more a buddy than a father" and his "best friend"—was less apparent in Pete's feelings toward him. Then he had a second chance to be "the man of the family" when his mother moved to Florida, but this turned out as badly as it had the first time, and his mother's living in her own apartment made little difference.

Levinson placed Bill with six other men in their thirties who were "declining or failing within a stable life structure," noting that Bill was a "moderate failure" in comparison with some of the others (152). He points out that Bill was not by any means unique, for most of the men in this category reached their "ceiling" in their mid- to late thirties. One received a "lateral promotion" that meant exile within the company, while several university faculty members were denied tenure in their late thirties and were forced to find employment elsewhere. Thus, these seven men were confronted with the "differential opportunity" to which Erikson (1963) refers in his discussion of the "technological ethos" of a given society (260).

Interestingly enough, Bill was spared almost certain future humiliation by not being promoted to a management position, for, as Levinson points out, "the structure of management in industry is pyramidal, with only one position in top management for every 15 or 20 in middle management," and because "the culture of management places a great value on upward mobility, most middle managers are doomed to personal failure, ranging in degree from moderate to devastating" (155). But this would have been small consolation to a man who, in his thirties, believed himself to be especially competent in mediating between middle managers and the clerical staff.

Bill's chest pains due to nervous tension when he was thirty-nine convinced him that he needed to do something about his situation. As Erikson (1958) notes in *Young Man Luther*, "Many individuals should not do the work which they are doing, if they are doing it well at too great inner expense" (220). Erikson also emphasizes that Luther had a "spiritual mentor" in Dr. Staupitz, the vice-general of the province of Saxony, who served as "fatherly sponsor for his identity" and "treated him with therapeutic wisdom" (17, 165, 37). Not so Bill Paulsen. As Levinson points out, Bill Paulsen never "found a mentor who could help him get established in the adult world" (135). In fact, from his early years to the present, "few people served as models for an adult life he could find inspiring" (127). He admired his grandmother's way of living but did not aspire to do what she did. He loved and admired his father but was critical of his settling for so little: "There was no admired teacher, relative or friend whose life Bill wanted to emulate. All in all, his world offered him little in the way of models" (127).

In the next chapter, when we continue Bill Paulsen's life story in his forties, we will see that he eventually made a reappraisal of his father's tendency to accept what he could take for granted and not strive for more. As Levinson puts it, "Like his father Bill would strive to make peace with the world and to settle for a modest place in it. Like him, he would come to love his pastimes and see them as a major source of pleasure and satisfaction in his adult life" (127). As Jesus said of the prodigal son (Luke 15:17), "But when he came to himself. . . ." As we will also see, however, the fifth decade of Bill's life was a period of great struggle and pain.

SALLY: "NO WORK I DID WAS EVER THAT PERFECT"

When we left Sally Wolford in chapter 3, she had been married for four years, had been working for a large banking firm for seven years, and had decided, at age thirty-two, to start a family. The decision to get pregnant was triggered by a longstanding personal timetable—"Thirty is as long as one can wait to start a family"—but also by the realization that her career was at an impasse. Daniel Levinson (1996) explains, "She had worked for almost ten years in a large firm, and she had not been promoted, despite recurrent promises. She was beginning finally to understand that she was in a dead-end job" (359). She stayed with the job for three more years, however, because she was unable to get pregnant: "Hovering on the brink of motherhood, she could not bring herself to quit the stagnant job and seek new work. When she finally got pregnant at 35, she was more than ready to leave the corporate world for awhile" (359).

When Sally was interviewed at age forty-four, she looked back on her days in the corporate world:

> I left the corporate race at 36, when my first child was born. I had worked in the same firm for thirteen years without getting recognition, title, or salary. There have been many blocks to my career development. If I let myself, I could work up a lot of resentment. (387)

She went on to talk about having children: "I don't think there's any way to know before you have children how fulfilling it is. When my son was born it was a wonderful feeling! No work I did was ever that perfect" (387).

At the same time, she said, "It was very boring to spend all that time with small children—their attention spans weren't very long," and it was also "very isolating being an older mother. The thing that gets to me is that it's so *confining*. It will still be a while before the light at the end of the tunnel, when I can leave them alone" (387). Feeling confined, she began her own firm when she was forty, and at this point in her life, she said,

> [I am] trying to combine the best of both worlds. Predominantly I feel like I'm a mother, and that's the first thing in my life. I also want to have a career and be respected in that world, but it's very hard. . . . I'd like to be seen as a professional and not lose status in the financial world, but they don't consider me professional. And the nonworking mothers don't fully accept me either. No one is quite sure where I belong. (387)

She concluded by saying, "[I hope] gradually to have more time to develop my career. I won't have a big career in the earlier sense, but I'll keep busy doing various things that interest me" (388).

Like Bill Paulsen, Sally Wolford was experiencing the inferiority side of the industry vs. inferiority conflict in her thirties. It was not that she felt her work was poor in quality or below average but that she was not receiving appropriate recognition in terms of rank and status. As she puts it, "There have been many blocks to my career development" (387). She does not say what these blocks were, but her comment that she could work up a lot of resentment if she allowed herself to indicates that she has been the victim of differential treatment by the firm's management. The fact that she referred to her newborn baby as "more perfect" than any work she had ever done suggests that she held herself to a high work standard, but good work does not necessarily result in recognition. In fact, the cynics among us would argue that good work has nothing to do with recognition, promotion, salary increases, and the like.

Sally decided in her early thirties to become a mother. In doing so, she took herself out of the "corporate race" and assumed a venerable social role that has high symbolic value but relatively low social status in today's world. Moreover, she was an "older mother" and therefore felt socially isolated because most of the mothers she knew were considerably younger. Wendy Lewis (the other woman in Levinson's study presented in chapter 3) had her first child at age twenty and was the mother of three children by the age of twenty-seven. Her first child was fifteen years old and in high school when Sally's first child was born. In addition, although Sally viewed motherhood as the "first thing in my life," she also found it confining.

So, as the decade came to an end, she decided to return to the work world but on her own terms. She recognized that there was no status in managing her own firm, but she wanted to be able to view herself as engaged in what Erikson (1964a) calls "the ethos of production" (124). Now, however, she would confine herself to "the various things that interest me" (388). Her relinquishment of dreams of having "a big career" recalls the following ancient poem (RSV translation):

Psalm 131

O Lord, my heart is not lifted up,
    my eyes are not raised too high;
I do not occupy myself with things
    too great and too marvelous for me.
But I have calmed and quieted my soul,
    like a child quieted at its mother's breast;
    like a child that is quieted is my soul.

Because this psalm was written by a woman who was also a mother,[1] it is not too much of a stretch to suggest that the change in Sally's attitude concerning a "big career" was inspired by her insight that no work she had ever done was as perfect as giving birth to her son. As new life began inside of her, a shift in the dynamic conflict between industry vs. inferiority was also beginning, and with it, a renewed sense of competence. As Erikson points out in his discussion of the first stage of the life cycle, the mutual recognition that occurs between the infant and mother is the model for all recognitions that follow. As the mother of her newborn son, Sally *was* recognized, and by one whose very life depended on this recognition. And if she could do *this* without the support of the managers, why, after all, would she not be able to manage her own firm?

---

1. Patrick D. Miller, a recognized expert on the Psalms, is persuaded that Psalm 131 was written by a woman, basing this view on the fact that in the Hebrew text the word for mother is self-referential (Miller 1993, 244–46).

THE COMPETENT SELF

In "Human Strength and the Cycle of Generations" (1964a) Erikson notes that his friend, Robert W. White, who was a professor of Clinical Psychology at Harvard University, has proposed that *competence* is "a principle active in all living" (122). Erikson adds, however, that a quality that "endows all living" should have its "crisis" during one stage of the life cycle, and proposes that this crisis occurs in the fourth stage. Following the same reasoning, I have placed competence in the fourth decade of life.

In his essay "Sense of Interpersonal Competence" (1963), White focuses on the need for competence in one's interactions with another person. He notes that "acts directed toward another are intended, consciously or unconsciously, to have an effect of some kind, and the extent to which they produce this effect can be taken as the measure of competence" (73). In causal interactions, the element of competence may be minimal, but when matters of importance are at stake, competence plays a much greater role: "If we are seeking help or offering it, trying to evoke love or giving it, warding off aggression or expressing it, resisting influence by others or trying to exert influence, the effectiveness of our behavior is a point of vital concern" (73).

The cases of Bill Paulsen and Sally Wolford show how important it was to them to be recognized by themselves and others as competent persons. These cases also reveal that a person in the fourth decade of life is expected to be competent with regard to various interpersonal relationships—familial and work related—and that competence in every one of these relationships is very difficult to achieve. Bill Paulsen was unable to achieve competence in his role of "the man in the family" and his interpersonal competence in the work place was thought by his superiors to be adequate for the work he was already doing, but not for the kind of position to which he aspired. Sally Wolford encountered difficulties in convincing her superiors that she was a highly competent professional who should be rewarded for it, and the other mothers seemed unwilling to view her as a competent mother because she had come rather late to motherhood. Recall, too, that in her late thirties Wendy Lewis had "had it" with her husband's business and began to seek out an outside job because she "needed a place where [she] would be free to be competent" (Levinson 1996, 131).

White concludes his article with the observation that the sense of interpersonal competence can be "richly gratifying and enormously frustrating" (93). Sally Wolford would certainly agree with the frustrating part: when she was interviewed at age forty-four, she said, "At this point I'm trying to combine the best of both worlds. Predominantly I feel I'm a mother, and that's the first thing in my life. I also want to have a career and be respected in that world, but it's very hard. My frustration rose to such a level that I'm overeating again after losing twenty pounds last spring" (Levinson 1997, 387).

Such frustration calls to mind Erikson's cautionary note in *Young Man Luther*

(1958) that good work is often done "at too great inner expense" (220). Thus, there are times when the maintenance of our sense of competence depends on our ability to recognize when we are living, psychologically speaking, beyond our means, and borrowing against future psychological resources that we do not yet possess. At such times, we prove ourselves to be competent selves through the very act of cutting back and letting go.

PART THREE
THE MIDDLE ADULT
DECADES

Chapter 5

The Fifth Decade:
The Faithful Self

Contemporary birthday cards for those who are turning forty tend to suggest that one is no longer young: for example, "Happy 40th, and remember, you're only young once. So, how was it?" Physical changes that tend to be associated with older adults are mixed in with changes that are more likely to occur during one's forties. For example, another card reads, "Ode to a 40-year-old—40 is fun, 40 is neat, 40 means bunions and corns on your feet! 40 is great, 40 is swell, 40 means body parts going to hell! 40 is nifty, 40 is cool, 40 means farting and starting to drool! I'd go on, but it doesn't get any more encouraging."

The idea that at forty one is almost as old as one is young is fairly well established. Even if this belief may seem a bit premature when one *enters* the fifth decade of life, it's pretty hard to dispute it as one *exits* the decade. This being the case, it may be useful to consider the numerous dictionary definitions of *young* and *old*. Here are some of the more relevant definitions for *young*: (1) "being in an early period of life or growth"; (2) "characteristic of youth in quality, appearance, or behavior; fresh; vigorous; strong; lively; active"; (3) "lately begun, not advanced or developed, in an early stage"; and (4) "lacking experience or practice, immature, raw, ignorant, green" (Agnes 2001, 1662). These are some of the more relevant definitions for *old*: (1) "having lived or been in existence for a long time, aged"; (2) "of, like, or characteristic of aged people; specifically, mature in judgment, wise, etc."; (3) "having been in use for a long time, worn out by age or use, shabby"; (4) "having had long experience or practice (an *old* hand at this work)"; and (5) "tiresome, annoying, etc., especially as a result of repetition or monotony (their incessant chatter has gotten *old*)" (1003–1004).

These definitions suggest that there are positive and negative features of both *young* and *old*. To be *young* implies strength, freshness, vigor, liveliness, being active, and so on, but it also implies lack of experience, immaturity, and igno-rance. To be *old* implies aged, no longer new, worn out, tiresome, monotonous, but it also implies maturity of judgment, wisdom, long experience and practice. Perhaps a good way to look at the person turning forty is that immaturity is no longer a convincing excuse for poor work or stupid actions, and it is no longer considered a sign of precociousness when one makes a mature judgment. But now let's turn to the issue of identity vs. identity confusion, the dynamic conflict that I assign to the fifth decade of life (the forties).

THE IDENTITY VS. IDENTITY CONFUSION CONFLICT

Webster's has two definitions of the word *identity*. The first focuses on the group or aggregate: *identity* means "the condition or fact of being the same or exactly alike; sameness; oneness (such as groups united by *identity* of interests)" (Agnes 2001, 708). The second, which focuses on the individual, has three meanings: (1) "the condition or fact of being a specific person or thing; individuality"; (2) "the characteristics and qualities of a person, considered collectively and regarded as essential to that person's self-awareness"; and (3) "the condition of being the same as a person or thing described or claimed" (708).

I would differentiate these three meanings of the second definition of *identity* as follows: The first one is the declaration "I'm me and anyone who might think otherwise is mistaken." The second is the affirmation "There are the things that make me the *me* that I am; if I were to lose them, I wouldn't really be *me*." The third is the confirmation "The person you are describing is me alright." The first would apply to issues of mistaken identity, identity theft, confusion over identi-cal twins, and so forth. The second would relate to situations where, due to job loss, physical or mental disabilities, or other traumatic or debilitating experi-ences, one feels that one has lost, either temporarily or permanently, what is essential or central to who one is. In other words, without these, I no longer rec-ognize myself. The third concerns a situation in which if someone were to say, "The one I am looking for to share my life with will be . . . ," and, on hearing the description, you step forward and declare, "That's me. *I'm* the very one you are looking for!" Or it might be a job description: "The successful applicant will have . . . ," and, on reading through the list of qualifications, you think to your-self, "That's me. It's as though they created the job just for me." Unfortunately for the one who thinks this, the third meaning shades over into the definition of *identity* that focuses on the group or aggregate, which means that several or many others could make the very same claim and not be mistaken or misguided.

Thus, the first two meanings of the second definition of *identity* are the most significant, and these, I believe, were the ones that Erikson had in mind when he introduced the word. Hence: *I* am *me,* and this is what makes *me myself.* On the other hand, he considered the group or aggregate aspect of identity equally important. In *Identity: Youth and Crisis* (1968) he presents two formulations "which assert strongly what identity feels like when you become aware of the fact that you do undoubtedly *have* one" (19).

The first, which focuses on the individual, is from a letter William James wrote to his wife in which he noted that "a man's character is discernible in the mental or moral attitude in which, when it came upon him, he felt himself most deeply and intensely active and alive. At such moments there is a voice inside which speaks and says: *This* is the real me!" (19). For Erikson, what James describes here is "a subjective sense of an invigorating sameness and continuity" (19).

The second formulation of identity focuses on one's affinity with a group. It is provided by Sigmund Freud and comes from a talk that he gave to the Society of B'nai B'rith in Vienna. Freud had joined the local chapter of B'nai B'rith in 1897 when he was feeling professionally isolated, and in 1924 the Society honored him with a birthday celebration when he turned seventy. He confessed that he has not shared the Jewish religious faith or its national pride, but other things continued to bind him to his ancestral people. There are, he said, "many obscure emotional forces which were the more powerful the less they could be expressed in words," plus "a clear consciousness of inner identity, the safe privacy of a common mental construction" (20). Those who have grown up in a particular church tradition, have subsequently left it, and yet continue to identify themselves with it will know what Freud is talking about. But so will those who, as adults, have found a church tradition in which they feel at home despite the fact that they did not grow up in this tradition.

Together, these two formulations make Erikson's point that when we try to understand what identity is about, "we deal with a process 'located' *in the core of the individual* and yet also *in the core of his communal culture*" (22). Significantly enough, *Webster's* definition of the *identity crisis* (for which term it credits Erikson) includes both elements. Thus, the *identity crisis* is "the condition of being uncertain of one's feelings about oneself, especially with regard to character, goals, and origins, occurring especially in adolescence as a result of growing up under disruptive, fast-changing conditions" (Agnes 2001, 708).

In *Identity and the Life Cycle*, Erikson (1959) emphasizes that the identity vs. identity confusion stage represents a major development in relation to the previous stages, for "in puberty and adolescence all sameness and continuities relied on earlier are questioned again because of a rapidity of body growth which equals that of early childhood and because of the entirely new addition of physical maturity" (88–89). Thus, "in their search for a new sense of continuity and same-ness, some adolescents have to re-fight many of the crises of earlier years" (89). He also notes that young persons in this stage are now "primarily concerned with attempts at consolidating their social roles" and "are sometimes morbidly, often curiously, preoccupied with what they appear to be in the eyes of others as com-pared with what they feel they are and with the question of how to connect the earlier cultivated roles and skills with the ideal prototypes of the day" (89). By "ideal prototypes" he means persons or roles that serve as models for youth to seek to emulate.

In *Childhood and Society* (1950) he emphasizes the importance of the inte-gration of one's sense of who one is and aspires to be with who one is thought to be and capable of becoming by one's society, and suggests that this integration typically centers around a career choice (228). In chapter 3, we saw how Sally Wolford's father squelched her aspiration to become an accountant (like him) because he felt that women in that profession are assigned to its more boring functions. We also saw how Erikson's own aspirations to become an artist were countered by his stepfather's desire that he become a local pediatrician like him-self. For such youth, the integration is likely to become protracted and continue well into the next decade of life.

Erikson used various terms for the negative tendency of this stage, beginning with *role diffusion* (1950), then *identity diffusion* (1959), then *role confusion* (1963), and finally *identity confusion* (1968). Despite these changes in terminol-ogy, his original emphasis on the difficulty of finding one's *role* in life remained a central component of the negative tendency and its threat to the development of a reliable sense of identity. As he noted in *Identity and the Life Cycle,* "Youth after youth, bewildered by some assumed role, a role forced on him by the inex-orable standardization of American adolescence, runs away in one form or another" (91). In other words, the core of the individual and the core of the com-munal culture fail to make contact, whether because there *is* no role that corre-sponds to one's inner core, or one is prohibited (external block) or inhibited (internal block) from taking the role that corresponds to one's inner core, or one is unable to decide between the various roles that correspond to different aspects of one's inner core.

In the third case, another William James citation is relevant. In "Great Men and Their Environment," James (1992) noted that "whether a young man enters business or the ministry may depend on a decision which has to be made before a certain day. He takes the place offered in the counting-house, and is *commit-ted*" (626). Then,

> little by little, the habits, the knowledges, of the other career, which once lay so near, cease to be reckoned even among his possibilities. At first, he may sometimes doubt whether the self he murdered in that decisive hour might not have been the better of the two; but with the years such questions them-selves expire, and the old alternative *ego,* once so vivid, fades into something less substantial than a dream. (626)

The adoption of one career trajectory over another equally plausible and possible may, indeed, seem like an act of partial self-murder and help to explain why there may be considerable vacillation, delay, and anguish over the decision.

This leads to the *moratorium* concept that Erikson (1963) introduced in the revised edition of *Childhood and Society.* He writes, "The adolescent mind is essentially a mind of the *moratorium,* a psychosocial stage between childhood and adulthood, and between the morality learned by the child, and the ethics to be developed by the adult. It is an ideological mind" (263). *Webster's* defines *moratorium* as "any authorized delay or stopping of some specific activity" and *ideology* means "the doctrines, opinions, or way of thinking of an individual, class, etc., specifically the body of ideas on which a particular political, economic, or social system is based" (Agnes 2001, 936, 708). Thus, Erikson suggests that "it is the ideological outlook of a society that speaks most clearly to the adolescent who is eager to be affirmed by his peers, and is ready to be confirmed by rituals, creeds, and programs which at the same time define what is evil, uncanny, and inimical" (263). The moratorium period allows the adolescent time to try out different ideologies, usually in company with other adolescents, and to come to some resolutions, however preliminary, as to what is believable and worth believing in.

In *Young Man Luther,* Erikson (1958) notes in the introductory chapter that he will be focusing not on political or economic systems but on religious systems, for religion was the basis of the social and intellectual milieu in which Luther sought his own identity (22). In a later chapter, he alludes to an earlier article, "The Problem of Ego Identity" (Erikson 1956), where he had pointed out that "ideologies offer to the members of this age-group overly simplified and yet determined answers to exactly those vague inner states and those urgent questions which arise in consequence of identity conflict" (42). Thus, if the corresponding cultural dimensions for the third and fourth stages are the *economic* and the *technological ethos,* the *ideological ethos* serves the same purposes in the fifth stage of identity vs. identity confusion.

THE VIRTUE OF FIDELITY

Erikson assigns the virtue of fidelity to this stage. *Webster's* defines *fidelity* as "faithful devotion to duty or to one's obligations or vows; loyalty; faithfulness" (Agnes 2001, 526). In "Human Strength and the Cycle of Generations," Erikson (1964a) states that fidelity "is the ability to sustain loyalties freely pledged in spite of the inevitable contradictions of value systems" (125). Questions that inevitably arise from this ability are, "To whom or what does the individual pledge loyalty and faithfulness?" and "What are the benefits and costs of such pledging both to oneself and to others?"

In his discussion of fidelity, Erikson emphasizes the adolescent's sexual development and the difficulties that result, noting especially that "a youth's ego-balance is decidedly endangered by the double uncertainty of a newly matured sexual machinery which must be kept in abeyance in some or all of its functions while he prepares for his own place in the adult order" (124–25). The alternation of impulsiveness and compulsive restraint in this period is well-known, yet an "'ideological' seeking after an inner coherence and a durable set of values can always be detected" (125). If identity essentially involves a sense of inner coherence, then fidelity, the cornerstone of identity, concerns the durable set of values without which there can be no genuine sense of identity (125). As identity's cornerstone, fidelity "receives inspiration from confirming ideologies and affirming companions" (125). In youth, the truth which is the bedrock of fidelity

> verifies itself in a number of ways: a high sense of duty, accuracy, and veracity in the rendering of reality; the sentiment of truthfulness, as in authenticity; the trait of loyalty, of 'being true'; fairness to the rules of the game; and finally all that is implied in devotion—a freely given but binding vow, with the fateful implication of a curse befalling traitors. (126)

Although identity and fidelity are necessary for ethical strength, they do not provide it in themselves. Adults must provide the content for the loyalty that youth are prepared to offer and worthy objects for their need to repudiate. As cultures enter into the fiber of youth, "they also absorb into their lifeblood the rejuvenating power of youth" (126). Thus, adolescence is "a vital regenerator in the process of social evolution" because youth selectively offer their "loyalties and energies to the conservation of that which feels true to them and to the correction or destruction of that which has lost its regenerative significance" (126). Youth can be loyal to an existing or prevailing ideology or decide to remain deviant or become revolutionary in loyalty to "an overdue rejuvenation" (126). Thus, *fidelity* can take various forms. But whatever form it takes, it requires a confirming ideology and affirming companions, companions who are drawn to the same ideology.

Readers of this book may have some objections to Erikson's use of the word *ideology* to apply to religious beliefs and practices. They may want to contend that religions are non-ideological because they affirm universal or eternal truths. To this argument, Erikson would respond that in order to be persuasive, any belief system, including a religious one, needs to "create a world image convincing enough to support the collective and individual sense of identity" (1958, 22). That is, it needs to make sense of the world in which the adolescent lives and to invest it with meaning so that the adolescent will, in turn, invest in it. An appeal to the eternal truth of a belief system is insufficient. The belief system needs to impress the adolescent as a *living* truth, and thus as worthy of fidelity—of faithfulness.

Erikson makes a persuasive case for locating the identity vs. identity confusion conflict in the second decade of the life cycle. I do not wish to challenge the idea that there is a rudimentary struggle with this conflict during this period. At the same time, I believe that the fifth decade of life (the forties) is one in which there is an effort to realize a lasting sense of identity. It is the decade when one undergoes a profound "identity crisis" as *Webster's* defines it: "the condition of being uncertain of one's feelings about oneself, especially with regard to character, goals, and origins" (Agnes 2001, 708). After all, one has lived long enough to have some rather distinct impression of who one is and has become, and these very impressions are likely to produce uncertainty as to how one feels about oneself, especially with regard to one's character (moral strength, self-discipline, fortitude, and so forth); life goals (how effective one has been in pursuing them, whether they should be altered or revised, whether they reflect the core of one's being, and so forth); and origins (how they have fostered or impeded one's development into the kind of person one aspires to be, whether they afford previously untapped resources that one may use more effectively in the second half of one's life, and so forth).

One stands, as it were, on the bridge between the young and the old, and the road one has traveled and the road ahead are of roughly equal distance. It makes sense, then, that one would stop for a moment and engage in self-reflection. Most personal autobiographies are written in middle adulthood and have as their purpose the exploration of one's past in order to lay the groundwork for the future. If any literary genre is fundamentally about the identity vs. identity confusion conflict, the personal autobiography is surely that genre. It is significant, therefore, that the very first personal autobiography, Augustine's *Confessions* (1960), which he wrote sometime between the ages of forty-three and forty-seven, focused on the author's *religious* struggles.

RETURNING VETERANS
WITH SYMPTOMS OF INSTABILITY

My proposal that the identity and identity confusion conflict is central to the fifth decade of life (forty to forty-nine) makes it noteworthy that Erikson was in his fifth decade when he began to employ the term "identity crisis." He notes in the prologue to *Identity: Youth and Crisis* (1968), "The term 'identity crisis' was first used, if I remember correctly, for a specific clinical purpose in the Mt. Zion Veterans Rehabilitation Clinic during the Second World War" (16–17). In his clinical view, most of their patients had neither become "shell-shocked" nor were they malingerers; instead, they had "lost a sense of personal sameness and historical continuity" (17). They were "impaired in that central control" for which only "the 'inner agency' of the ego could be held responsible" (17). Thus, they were suffering from a loss of "ego identity" (17).

Erikson began working at the Veterans Rehabilitation Clinic in 1943, when he was forty-one years old. The clinic's purpose was short-term treatment of American veterans who had been discharged for "nervous instability," "shell shock," and/or "psychoneurosis." Federal and military officials and large segments of the public had been deeply distressed by the high incidence of these mental illnesses among seemingly healthy GIs. Several Bay Area analysts were recruited for part-time services, and Erikson was appointed as a consultant in psychology and child guidance.

During staff conferences he disagreed with pathological diagnoses for most of the veterans and suggested that their problems stemmed from their experience of "dramatic historical changes" (Friedman 1999, 160). Their careers had been disrupted; they had been separated from families and loved ones, transported from familiar communities to strange distant locations, and had to deal with military procedures, including the sights and sounds of deadly combat. As his biographer Lawrence J. Friedman puts it, "Reduced to its essentials, they had 'lost a sense of personal sameness and historical continuity' and were experiencing 'identity crises.' They could not rely on ego synthesis—the intact ego's capacity to organize thousands of diverse stimuli so that the important ones could be addressed and the others ignored" (160–61). Thus, an "identity crisis" represented the absence of a sense of what one is, of knowing where one belongs, and what one wants to do (161).

In a paper written in 1945 Erikson (1987d) pointed out that the very diagnosis of "psychoneurosis" has, in many cases,

> caused the patients inferiority feelings, doubts regarding their sanity, and guilt feelings toward their buddies who stayed to finish the job. For some individuals and groups of the community it has led to an economic stigma—unreasonably, since innumerable undiagnosed neurotics do acceptable peacetime work. (614)

He also noted that there is "a whispering campaign which suspects all psychoneurotic discharges as weaklings" (615). In wartime, there is "a general inclination to condemn all weakness in the prosecution of the war as a danger to morale" and in the armed forces a high premium is placed on "the determination to 'finish the job'" (615). But even among the soldiers who stuck with it to the end, "much of the most venomous and heated condemnation of 'weak sisters' or 'cowards' has come from those who have been closest to a breakdown themselves and do not want to admit it" (615). During the war, this condemnation served a purpose, but "now that the war is over, condemnation or suspicion becomes senseless. The conscience of the strong who broke is already overburdened—and the weak will not learn from condemnation" (615).

He warned that although "American family life and American economic resiliency will gradually reabsorb the vast majority of those who have suffered dislocation," any geographic dislocation or interruption of a career is a dangerous thing "in a competitive system" (615–16). A man who was called to serve in the armed forces wanted "to finish the job (as long as he was convinced that there was a job), and he wanted to avoid letting his buddy down (as long as he was convinced his buddy felt the same)," but the one thing he hated was "to be a sucker" (616), and many who returned to find that their old jobs had been given to others, that others had, in the meantime, purchased homes that they themselves could not afford, caused many to feel that they had, in fact, been "suckers." Thus, on returning home, only a small number of the veterans "have been able to avoid serious doubts in this war," and not every veteran who, in order to forget these doubts, simply wants to get home or get his old job back "will be able at first to make the best of either" (616).

Erikson's report concludes with a list of the common symptoms of the veterans' unrest. In addition to restlessness, sleeplessness, sexual anesthesia or even temporary impotence, and unusual bursts of anger, they may have "a mildly confused feeling of unreality," including lapses of memory, indecision, and inefficiency in regard to simple tasks well mastered before the war, with these symptoms often lasting into the first job, even if this happens to be the prewar job. There may also be puzzling contradictions and ambivalences: "Some men will be excessively active, aggressive, talkative; others will be silent, moody, and passive; others will oscillate between these extremes. At one moment they will pour out their experiences and at the next will resent a simple little question" (616). Furthermore, some may not know what to do with themselves, yet be upset by any suggestion as to what they *should* do. Some may also become quite dependent, especially on their wives, yet be angry at any recognition of this dependency. Some may want to find things as they left them, yet complain that nothing has been done since they were away. Some may hate the army, yet resent disparaging remarks, especially against their particular outfit. Some may crave continuity, yet be shiftless; some may be very jealous, yet indicate that faithlessness has not been beyond them; and some may act young, yet appear old (616).

I suggest that these veterans were experiencing, in an acute and extreme form, what is more chronic and less extreme in the fifth decade of life. If the veterans were experiencing a sense of *historical* discontinuity between the worlds they experienced before and after the war, the fifth decade ushers in a period of *chronological* discontinuity due to the simple but inevitable fact that one has crossed the divide between being unconditionally young to being incipiently old. As one crosses this divide, one engages in a review, however informal, of where one has been (origins and subsequent development) and contemplation of where one is going (goals). One experiences a "crisis" for, as Erikson (1968) notes, "crisis" does not mean an "impending catastrophe" but instead designates "a necessary turning point, a crucial moment, when development must move one way or another, marshaling resources of growth, recovery, differentiation" (16).

In *Childhood and Society*, Erikson (1950) presents a case titled "A Combat Crisis in a Marine." It concerns a thirty-year-old teacher who was discharged from the armed forces as a "psychoneurotic casualty" (34). A medical corps man, he had broken down during combat when someone thrust a submachine gun in his hands. Erikson spoke with him in the Veterans Rehabilitation Clinic and learned that he had not seen his mother since he was fourteen years old, when, in a drunken rage, she had pointed a gun at him. He had grabbed the gun, broken it, and thrown it out the window, then left the house and never returned (36–37). Soon thereafter, he made a solemn vow never to drink and never to touch a gun again. The second vow was inadvertently broken the night when his platoon was under intense enemy fire on a beachhead in the South Pacific.

Persons in their fifth decade of life are not undergoing a "combat crisis," but there are similarities between what they are experiencing and what this marine was undergoing in an acute form: his experience that night had created a rupture in the self that he had carefully fashioned following his traumatic experience at age fourteen and the man he was forced to become due to the exigencies of war. This rupture was more severe than the breach that occurs in the fifth decade of life, but this breach is no less threatening if one is unable to cope with its challenges. The fifth decade of William Paulsen's life illustrates some of the challenges it presents.

BILL: "I FEEL AS THOUGH I'M A LITTLE TOO OLD RIGHT NOW"

When we left off with Bill Paulsen's story (Levinson 1978) in the preceding chapter, he had decided to leave his dead-end job at Bowles & White and he, his wife Ruth, and their son Pete had moved back north. He left Florida full of self-doubt yet determined to try again.

The move began well. The family moved into an apartment in the New York City area, and he got a good job at the Bing Company in the computer section of a plant that built aerospace simulators. His boss, a young engineer, liked him, and when his boss was transferred to another plant in Hampton, New York, he invited Bill to join him. In Hampton, he was in charge of all documentation for computer application and purchased the software. During his first three months at Hampton, he was involved in developing the simulation for the Apollo spacecraft. He and his family spent eight months in Texas while he worked on the Lunar Excursion Model, and he then went to Cape Kennedy for the installation of a second LEM simulator. This was an exciting time for him and was in many ways the high point of his career. At forty-two, he felt that his gamble in leaving a secure but essentially dead-end position in Florida had paid off (285–86).

But then everything suddenly turned sour. His boss was made the managing director of a program to develop a simulator for the F-111 fighter plane, and he asked Bill to join him. After a few months on the project, Bill realized that he had made a mistake. The project was failing, he was not promoted to supervisor as he had hoped, and his boss left the company. In serious corporate difficulty, Bing Company merged with Western Corporation; a number of employees were laid off, and Bill was among them. At forty-two, he was without a job. Desperate, he found a job with the P-E Company in Connecticut, but after seven months, its government contract expired, and he was laid off again. At the time, Bill thought, "This can't go on" (286).

Then, however, a man who lived in his apartment complex said to him, "I understand that you are looking for a job" (286). That evening they sat down together, and the other man wrote a resume for Bill that he could sell his own company on and get Bill hired. The plan worked. At forty-four, Bill got a job at United Electronics. The resume had given the impression that he had experience in quality control, and he was hired as a quality-control engineer. He was placed in a position for which he lacked the requisite experience, and the company had no quality-control program when he started, so he was "running around the plant like a madman" (287).

Moreover, the company was new and struggling to establish itself, and there was considerable conflict between the workers and their bosses. Bill pictured himself as the man in the middle, trying to make peace between workers and managers. He believed that his skills as a mediator would get him promoted and felt that his boss was grooming him to be the manager of quality control. He felt that he was "the logical choice" for the job, but he also acknowledged that his personality might get in the way:

> I'm afraid there is something that may keep me from it—my own personal makeup, the way I talk to people. I think I give the impression to some people that maybe I'm above them because of my position. If I do this, and I was told this once before, it's not my intention. (287)

He also recognized that he tends to "think and administer from the working man's class, the subordinate class, as opposed to orienting myself to management's point of view," and noted that when one goes "toward the lower people" instead of "the big ones," you get put into that slot and are given "more responsibility than you've had to cope with before" (287). In Levinson's view, his self-reassurances that, if asked, he could handle the position as manager of quality control "seemed shallow and unconvincing, even to Bill" (287).

His marriage and family were also a concern. Ruth told the interviewer that she knew how much Bill wanted to build a better life for the three of them, but that she was beginning to feel that he would not be able to work things out. The turmoil of their entire life was beginning to erode their marriage. One evening they were visiting friends, and they got into an argument. Bill got angry and stomped out of the house. Ruth knew that if he walked out for good, this "would be the end of everything" (288). Fortunately, he came back ten minutes later, but, for Ruth, this incident demonstrated how close they were to breaking up their marriage.

Another problem was that they deeply missed their home in Florida. They especially disliked the fact that they were living in an apartment complex because Bill's income level and job instability meant that they were unable to buy a home of their own. Ruth, who was also working, no longer looked forward to going to work or coming home and fought feelings of despair: "At this stage I just accept it. I guess that's something you have to go through. I don't count on things anymore because perhaps I'd be too disappointed if they didn't work out" (288).

Bill's health problems were also a major concern. His doctor examined his lungs and told him that "things don't look very good down there," but he had difficulty quitting smoking. Then, after working just a few months for United Electronics, he was laid off and again began the agonizing search for a job. Four months later, he found a job and took it even though it was sixty miles from home. Given the job market at the time (1970), he was lucky to find work at all. It was a small plant, and he was the only worker in quality control. There were tensions on the job; the daily commute was difficult; and he began drinking heavily for the first time since the difficult years after his father's death.

Just before his forty-fifth birthday, he woke up at 5:30 on a Monday morning and felt a burning sensation in the back of his head. Ruth drove him to the hospital, and a neurosurgeon was called in. A couple of angiograms indicated that he had experienced a brain hemorrhage, but they could not locate it. After a month in the hospital, and no success in finding anything, he was sent home. He was home for about a week when he collapsed on the living room floor and returned to the hospital. This time they found out what the problem was, and the neurosurgeon operated and was able to patch up the rupture. He remained in the hospital for almost three months. The surgeon later told him that he was "very fortunate and that he thanked God that he was able to repair it" (289). He had operated on Bill in March and told him that November would be the earliest that he would even think of letting him go back to work.

Bill now faced a multitude of problems. He had hospitalization insurance but had to pay the $3,000 surgeon's bill himself. He was ineligible for social security insurance or a veteran's pension. He couldn't get unemployment compensation because he was still employed by his company. His supervisor promised to hold his job until he could return in a few months, but when he finally told the company that he was ready to come back, they said that they had replaced him and had no other openings. On learning this, he applied for unemployment compensation, but it didn't begin until Christmas Eve. More than a year later, he was still unemployed.

When he was interviewed for the last time at age forty-six, Bill was painfully blunt in assessing his situation: "It's on my nerves that I haven't got a position yet. And it doesn't look as though there's going to be anything in the near future" (289). He went on to say that his wife was working and that if it weren't for her "the family would have just gone to hell" (289). But he found it demeaning to know that she was the one who was holding the family together and he was doing nothing to support the family: "I feel that I'm not contributing to the welfare of the family. I have no income except unemployment and to me this is not a source of income. I just do not like being on it" (289).

Bill acknowledged that local newspapers advertised lots of jobs, but he then lamented, "These companies don't want to touch people like myself. They won't take you on and you can't get a reason as to why. Well, there are three things I can think of: I don't have the background, I don't have the degree, or I'm too old" (289). Also, "You tell them you had cerebral hemorrhages and enjoyed full recovery, but all they see is cerebral hemorrhage. They don't want to take a chance. I don't know what the hell I'm going to do. I'm running into a blank wall" (289).

By this time Bill had been on unemployment for more than a year. He was almost forty-seven years old. Levinson comments, "He had been hunting for a job energetically but without success, and his chances of getting what he wanted were slim. He struggled to accept the idea of taking a lower-level job. An important shift was taking place in his feelings about himself and his future" (290). Bill described his current thinking in this way:

> I'm living for the present now. God willing, if a good job comes along then it may be that I'm going to want to stay with it for the rest of my life. I don't know. On the other hand, I may work there for a month or so and then say this is not for me and go looking someplace else. But I don't like that. *I feel as though I'm a little too old right now* to go from one job to another in a short time. This has happened in the past three or four years. I don't like the feeling because I'm not only upsetting myself but I'm fouling up the well-being and the harmony of the family. (290, emphasis added)

He went on to talk about how he has made his wife "a nervous wreck by going from one job to another" and "by moving to a different area, maybe two, three times a year" (290). He also noted that his son's "education right now is more important than a lot of other things. If I keep moving him around, his education is going to suffer, and I don't want that to happen" (290). He added, "The only way I can work on something like that is to locate a good position someplace in a small company, or even a large company for that matter, where I can function with no lying about it, shall I say, no bluffing" (290). He had learned his lesson about bluffing at United Electronics.

Although Bill's current situation seemed dreary and hopeless, Levinson thinks that he had undergone some important changes in his outlook on life and had come to a more realistic—and hence hopeful—self-assessment:

> For the first time he talked of settling for a small job that he knew he could do, rather than overreaching himself. His major concern was not advancing to a managerial position; that Dream was gone. He was ready to settle for a good deal less—a job with a stable income that would give his family a settled life. (290)

To be sure, "He felt rootless, lonely, defeated" and his "feeling of desperation turned to despair" (291). At the same time, "important developments were taking place" because he "was making a critical evaluation of himself and his capabilities" (291). In his job at United Electronics, "he had begun to come to terms with the fact that he would never be a manager, that he had lost the bet he made at age 40," but relinquishing this aspiration

> carried with it the hope that he might be able to settle for more limited goals and seek other satisfactions. There is evidence that Bill Paulsen at 47 was planning for a modest future. It was as if his illness had both forced and enabled him to come to grips with the reality of his life. He seemed ready to make his peace with the world, to live with fewer illusions and to provide a stable life for his family. (291)

From Levinson's perspective, Bill was down, but he was not out.

BILL'S IDENTITY CRISIS

Many would call what Bill had gone through the last several years a "mid-life crisis," and Levinson, for one, would not disagree. He notes that "various discussions of 'mid-life crisis' refer to times of great difficulty in 'the middle years,' which may cover any part of the span from 35 to 65," but he then goes on to say that he prefers to reserve this term for a crisis that occurs in the early forties, a period that corresponds to what he calls the "mid-life transition" (Levinson 1978, 159). There is no reason that we should challenge this terminology for what Bill had been going through. At the same time, we gain some important insights into his experiences in his forties if we view the changes that Levinson himself describes as evidence of an "identity crisis."

As we have seen, Erikson (1968) does not view "crisis" as an "impending catastrophe" but as "a necessary turning point, a crucial moment, when development must move one way or another, marshaling resources of growth, recovery, differentiation" (16). Following his cerebral hemorrhage and narrow escape from death, Paulsen has come to that "turning point" or "crucial moment," and his "painfully blunt" assessment of his situation indicates that he is fully aware of this fact. This crisis has all the hallmarks of an "identity crisis." Among *Webster's* various definitions of *identity*, the one most central to this crisis is the one that focuses on "the characteristics and qualities of a person, considered collectively and regarded as essential to that person's self-awareness" (Agnes 2001, 708).

Before his hospitalization, Bill was prone to a certain amount—some would say a great deal—of self-deception as far as his abilities and prospects were concerned. Levinson notes his tendency toward self-deception when he was working for Bowles & White in Florida:

> Soon he aspired to become the supervisor of the entire data processing section. *A thread of self-deception ran through Paulsen's description of his life.* He exaggerated his talent for mediating between workers and management. Not wanting to think of his job as clerical, he was overly optimistic about his chances for advancement. So, as he established himself in the job, he was sowing the seeds of future problems. (Levinson 1978, 282, emphasis added)

But in the wake of his hospitalization and recovery, he seems much more concerned to *see* himself as he really is, and to try to *know* who he essentially is.

This truer understanding of himself—as a person and as a worker—had become a practical matter when he was laid off by United Electronics and was hired at the other company as a quality-control specialist, only to lose this job as well. *Webster's* also defines *identity* as "the condition of being the same as a person or thing described or claimed" (Agnes, 2001, 708). Bill, of course, was well-aware that his United Electronics resume misrepresented his training and experience. He was *not* the person his resume said that he was. Now, after losing both jobs, he hopes to locate a good position: one, he says, "where I can function with no lying about it, shall I say, no bluffing" (290). Having worked the past couple of years—when he was able to work—on the basis of a feigned identity, he is now hoping that he can find work on the basis of who he *really* is. As Erikson (1950) puts it, he is recognizing the importance of the integration of his own sense of who he is and aspires to be with who he is thought to be and capable of becoming by his society (228)—in his case, the companies that he hopes will extend him a job offer.

Another change taking place in Bill concerns his family. He seems genuinely worried about Ruth and the difficulties she confronts in being the only wage earner in the family. He is also concerned about his son Pete and the effect that their frequent moves could be having on his education. Having long since relinquished the idea—and responsibilities—of being the man of the extended family, he has begun to focus his loyalties on his immediate family, loyalties growing out of his awareness that were it not for Ruth, his family "would have just gone to hell" (285). There seems, in other words, to be a newly discovered sense of fidelity—of faithfulness—arising out of his awareness that he has *not* been able to support his family as he had felt obligated—as the husband and father—to do. This experience has been humbling but has also taught him that fidelity is a strength. Despite their conflicts and problems throughout the years, he and Ruth have been faithful to one another.

In a sense, he is coming to understand, more than ever, his father's wisdom. As a younger man, he had cherished his father's common sense and generosity with his attention and advice, but he had also been bothered by the fact that his father worked in the same job all his life and never received more than a $10-a-week raise. Now, in his mid-forties, he is beginning to come around to his father's preference for security over risk taking. To be sure, he is somewhat uncertain on this point, as he says that "if a good job comes along then it may be that I'm going to want to stay with it for the rest of my life," or "I may work there for a month or so and then say that is not for me and go looking for someplace else" (290). But for the first time in his life he has been able to say that he does not like the latter prospect because "I feel as though I'm a little too old right now to go from one job to another in a short time" (290). In this case, the association of the word *old* with mature judgment seems altogether appropriate.

A SECOND BIRTH?

If Bill really believes that he is too old to go from one job to another in a short time, then I would conclude that this is one of the true blessings of coming to realize that one is no longer young. Moreover, his "identity crisis" has led him to share, in spirit at least, the views of the ancient poet cited earlier (Ps. 131 RSV):

O Lord, my heart is not lifted up,
    my eyes are not raised too high;

> I do not occupy myself with things
>   too great and too marvelous for me.
> But I have calmed and quieted my soul,
>   like a child quieted at its mother's breast;
>   like a child that is quieted is my soul.

The image of a child at its mother's breast suggests that Bill may also be at that "crucial moment" in his life when he is asking, implicitly, the question that Nicodemus asked when Jesus told him that one needed to be "born anew": "How can a man be born when he is old? Can he enter a second time into his mother's womb and be born?" (John 3:4).

Surely this was a rhetorical question, for Nicodemus knew full well that entering one's mother's womb again is physically impossible. But Jesus responded, "Very truly I tell you, no one can enter the kingdom of God without being born of water and Spirit. What is born of the flesh is flesh, and what is born of the Spirit is spirit" (5–6). The first birth was by water (intrauterine); the second is spiritual.

In "Issues in the Psychology of Religious Conversion," James R. Scroggs and William G. T. Douglas (1977) discuss the "ripe age" for conversion, noting that there "has been more research on age of conversion than on any other aspect. Early writers were unanimous in regarding adolescence as the most probable age for conversion" (259). But they also cite three studies by Robert Ferm, all published in 1959, which reported average ages of conversion of forty-one, forty-three, and forty-six. In an attempt to resolve the conflict between these two sets of findings, Scroggs and Douglas cite Erikson's life-cycle model and suggest that the identity crisis "is repeated during middle age in the form of the integrity crisis," so "it is probably fair to conclude from Erikson's theories that both the identity crisis in adolescence and the integrity crisis in the middle years constitute ripe moments for conversion" (260).

They are mistaken, of course, when they assign the integrity crisis to the middle years, for Erikson located integrity in old age. But my relocation of the identity vs. identity confusion conflict to the fifth decade of life reconciles these two sets of findings, for it suggests that the forty-year-old is struggling with identity concerns and is therefore at a "ripe age" for some sort of spiritual rebirth. Recall that Nicodemus asked Jesus, "How can a man be born when he is old?" One is unlikely to think of oneself as "old" before the fifth decade. So this may be the first time in one's life when Nicodemus's question has existential relevance.

The first half of Bill's life was spent as his mother's son. In his late thirties he was still trying to prove to her that he loved her, but when she entered a nursing home, his days of caring for her were over. His fifth decade, then, was a time when he could, indeed, be born again. And the most direct evidence that this was possible was the fact that he had survived cerebral hemorrhages—his own surgeon gave thanks to God that he was able to repair it—and had completely recovered.

One does not need any stronger empirical evidence than this that the "Good Lord" (Levinson 1978, 290) was watching over him.[1]

THE FAITHFUL SELF

In his essay, "The Galilean Sayings and the Sense of 'I'" (1981) Erikson comments on the story of the woman who had been afflicted with a hemorrhage for twelve years. He notes that Jesus responded to her touch by saying, "Your faith has made you well" (Luke 8:48), adding that the King James version says that he called her "daughter," and said that her faith had made her "whole" thus underlining "the loving as well as the holistic character of all healing" (342). Erikson also mentions Jesus' parable of the prodigal son (Luke 15:11–32) and notes that "the two distinct parts of the parable make us alternately sympathize with the lost son and with the older one who was so concerned over all the excessive attention to his younger brother" (354). Then, however, he wonders if there isn't another way to view the parable: "Yet the parable is so evenly constructed that we can end up only realizing that both brothers are at odds within us, too" (354–55). A similar point could be made concerning the story of the two sisters, the attentive Mary and the distracted Martha (Luke 10:38–42).

If we combine Erikson's comment on the "holistic character of all healing" with the suggestion that the two brothers "are at odds within us, too," we can see how the faithful self is the self that ensures that we are being true to ourselves, that we are neither claiming to be what we are not, nor acting as though we were two different persons. Thus, the faithful self is the self that enables us to be faithful to who we are—to our essential identity—and therefore capable of faithfulness to our commitments to other persons and to the tasks that are integral to the social roles that we have made our own.

That the faithful self should come to prominence in the fifth decade of life is especially appropriate, for, as noted earlier, this is the decade when we first confront the implications of the fact that we are both young and old. Like two horses of unequal ages harnessed to a wagon or carriage, the question of whether they will pull together depends on the ability of the faithful self to convince the younger one and the older one that fidelity to oneself manifests itself in "faithful

---

1. In "The Mind of Paul: A Psychological Approach," C. H. Dodd (1933) argues that St. Paul experienced a "second conversion" that completed the process that the first conversion had initiated. Dodd notes that 2 Cor. 12—"I am strong just when I am weak"—"shows how in the depth of his humiliation he found firm ground" and that it expresses a "profound psychological truth," for as long as Paul "chafed against unavoidable disabilities and reverses which wounded his prestige, he was losing the spiritual liberty and power which came from the abandonment of personal claims. But when he accepted his limitations he was liberated afresh" (104). In his 1903 address at the centenary observance of the birth of Ralph Waldo Emerson, William James (1986) said of Emerson, "Rarely has a man so known the limits of his genius or so unfailingly kept within them" (1119).

devotion to duty or to one's obligations or vows" (Agnes 2001, 526). The one cannot afford to let the other one down, especially when the other one is an integral part of who one is. The faithful self is that self within the composite Self that never fails to remind us of the importance of being true to ourselves.

Chapter 6

The Sixth Decade:
The Loving Self

Milestone birthday cards make a habit of attributing to persons entering a new decade physical changes that are more likely found among persons a couple of decades older. Here is a typical birthday greeting for persons turning fifty: "Groans when getting out of bed, hairs of gray atop your head. Wrinkles, 'roids, and cellulite, peeing several times a night. Nagging pains and trouble pooping, body parts that now are drooping. Causing smells that ain't too nifty, welcome to the world of 50!" Or this: "50 is when you bend over to tie your shoelace and wonder 'What else can I do while I'm down here?'" Or this: "What do you call a group of 50-year-olds who sit around thinking about sex all the time? Nostalgia buffs!"

Other cards seem to tell it like it is: "You're 50! The bad news is you've reached the age where you have to expect a few gray hairs and a few wrinkles on your birthday. . . . The good news is all your friends have reached the age when they're too nearsighted to notice!!" Or this: "Fifty is the new forty! And I'm the queen of England." We assume, of course, that those who are unlucky enough to receive this birthday greeting are not on the queen's birthday card list, and that if there are any who believe that they are, this may itself be a sign that they have reached fifty. And, finally, a card that suggests that some signs of aging are irreversible: "Happy Birthday from the 50th Birthday Fairy. I will grant you one wish . . . I said a wish, not a miracle!"

If birthday cards use rather strained humor to assuage the pain of turning fifty, the poet Billy Collins (1995, 46–47) turns to irony:

Fiftieth Birthday Eve

The figure alone is enough to keep me awake,
the five with its little station master's belly
and cap with the flat visor, followed by the zero,
oval of looking glass, porthole on a ghost ship,
an opening you stick your arm into and feel nothing.

I want to daydream here in the dark, listening
to the trees behind the house reciting their poems,
bare anonymous beings, murmuring to themselves
in lines that reach out like long branches in spring.
I want my mind to be a sail, susceptible to any breeze
that might be blowing across the lake of consciousness.

But I keep picturing the big number, round and daunting:
I drop a fifty-dollar bill on a crowded street,
I carry a fifty-pound bag of wet sand on my shoulders.
I see fifty yearlings leaping a fence in a field,
I find the five decades before me like a poker hand.

I try contemplating the sufferings of others, Rossini,
for example, considered by many to be the Father
of Modern Insomnia for his prolonged sleeplessness
during the composition of the *William Tell* overture.

But even a long meditation on the life of Brahms,
widely recognized as a Father of Modern Lullaby,
will not dispel the fives and zeros, gnomes in the night,
perched on the bedposts, one straddling a closet doorknob.

By dawn, I have become a Catholic again,
the oldest altar boy in the parish, complete
with surplice and cassock, cruet, thurible, and candle.
And this day, whose first light is gilding the windows,
has become another one of the sorrowful mysteries,

following the agony in the garden of childhood
and preceding the crucifixion,
the letter X removed from the word and nailed to a cross,

the rest of the alphabet standing witness
on the rocky hillside, marveling at all the lightning
that is cutting across the dark sky.

Collins conveys the idea that the thought of turning fifty is grounds for a sleepless night, one in which he obsesses over the very number "50," and thinks of all the ways that it has insinuated itself into his life. As dawn approaches, he feels as though he has returned to the religion of his childhood, but this does not bring him any sense of peace; rather, it reminds him of the suffering and agony at the very heart of the tradition. While some readers of this poem may feel that the association of turning fifty with the crucifixion is rather extreme, and the poet's rational mind may well agree, his internal master is telling him that more than half of life's journey is behind him.

In "Turning Fifty," Stephen Dunn (1994, 264–65) doesn't say anything directly about himself or his thoughts about what it means to enter another decade in life. But he invites us to infer how he feels about it from his accounts of two incidents that occurred on the day that he, like Collins, turned "the big number":

Turning Fifty

I saw the baby possum stray too far
and the alert red fox claim it
on a dead run while the mother watched,
dumb, and oddly, still cute.
I saw this from my window
overlooking the lawn surrounded
by trees. It was one more thing
I couldn't do anything about,
though, truly, I didn't feel very much.
Had my wife been with me,
I might have said, "the poor possum,"
or just as easily,
"the amazing fox." In fact
I had no opinion about what I'd seen,
I just felt something dull
like a small door being shut,
a door to someone else's house.

That night, switching stations, I stopped
because a nurse had a beautiful smile
while she spoke about triage and death.
She was trying to tell us
what a day is like in Vietnam.
She talked about holding a soldier's one remaining hand,
and doctors and nurses hugging
outside the operating room,
And then a story of a nineteen-year-old,
almost dead, whispering, "Come closer,
I just want to smell your hair."

When my wife came home late, tired,
I tried to tell her

about the possum and the fox,
and then about the young man
who wanted one last chaste sense
of a woman. But she was interested
in the mother possum,
what did it do, and if I did anything.
Then she wanted a drink, some music.
What could be more normal?
Yet I kept talking about it
as if I had something to say—
the dying boy
wanting the nurse to come closer,
and the nurse's smile as she spoke,
its pretty hint of pain,
the other expressions it concealed.

This poem beautifully expresses the intimacy vs. isolation conflict that Erickson locates in young adulthood but that I have assigned to the sixth decade of life (the fifties). Dunn is spending his birthday alone and is waiting for his wife when she returns home late and tired. He is also observing the loss of life: first the baby possum, whose mother merely watches the fox's attack; then the young nineteen-year-old soldier and the seeming anomaly of the nurse's beautiful smile as she tells of being with him as he was dying, a smile that has a "pretty hint of pain" that seems to hide other expressions that might have been revealed had she herself not seemed so far away from where Dunn was watching. He is aware of the fact that he was a witness and a listener to scenes and events that he could do nothing about. As he describes them, he is also aware that what interests him about the stories is not what interests his wife, and that there is no real reason why their interests should be the same. After all, she was tired and wanted to relax, a perfectly normal desire at the end of a long day.

So what does this poem have to do with turning fifty? It reflects the poet's sense of having reached a stage in life in which he knows that there are situations he cannot do much, if anything, about—situations about which he's not even sure he has an opinion. His wife's question of whether he or the mother possum did anything about the plight of the baby possum is a reasonable one, but it seems not to have entered his mind that either of them could have done anything. Nor was there anything he could do for the young man who was dying except to bear witness to his desire for "one last chaste sense of a woman." Turning fifty meant that if the younger Dunn had thoughts of righting wrongs and fighting against injustice and pain, the older Dunn is only able to bear witness to what he observes, and what he observes is a mixture of revelation and concealment. He sees *intimacy* and *isolation* as he watches these scenes, first through a window, then through a television screen, and as he tells his wife about them, he experiences what he has witnessed: their own intimacy, but their isolation, too.

THE INTIMACY VS. ISOLATION CONFLICT

Webster's defines *intimacy* as "the state of being intimate" and notes that the word is sometimes used to suggest a sexual act ("intimacies" between two persons) (Agnes 2001, 748). The relevant definitions of *intimate* are (1) "most private or personal (his *intimate* feelings)"; and (2) "closely acquainted or associated; very familiar (an *intimate* friend)" (748). Thus, *intimacy* connotes that which is private, personal, and close—the opposite of public, impersonal, and distant. *Webster's* defines *isolation* as an isolating action or being isolated (Agnes 2001, 758). The relevant definitions of *isolate* are (1) "to set apart from others; place alone"; and (2) "a person who is separated from normal social activity, as through choice, rejection, psychological problems, etc." (758). Thus, *isolation* has the connotation of being alone or separate. When paired with *intimacy,* the word *isolation* suggests that this aloneness or separateness is experienced in relationships that are personal and close, not public and distant. Thus, its central meaning is not that a person feels alone in a large crowd but alone in a relationship or setting that is personal and private (hence, in a marriage or in one's own home).

In *Identity and the Life Cycle*, Erikson (1959) begins his discussion of this stage by noting that "it is only after a reasonable sense of identity has been established that real *intimacy* with the other sex (or, for that matter, with any other person or even with oneself) is possible" (95). He emphasizes that sexual intimacy is only part of what he has in mind, "for it is obvious that sexual intimacies do not always wait for the ability to develop a true and mutual psychological intimacy with another person" (95). He adds that the youth "who is not sure of his identity shies away from interpersonal intimacy; but the surer he becomes of himself, the more he seeks it in the form of friendship, combat, leadership, love, and inspiration" (95). In addition, unless the social and cultural mores *demand* overt sexual behavior, the attachments that young persons form are "often devoted to an attempt at arriving at a definition of one's identity by talking things over endlessly, by confessing what one feels like and what the other seems like, and by discussing plans, wishes, and expectations" (95).

Erikson does not disparage these experiences of intimacy. On the contrary, he notes that if a youth "does not accomplish such intimate relations with others" and "with his own inner resources" in late adolescence or early adulthood, he may either "isolate himself and find, at best, highly stereotyped and formal interpersonal relations (formal in the sense of lacking in spontaneity, warmth, and real exchange of fellowship)" or "he must seek them in repeated attempts and repeated failures" (95). Unfortunately, many young people marry under such circumstances, "hoping to find themselves in finding one another," but "the early obligation to act in a defined way, as mates and as parents, disturbs them in the completion of this work on themselves" (95). A change of mate is rarely the answer. Rather, what is needed is "some wisely guided insight into the fact that the condition of a true twoness is that one must first become oneself" (95).

Clearly, for Erikson, identity formation and the ability to engage in genuine intimacy are themselves intimately related.[1]

In the revised edition of *Childhood and Society* (1963), Erikson notes that the "strength acquired at any stage is tested by the necessity to transcend it in such a way that the individual can take chances in the next stage with what was most vulnerably precious in the previous one" (263). Thus, if the young adult has been fortunate enough to have established a secure-enough sense of identity, he "is eager and willing to fuse his identity with that of others. He is ready for intimacy, that is, the capacity to commit himself to concrete affiliations and partnerships and to develop the ethical strength to abide by such commitments, even though they may call for significant sacrifices and compromises" (263).

In suggesting that true intimacy involves commitment and the ethical strength to abide by these commitments, Erikson anticipates his discussion of the virtue of love, the human strength that he assigns to this stage of the life cycle.

In his presentations of the earlier stages in the revised edition of *Childhood and Society*, Erikson (1963) identified the social domain that provides an institutional safeguard of the positive tendency of a given stage dynamic. In this case, he briefly mentions a "culture's style of sexual selection, cooperation, and competition" (266) but does not indicate that it is an institutional safeguard as such. In his discussion of the virtue of love, however, he implies that affiliations, especially those that lead to the creation of families through marriage or partnerships, provide this institutional safeguard. In *Toys and Reasons* (Erikson 1977), he makes this point more explicit when he notes that "*marriage ceremonies* provide for the young adult the 'license' to enter those new associations which will transmit a way of life to the coming generation" (110).

THE VIRTUE OF LOVE

As one might have guessed, *Webster's* has many definitions of the word *love,* but in its effort to distinguish *love* from words that might be considered synonyms, it says that *love* "implies intense fondness or deep devotion and may apply to various relationships or objects" (Agnes 2001, 850). *Affection* suggests "warm, tender feelings, usually not as powerful or deep as those implied by love," and *attachment* implies "connection by ties of affection, attraction, devotion, etc., and may be felt for inanimate things as well as for people" (850). Thus, the distinguishing feature of love is not its object or even its devotion—for attachment may involve devotion—but the depth or intensity of the feelings or emotions involved.

---

1. In *Identity and the Life Cycle*, Erikson (1959) calls this the intimacy and distantiation vs. self-absorption stage. But in all other writings, including the earlier version of *Childhood and Society* (Erikson 1950) he calls it the intimacy vs. isolation stage. He states that distantiation is "the readiness to repudiate, to isolate, and, if necessary, to destroy those forces and people whose essence seems dangerous to one's own" (95–96). The distantiation issue—but not the word itself—reappears in his discussion of the virtue of love in "Human Strength and the Cycle of Generations" (Erikson 1964a).

In "Human Strength and the Cycle of Generations," Erikson (1964a) states that love "is mutuality of devotion forever subduing the antagonisms inherent in divided function" (129). He presents this definition, however, after having first discussed the fact that because love is considered "the greatest of human virtues, and, in fact, the dominant virtue of the universe," it *could* be argued that love binds every stage of the life cycle together, and therefore ought not be assigned to a single stage. He does not disagree with this argument, but he suggests that if we consider love's "evolutionary rationale," we will understand why it "is here assigned to a particular stage and a particular crisis in the unfolding human life cycle" (127). Surely, it "must be an important evolutionary fact that man, over and above sexuality, develops a selectivity of love," a selectivity that expresses itself in "the mutuality of mates and partners in a shared identity, for the mutual verification through an experience of finding oneself, as one loses oneself, in another" (128). Because identity proves itself strongest where it can take chances with itself, "love in its truest sense presupposes both identity and fidelity" (128), the positive tendency and the virtue of the preceding stage.

Thus, while many forms of love can be shown to be at work in the formation of the various virtues, the uniqueness of the love of young adulthood is that it is, above all, "a *chosen,* an *active* love, no matter what the methods of matrimonial selection are which make such a choice a precondition for familiarity or lead to it by a process of gradual familiarization" (128). In either case, "the problem is one of transferring the experience of being cared for in a parental setting, in which one happened to grow up, to a new, an adult affiliation which is actively chosen and cultivated as a mutual concern" (128).

He discusses the fact that the virtues acquired in the earlier stages have contributed to both the differentiation and commonalities of the sexes, with competence and fidelity being the most notable as "intersexual virtues" (129). In the young adult stage, it would appear that "the sexes are less different in regard to the capacities and virtues which further communication and cooperation" and more different "where divergence is of the essence, that is, in the counterpoints of love life and the divided functions of procreation" (129). This difference, which is perhaps most self-evident in the divided functions of procreation, is thus a key factor in the way he defines *love,* that is, as "mutuality of devotion forever subduing the antagonisms inherent in divided function" (129). Thus, mutuality—which has connotations of reciprocal relations and shared interests—plays a vital role in Erikson's understanding of love, for it is the mutuality of devotion that enables the sexes to emphasize sameness over difference, cooperation over competition. Therefore, love "pervades the intimacy of individuals and is thus the basis of ethical concern" (129–30).

On the other hand, Erikson also notes that the very *selectivity* of love has a regrettable, if inevitable side effect: "Love can also be joint selfishness in the service of some territoriality, be it bed or home, village or country. That such 'love,' too, characterizes his affiliations and associations is at least one reason for man's clannish adherence to styles which he will defend 'as if his life depended on them'" (130). In a sense, however, his life *does* depend on them, because his very "certainty of orientation" in space and time requires it, and this explains, while it does not justify, the fact that man can become blinded by rage "in the righteous defense of a shared identity, to sink to levels of sadism for which there seems to be no parallel in the animal world" (130). Yes, love is the greatest of all virtues, but the very aspects of love that make true intimacy possible—selectivity, commitment, devotion—may also create "the readiness to repudiate, to isolate, and, if necessary, to destroy those forces and people whose essence seems dangerous to one's own" (Erikson 1963, 95–96). Such threatening forces are not only outsiders, strangers, and foreigners, but also members of one's household—products of the intergenerational process of procreation.

As we begin our consideration of the relocation of the intimacy vs. isolation conflict from young adulthood to the sixth decade of life (the fifties), I want to expand Erikson's understanding of this conflict to include what William James (1982) terms "the divided self"(166). Viewed in this light, intimacy concerns not only interpersonal relationships but also intrapersonal relationships, especially the peaceful reconciliation of aspects of oneself that have been at odds with another. This is not the same as self-absorption, a preoccupation with one's own interests at the expense of relations with others. On the contrary, such self-reconciliation would manifest itself in becoming more aware of the desires and impulses within oneself that threaten intimate relations with others, and in recognizing the fact that one's tendency to repudiate and isolate forces and people whose essence seems dangerous to one's own is a projection of conflicts within oneself. Thus, intimacy would involve recognizing and embracing that aspect of oneself that one has treated as foreign to oneself, and would be viewed as an internal process, one that is likely to pay dividends in one's relations with others. This is a process that seems to be occurring in the life of Bill Paulsen, as his reconciliation with himself seems to be making a perceptible difference in his feelings toward his wife, Ruth, and his son, Pete.

BARBARA: "I WAS JUST A LITTLE GIRL"

In chapter 1, I discussed Barbara J. Scot's (1995) experience of her father's suicide when he was thirty-eight and she was eight. In this chapter, I will discuss her struggle with the intimacy vs. isolation conflict when she was in her fifties. This was the decade when, with the encouragement of her therapist, she returned to her childhood home in Scotch Grove, Iowa, in hopes of uncovering the mysteries of the tragedy and its meaning for her own life. She had barely known her father because he had left his wife and two children when Barbara was two years old and her brother Robert was four. Born in 1942, she had returned with her husband and two young sons to Scotch Grove in 1983, when she was forty-one-years old, intending to share with them her love for the place of her childhood. But it was too soon, because she showed them mostly her pain (3).

But while she was there, her Uncle Jim showed her a black-and-brown trunk in her mother's bedroom in their brown Victorian farmhouse. He told her that her mother had meant for her to have it and that he'd saved it until she returned. She looked through the contents of the trunk to decide whether she should carry it back to her home in Portland, Oregon, and immediately saw that her uncle was right. It had definitely been left for her. She wondered why she had not claimed it when she moved away, but, in fact, she had taken nothing from the house. "We had never belonged there, my brother and I, and nothing there was really ours," she explained (3).

At the bottom of the trunk she found her mother's wedding gown, pictures and letters (mostly from her father plus her mother's first drafts of her own letters) that immediately told her that her mother had left her the story of her brief marriage and its painful unfolding. At the bottom of the trunk was a note her mother had written containing three evenly spaced lines: *What do you think? You don't understand. You'll never know how much.* After returning home, she left the trunk unopened for several years. Then, in the spring of 1993, when she was fifty-one years old, she "reopened the trunk, carefully read all the letters, and puzzled over the note." "I felt the pain, I felt the love," she said. "I also felt a confused resentment that I needed, at last, to resolve. So in early summer I returned again to the brown Victorian farmhouse" (4).

Visit to Her Father's Grave

Barbara's trip began with a visit to her father's grave near Luzerne, Iowa. As she drove toward Luzerne, where her father had lived with his second wife and three young daughters, she calculated that it had been twenty-three years—when she, too, was thirty-eight—that she had become deeply depressed and a danger to herself:

> Pregnant, and in a marriage that was sliding precipitously downhill, I had tried to die—like him, I thought, with an old rise of anger. He was not going to usurp my mother as the primary object of my search, I promised myself firmly. To understand my mother's loyalty, however, I would have to know more of him. (8)

She found the simple gravestone with his name and the dates 1912–1950. Nothing more. She decided to have lunch at the graveside—"Lunch with my father" she said to herself, "more amused than sad" (10). She then reflected,

> I had come to this grave to honor my mother. Her love for this man had been deep, unconditional, and maddening, as far as I was concerned. I felt a rise of anger as I thought of it. To bear humiliation was a virtue, I would grant that. But to continue to love a man who humiliated her? Never to speak ill of him, indeed never to speak of him at all for almost twenty years, carrying that love to her grave in dignified silence—was that a virtue, too? (16)

A rush of guilt at her disloyalty to her mother for even thinking these thoughts swept through her as she stood up to return to the camper, for she "had loved her mother intensely. Nevertheless, as [she] drove along thinking of her, [Barbara's] mind repeated the question: Was it a virtue—or was she merely playing the fool?" (16).

Family Reunion

The next day Barbara attended a Hughes family reunion (her mother's relatives) in Cedar Rapids. She asked questions about her mother and her father, but none of the responses added to what she already knew or had intuited. Her mother? "A wonderful woman." Her father? It was said back then that "Bob wasn't good enough for Kate," and there was this story about how her father "had been gone for a long time and had come back with a short haircut. The story he told was that he had been in the military, but [the aunts] found out he had been in jail" (24–25).

The following afternoon she headed toward Scotch Grove, but as she was not expected for another day, she stopped in Anamosa for the night. As she lay in her motel room, she was keenly aware of her unresolved edge of anger whenever she thought of her mother's quiet loyalty to her father. She wondered resentfully, "Was quiet loyalty the best example for a daughter who would later be left by a husband of her own?" (29). And how was she ever going to decipher her mother's mysteries when she herself had chosen "to dissociate [herself] early in life from the farm, the church, and the traditional woman's role—with its deference to men—which had been her existence?" (29).

She left for Scotch Grove by midmorning. Just north of Anamosa she saw a sign announcing the Jones County Care Facility, which had been the county "Poor Farm" when she was a child. The site of the Poor Farm was the place where the first party of Scots had planted tentative roots before they built the more substantial Scotch Grove Presbyterian Church a short distance to the east. As she approached her grandmother's farmhouse where she, her mother, and her brother had lived, she was jolted once again to find that it was a bed-and-breakfast named "Sweet Memories" run by her cousin Vaneta, whose father was Barbara's Uncle Jim. She and Vaneta, seven years older than Barbara, had enjoyed each other's company on her earlier trip to Scotch Grove, and this time was no different. Vaneta had decided to put Barbara in her mother's old room.

Her Mother's Room

As they entered the room, Barbara glanced at a picture on the bureau and asked, "Who's this?" Vaneta expressed surprise. "That's your *mother*," she said. "Don't you recognize her?" Barbara sat down on the bed: "Perhaps I did not know her. I was only twenty-one when she died" (42). True, she knew a lot about her mother, "but not what she'd gone through with the marriage. She'd spoken of that only once." "I was home from graduate school preoccupied with my own pain over a broken engagement," said Barbara. "That was shortly before she died" (42).

That evening, sitting on the bed in her mother's room, she thought of the note she had found at the bottom of the trunk her mother had left her: *What do you think? You don't understand. You'll never know how much.* She pondered the first sentence:

> What do I think? I think you were a loyal, sensitive woman who loved a man deeply. A man who was a crook and took you for every penny he could. And when he left, you were humiliated and retreated in silence. And covered his bounced checks, paid off his notes penny by stinking penny, until you had saved that damn farm for my brother and me to lose in our own divorces later. You lived your life quietly, traveling only to town for groceries, to the woods for picnics with your children, and to church. For twenty years every Sunday unless the road was blocked by snow. Ladies Aid. Sunday school. You were a Presbyterian nun. Never saying a word against him. (42)

Then she reflected on the second sentence: *You don't understand.*

> You're right. I loved you. But I don't understand. I really don't. Why did you stay? You had a college degree at a time when many teachers didn't. You drove a car when many women were afraid or too controlled by their husbands. I don't understand the whole lot of you. Why was it so important to stay on the farm? The farm. That hallowed ground. . . . Were you trapped or were you here by choice? (42)

Finally, the third sentence: *You'll never know how much.* She turned out the light. "Until I understood, I could not possibly know how much" (43).

The Holy Farm

The next day her mother's last remaining sibling, her mother's younger sister Aunt Em, and Aunt Em's daughter Marge arrived. Barbara had timed her trip so that she could see them. They had driven over from Indiana and would be staying just a day. Aunt Em talked briefly about Barbara's mother, about the fact that she was college educated and this was probably why men were afraid of her, and that she was shy, which probably made her seem kind of standoffish (46). What about her father? Well, he was a talker, full of big ideas. Anything else? Aunt Em fell silent: "Whatever else she knew, she wasn't telling" (47). The conversation shifted to Uncle Jim, Vaneta's father. Aunt Em asked Barbara to read the poem she had written for Uncle Jim's funeral. Cousin Marge produced it, and Barbara reluctantly read it.

The first stanza described her Uncle Jim coming across the field in the first light of morning, yodeling. As she began the second stanza, which listed the things she had learned from him as a child, she hesitated, embarrassed, not wanting Vaneta to feel that Barbara had had "more of her father than she had" (49). Vaneta smiled at her, because she knew what Barbara was thinking. Aunt Em said, "Go on, there's more," so Barbara continued. This stanza concluded with her uncle's decision to return much of the farm to grasses, to resist the use of chemicals and heavy farm equipment. In his own reversal of history, he had worked backward to more antiquated farming methods as his life progressed. As she finished, her relatives were smiling approvingly "at what seemed a validation of my Uncle Jim's turning back to the time when farming made sense, when people were in touch with the land and were at least minimally integrated with nature" (50). But she herself felt a "claustrophic tightness" in her chest: "I wanted out of the room, out of the house, out of the farm. Had the horse not been dead long since I would have bolted, leaping the porch steps the way I had as a teenager" (50).

That night in her mother's room she read her great-uncle's lyrical account of Scotch Grove life in the late 1800s in his own memoir, *Iowa Sketches,* which graced the coffee table at Sweet Memories. She read the slim volume twice, the second time resenting his romanticism about agricultural ties and his equation of good farming with "a good course through life" (52). But what especially surprised her in the reading was the brevity of the family's ties to the land. Before her grandfather Gideon's generation, they were shipwrights, not farmers. Most other farmers had some eighty acres of land, enough to support their families. Not Gideon. As a young man, he had purchased a hundred acres with his father as cosigner. In the course of his lifetime, he had amassed eleven hundred more. He was the family's

> ticket into the new culture's complicated agrarian myth with its biblical imagery. The most dignified and worthy of callings was the land—a land rightfully assumed because of a promise to people far distant in time and succession that was not only grounded in the Bible, it was meant to endure until Judgment Day. The family farm. (54)

She recalled coming home from college and mentioning to her mother what she had been learning about the "agrarian myth." She might as well have been attacking the church. Her mother dismissed those professors from the cities: "The farmers are the backbone of the country" (55). "It was a religion with her—or rather, part of the religion that she lived. 'You must always be proud of your heritage from the farm.' And I was. I pictured fathers passing their farms forever to their sons in some sort of holy ceremony that went back to Abraham and Isaac" (55).

But because her mother's father had amassed so much land, a different ceremony had taken place, one that had far-reaching consequences for her parent's marriage. When her mother married, her father had given her a farm—the old Livingston place—as a wedding present. It was free and clear of debt. But the old letters in her mother's trunk had revealed an embarrassing story: Two years after her marriage, her mother's uncle, the author of *Iowa Sketches* and well-known Des Moines lawyer, had written her mother an unsolicited letter asking if he could be of financial assistance to her. Uncle Jim had alerted him about a notice for delinquent taxes, a lawsuit brought against the farm by a lumber company, and a rumor of an impending mortgage. Her mother had responded with an outline of the debt that her husband had incurred against the farm but said in her husband's defense that they were happy together when they didn't think about business and that she could never do anything that would "be disloyal to him or hurt his pride" (56). The lawyer uncle worked out a plan whereby Barbara's mother would place the farm in trust to Barbara's Uncle Jim to be passed down to Barbara's brother Bobby when her mother died. This way, the land would stay in the family and could not be subject to being sold for debts incurred by Barbara's father, who had a penchant for high-stakes gambling. But her father didn't stay around long enough for his mother's uncle's fears to be realized, and when her mother died, the land passed into the hands of Barbara's grandmother, then passed to Barbara, and was rented out to a neighboring farmer.

Barbara had subsequently sold the farm to her brother when she was a thirty-year-old single parent trying to raise her two children while working for minimum wage in a doctor's office. At the time, she was "so deep in personal pain" that she could not see that her brother "was tottering on his own abyss of alcohol and financial ruin," living in a fantasy world that was some confused cross between the grandiose schemes of their father and the land empire of their grandfather. Within a few years her brother sold the farm, including family relics, and disappeared (74).

That night, reading *Iowa Sketches,* Barbara was reminded of the religion of the farm in which she had been reared:

> The most worthy of callings was to till the soil, and it was the natural order ordained by God that the farm would pass from father to son. My brother and I grew up in the fierce shadow of those beliefs, knowing that our father had failed, that our Uncle Jim had failed, and that maintaining the family farm was that duty-at-which-we-were-all-failing. And we were very, very sorry for it all. (57–58)

She recalled the time when she was a little girl and had taken her mother's broom to the barn and was sweeping down the cobwebs that had formed above the horse stalls. Her Uncle Jim came in: "What are you doing?" he asked. "I am helping us get less behind," she replied. He took the broom from her gently. "This is a house broom," he said. "Take it back to the house." She did not try again.

Then her mind went back to her psychiatrist's puzzlement when she said that she was thinking of returning to the farm where she had grown up. This was before she had sold it to her brother. She had dreamed of the old farmhouse three nights in a row. Her psychiatrist had asked, "Why would you ever think of going back? You make it sound like the Museum of American Farming." She admitted, "I don't know." The thought of returning, the thought of becoming her mother completely, terrified her. She, too, had gone to Coe College. She, too, had become a teacher, had married a profligate spender, and had been left alone with two babies and no money. "Surely she is living her life over through me. She is trying to get it right through me and validate her own choices" (59), Barbara thought.

The next day she and Vaneta had coffee together after Aunt Em and Marge left for Indiana. Talk got around to the fact that Barbara had changed her last name to Scot after her husband left her and her two babies and a $90 phone bill that she couldn't pay. She needed a phone, so she decided to change her name. Why not take her father's name? She never knew him, and, besides, it was a name that immediately identified her as an abandoned child. Though she was from Scotch Grove, Barbara Scotch was out of the question, and she had no right to claim Scott, so she decided on Scot.

They struck a deal that morning: if Vaneta would address her mail to Barbara Scot, she would give Vaneta her cemetery plot in the church cemetery. To Vaneta, it was a very generous gift. To Barbara, it was a relief: "I don't want to be buried here. I feel as if it's taken me thirty years to get beyond all the parochial views I got from living here. I don't want my body trapped in a cemetery with a bunch of Calvinists." Vaneta countered, "Your mother's there." Barbara responded, "She was trapped, too" (61).

Meeting Her Father's Cousin

Barbara was not descended from the Scottish immigrants who came to the area and established the Scotch Grove Presbyterian Church, but her father's cousin, Eloise Clark, was, and she and her husband had returned to Scotch Grove for the summer from their retirement community in Arizona, where they lived most of the year. Eloise had been the church organist when Barbara was a child. She knew that Eloise would tell her the truth about her father.

Eloise told her about her father's difficult birth: two days of hard labor, the doctor's fear that they would lose both mother and child, and his "most awful misshapen head" (69). There was also the fact that his grandfather had given him $1,000 when he was born, but his father refused to pass the money along to him. Said Eloise, "I always wondered if that didn't have something to do with his irresponsible attitude toward money" (69).

Other facts emerged: he attended agricultural college for a year, perhaps less, then joined the Civilian Conservation Corps. He was always extremely considerate and polite, and told funny stories about himself. His parents considered the stories untruthful, and he was severely punished for them, but to Eloise "he was really a very creative dreamer." In fact, "I think your mother fell in love with him because he was so creative and so much fun," unlike her father, who "was a severe man" (71).

Then there was the Colorado misadventure: The year that Barbara was born, the four of them had left Scotch Grove in a house trailer, planning to make their home in Colorado. But before they got settled there, her father got into serious financial difficulty, probably due to high-stakes gambling, and her mother returned to Scotch Grove several months later with the two children. Her father spent a part of the time in Colorado in jail. He returned at Christmas, got a job in a hardware store in Monticello, and he and his young family rented a house there. Barbara knew about her father's return. When Barbara, then in her early twenties, had returned home from graduate school heartbroken over her broken engagement, her mother opened up to her for the first and only time in her life, telling her daughter that she knew her husband had not returned because he loved her but because *she* loved him and he was out of money. What she did not seem to know was that this was also when he began to get together with the woman who worked in town, where he would hang out in bars in the evening after work. She later became his second wife.

Her mother had thought their situation was improving and shook her head at her own naivete. When he began talking about a good job offer in Colorado but didn't ask her to come along this time, she assumed it was that he knew she wouldn't go again. She did not suspect that this was a ruse to leave her and their two children. Before she even knew what was happening, he loaded everything in the car to move them to her mother's home, claiming that he could make more money this way and they could return to the farm the next year. Her mother had said, "I didn't believe him, but I was so taken by surprise I could barely object" (168).

Barbara asked Eloise why, if her father had wanted a life of adventure, did he marry her mother and try to farm? Eloise said she thought he

> was probably trying to live the life that was expected of him. And the chance for farming fell in his lap with the situation with your mother. He wasn't cut out for it. He wasn't the kind who could wait for crops to grow. He liked new things and changes. He always had a crazy scheme—I will say he exaggerated. And he did seem to feel that money was there for the taking. (71)

Barbara brought up the matter of his death. Eloise was reluctant to talk about it, but said, "Barbara, it was the saddest funeral I have ever attended. And by now I've been to more than a few. I just kept thinking, What a wasted life. Your mother sat alone in the back" (72). Then Barbara said, "I know it was in Luzerne. But that seems odd to me, because I'm sure my mother said that he left Edith, too." Eloise said, "Well, I don't know. There was something about yet another marriage," adding, "It was said that the car he used when he killed himself belonged to a woman in Colorado. And on the seat was the marriage license. He'd been married again and would have been arrested for bigamy" (72).

Barbara now felt she knew the full story of her father. "But why," she asked Eloise, "didn't he just have affairs instead of getting married?" Eloise's eyes brimmed with tears for a cousin she had truly loved:

> Because, Barbara, in his heart he believed all the same things as the rest of us. You don't kill yourself at such a young age because you're irresponsible. You kill yourself because you have a moral code you have violated—or a strict vision of what your life should be and you think you can never attain it. And your father wanted so desperately to get it right. (72–73)

Scotch Grove Presbyterian Church

Barbara's great-uncle's *Iowa Sketches* credited much of the family's mental and moral fortitude to the guidance of the Scotch Grove Presbyterian Church. Barbara had to agree: "We went every single Sunday of my life. I could picture in detail the shift of light and shadows at the front of the sanctuary as the seasons changed. How could I hope to understand my mother without understanding the church?" (75).

There was a story in *Iowa Sketches* about a church trial in 1859 of a young man named William Clark whose primary crime was prenuptial fornication. Her great-uncle had taken the account of the trial from the Scotch Grove Presbyterian Church records, and his objective in telling the story was to illustrate the "church's effectiveness in restoring wayward youth to the fold" (85). She decided to peruse the church records herself. She wanted to dig deeper into the story as a way to place her father's scandalous behavior in context. She found the episode in the church records and discovered that the young man had been cautioned by the elders in February for dancing. Now, in October, he was not only being accused of fornication but of having taken communion in July without confessing his sexual misconduct. In November, however, he was "'restored to the communion and Christian fellowship of the church'" after he acknowledged his sin to the elders and consented to the reading aloud of the minutes of the trial proceedings to the entire congregation" (85).

What bearing did this case have on her father's scandalous behavior? After all, despite the fact that he had been accepted into membership in the church a month after Barbara's brother Robert had been baptized, his flamboyant departure with another married woman was not noted in the church session's monthly minutes. What made it relevant came out in a conversation with Vaneta a few evenings earlier. The one time when her mother had opened up to her, her mother had said that she was humiliated to think that her husband had left her for a woman who, although married, was not living with her husband at the time and had been denied custody of their three-year-old daughter. She was not furious, just bewildered. Barbara had voiced the same bewilderment to Vaneta: "I don't get it either. She certainly sounds like a total switch from my mother."

Vaneta "Of course she was a switch. The guy had screwed up royally."

Barbara "But she took him back. So why did he leave her, then, if she was willing to take him back, lies and all?"

Vaneta "Barb, he was living with a saint. Saint Kathleen. Think of it. Has anyone ever said anything negative about your mother to you?"

Barbara "No. Never."

Vaneta "So here's your dad, who has just put the nicest woman in the world

through all sorts of grief, only to be forgiven, and he surely hates himself, right?"

Barbara "I hope so."

Vaneta "So he finds a woman who is at least equally screwed up who tells him
he's wonderful. No wonder he runs away with her. As long as your dad
was with Aunt Kate, he was trapped into trying to be the kind of person he just couldn't be." (93)

This seems also to have been the fate of the young man who was forgiven
by the Scotch Grove Presbyterian Church elders. Barbara's great-uncle assumed
that the man named William Clark of the church trial was the same William
Clark who served as an elder of the church when he was a child. But Barbara
discovered that the William Clark of the church trial had transferred to the
"Four-Horn" United Presbyterian Church of Wayne Township west of Scotch
Grove in 1861 and was killed in the Civil War in 1862 (86). Of course, unlike
Barbara's father, he died a hero's death. But her great-uncle's assumption that
the forgiveness and restoration extended by the church had worked wonders
in the soul of William Clark was probably wishful thinking. And so was Barbara's mother's belief that her acceptance of her husband had changed him for
the better. The church had taught her mother well, but she was completely
unprepared for his response: suicide in an automobile belonging to another
woman.

Mother Opens Her Soul to Her

Four months before her mother died she opened her soul to Barbara in a conversation that began in the evening and continued until daybreak. As noted earlier, as she was just beginning graduate school at the University of Iowa, Barbara
had come home heartbroken because the young man to whom she had become
engaged three years earlier had broken their engagement. He had been attending
a prestigious school on the East Coast and had become attracted to a young
woman from another prestigious East Coast school. As her mother shared her
pain in an attempt to absorb some of it, Barbara began to question some of the
circumstances her mother had endured in such dignified silence for twenty years.

But now, occupying her mother's room at Sweet Memories, she began to try
to recreate the reality of her mother's marriage by combining the memory of that
conversation with the letters her mother had left for her. She regretted her youthful preoccupation with her own pain, realizing that it had interfered with her
understanding of her mother, and, for that reason, her understanding of herself
as well.

Her mother told Barbara about the night that she gave birth to her. She simply couldn't stop crying. It was such a terrible time to bring a child into the world.
Then she confessed,

> Barbara, I never thought I'd tell you this, but one night I honestly thought
> we would both be better off dead. You had cried for hours. . . . Bob was
> gone—he was often gone at night, and I didn't know where he was. I had
> been crying myself and all I could think was that we were both too miser-
> able to live. It was lucky for us that we had Bobbie to think about. (158)

Toward morning, her mother looked out the window and referred to the day
when she was told her husband was dead:

> What died in me was not the love for your father. It was the hope that he
> would someday come back. I understood then what I knew all along but
> didn't face. Bob had the same inner core of goodness all of us have—even a
> deeper core than many people, for it drove him relentlessly in ways that were
> hard to understand. (169)

Then she added, "Life is much deeper than just loving men, Barbara" (169). At
that moment, the sun began to rise, and she quoted from the last two lines of
Gerard Manly Hopkins's sonnet "God's Grandeur": "The Holy Ghost over the
bent / World broods with warm breast and with ah! bright wings." "It's all part
of God," her mother said, then turned from the window and put her arms around
the daughter who was to have the same experience a decade hence. As if her life's
work was now complete, she suffered a heart attack less than four months later
and was gone.

The Land and the Fathers

In the concluding chapters of *Prairie Reunion* Barbara relates her visits to the
Mesquakie settlement, a Woodland Native American community on the Iowa
River, a two-hour drive west of Scotch Grove; and to Hadfields Cave, the site of
an archeological dig on the North Fork of the Maquoketa River, less than fifteen
miles northeast of Scotch Grove. On the return trip from the Mesquakie settlement, she saw a sign—Luzerne, 4 miles—and pulled to the side of the road.
Should she visit her father's grave again, "now that I knew more and felt at least
some personal connection with the man who had been my father?" (185). However, it was raining and getting dark. Instead, she just sat there for a moment,
thinking:

> I'd always felt a special outrage because my father had forced a mortgage
> on my mother's land. Land was sacred in our family. . . . My mother had
> been given her farm by her father, who bought it during the Depression
> from a bankrupt Livingston of the same family who had come in oxcarts.
> The list of recorded owners seemed ridiculously short. I worked backward.
> Norris . . . Hughes . . . Livingston. Then who? The Mesquakies who had
> come in the 1600s from the north? Before them? (185)

Having sold the farm to her brother Bobby, she had held herself responsible for
losing what had been a sacred trust. But now, as she sat in her camper in the rain

and leaned her forehead against the steering wheel, she felt an unexpected wave of relief: "*The land was never ours to lose*. No matter that I had argued that fact intellectually for years—only then did I feel it emotionally" (185). She pulled the camper back on the highway: "I wasn't going to stand in a cemetery in this downpour, but I momentarily felt a certain sinful camaraderie with my father, anyway. We had both betrayed my mother with the farm" (185). *But the land was never ours to lose.*

As Barbara pulled into the entrance to Hadfields Cave a day or two later, she was advised by the woman responsible for granting permission to enter the land against going in it. There were rattlesnakes, and she might fall. She proceeded despite the warning. But why was she so determined to see the cave? "For the same reasons I had galloped my horse furiously toward the woods whenever I was engulfed by lonely questions" (187). To her mother, the land had meant self-sufficiency and security, a way of life integrated with God:

> But her myths were not mine. I needed to find my own integration with the land, with the past, with the place of my childhood. And whenever I went to the Iowa woods, I went with the ghost of Uncle Jim. Maybe, I thought with a stab of surprise, the same questions about the land we called home had haunted him, pushing him back in time, sending him to the river and the bluffs. (187)

It was Uncle Jim whom she had followed into the woods when she was a child. He had been the one who taught her what to look for and what to look out for. As she walked along the river, she thought of him: Had he ever seen anything in all his forays in the woods "that might not fit comfortably in his Presbyterian elder's consciousness?" (190). If he had, he hadn't told her or Vaneta. Yet it suddenly seemed quite likely:

> He'd been so out of step with the agricultural race toward new technology and chemicals, so much more interested in wildflowers and weeds than in whether the corn was in the crib before the snow. I imagined him striding swiftly in front of me. (190)

As she emerged from the cave, she knelt to tie her shoe and accidentally bumped her pack: The binoculars that she had set on her pack began to bounce downhill, and as she reached for them, she lost her balance and began tumbling as well down the steep, slippery incline. She stopped falling halfway down the slope and was unhurt due to the foliage and the soft ground. But as she reached toward a small rock outcropping for assistance, she recalled the time when she had fallen, had reached out for support, and a rattlesnake had reared up and hissed at her. Uncle Jim had pulled her other arm. "Never, never do that again."

So this time she pulled back her arm, stood up slowly, and noticed that two harmless blue racers slid off the rock into the undergrowth. The shelf was a perfect place for snakes to catch the late-afternoon warmth. A timber rattler might well have been there. She was shaking:

So I did have a father. Uncle Jim had tried to keep me safe. He taught me to pursue the lonely questions. Through him I had learned of nature and time. . . . I put my head down on my arms. My shaking turned to genuine sobs. I had been looking for a man who threw the stick for Spot in the reading-book picture, the Dick and Jane father. But how could I have known then? I was just a little girl. (192)

Visit to Her Mother's Grave

Before she returned to her home in Oregon, Barbara stopped by the cemetery in Scotch Grove. She laid some strips of cedar bark on Uncle Jim's grave and a bundle of wildflowers on her mother's grave. She told her mother that she now understood, that staying there had been more than loving her husband and more than loyalty to the farming way of life. To move would have been to lose herself, and so she remained. Suddenly, Barbara felt "an acute sense of loss, and the thirty years since her death melted. . . . I loved her then even more than I had loved her as a child" (220).

INTIMACY WITH THE SELF WE USED TO BE

As we have seen, *intimacy* concerns that which is most private, personal, and close to oneself, while *isolation* suggests separation and aloneness. A common theme of personal memoirs—*Prairie Reunion* is a wonderful example—is the desire to connect with one's past, especially the childhood years. Without having to be told by experts in child psychology and human development, we know, intuitively, that these were formative years. Yet we also sense that we know little about them: we have a few actual memories and a lot of general impressions, but as a whole the childhood years seem rather isolated from our adult years. This typically means that we, too, feel disconnected.

We are especially troubled by this disconnection at those times in our lives when we have reason to believe that our present difficulties are due, at least in part, to childhood experiences of which we know too little about. To reconnect with that earlier time, then, is more than an expression of nostalgia for bygone years—though it is partly that. It is the attempt to understand ourselves so that we become better at living in the here and now. As Barbara Scot puts it, "The quest began as an attempt to understand my mother. It developed into a quest to understand myself" (4).

Her story also makes clear that there was a time when she needed to distance herself from her life in Iowa. Her own survival as a person depended on her capacity to put these experiences at an emotional and intellectual distance, even to place herself in opposition to them. (Erikson [1959] refers to "distantiation" and calls it the counterpart of intimacy [95], but the word "distancing" seems less daunting.) Such distancing is not, however, the enemy of intimacy but instead makes new forms of intimacy possible. Thus our disconnection from our childhood years is due not only to our inability to recall or recollect so much of it but also to our need, especially in the third and fourth decades of our lives, to *oppose* it. In Barbara's case, this process of distancing began when she was in college and read about the agrarian myth. When she returned in her fifties to gain a deeper understanding of herself and her own connections with the people and place of her childhood, she found no reason to question her opposition. In fact, it received further confirmation.

But something else also occurred: Especially through conversations with relatives, but also through her solitary visits to cemeteries, to the church that she had attended every Sunday, to the Mesquakie settlement, and to Hadfields Cave, she was able to set the letters in her mother's trunk and her own memories within a meaningful framework and to see what she had not—and could not—have seen before. She was also able to experience in her heart what she already knew in her mind to be true. Most important, she had discovered new reasons to *love* and to feel that such "selectivity of love" did not require her to compromise her commitment to her deeply held belief that the land that had played such an important role in the lives of her parents—her father's defeats, her mother's security—does not belong to anyone in particular. Such love could be fully experienced when her own guilt had been absolved. The church had taught about forgiving others, but it was her reunion with her childhood that enabled her to forgive herself and to experience the peaceful reconciliation of aspects of herself that had been at odds with one another.

Although I have focused here on reconnecting with one's childhood, the intimacy vs. isolation conflict may play itself out in various ways in the sixth decade of life: One may experience it in relationship with one or more of one's children, an aging parent, one's spouse or a lifelong partner, a long-time work associate—and the outcome of this conflict may not lead to new intimacy but to increased, even irrevocable, isolation. But Barbara Scot's story is paradigmatic of the intimacy vs. isolation conflict of the sixth decade because it is so intertwined with the identity vs. identity confusion conflict of the fifth decade, as reflected in her earlier and largely unsuccessful trip to Iowa at the age of forty-one. As Erikson makes clear in his writings on the life cycle, these two are the most interactive of all the stages, including those of early childhood. So we should not be surprised that the first two decades of the middle adult years seem at times to coalesce, especially around the age of fifty.

THE LOVING SELF

As we have seen, Erikson recognizes that even as the human strength of love may be assigned to a specific life stage, this human strength may also be said to bind all the stages of the life cycle together. Thus, among the various selves that comprise our composite Self, love is the most responsible for maintaining the coherence of the Self. We have seen the role that love played in the healing of Barbara

Scot's wounded Self, both in her discovery of new reasons to love her mother and in her realization that, in her Uncle Jim, she had in fact experienced a loving father.

Also, despite her ambivalence toward the church of her childhood and youth, one cannot help but imagine that at some point she had heard or read St. Paul's hymn to love in his first letter to the Corinthians. Significantly, this hymn is written in the first person singular, and for that very reason it is an expression of the loving self. She would have learned that the qualities of the loving self include patience, kindness, and deference, as well as the absence of envy, boasting, arrogance, irritability, and resentment (1 Cor. 13:4–5).

But she would also have learned that St. Paul seems to have felt that a child's ways of expressing and thinking about love is somehow inferior to the ways in which adults express and think about love. For in the very midst of his reflections on the loving self he wrote that when he was a child, he "spoke like a child," he "thought like a child," "reasoned like a child," but that when he "became an adult," he "put an end to childish ways" (v. 11). She would have found this puzzling, I believe, because she had every reason to wonder whether the ways in which the adults she knew most intimately expressed and reasoned about love were superior to her own. But that evening—and morning—in which her mother unburdened her soul to her taught her that an adult's love for another can be as unconditional as the love that God has for us. It was not until she made her second trip to Iowa, however, that she felt that she finally—and truly—understood.

Chapter 7

The Seventh Decade:
The Caring Self

If contemporary birthday cards are at all trustworthy, the person entering the seventh decade (the sixties) is sort of at a crossroads. You are encouraged to look back and to consider where you've been. At the same time, you are encouraged to look ahead and consider the future. Here's a card that invites this dual perspective: "You've done a lot of living in your first 60 years. You're loved by friends and family, respected by your peers. You've made some special memories, but look forward and you'll see the future looks just wonderful—the best is yet to be." Because it has to be rather general and unspecific, it says that "you've done a lot of living" and have "made some special memories" but leaves it to the recipient to fill in the blanks. Though it does not specify what's "just wonderful" about the future, it wants you to think that your best years are out in front of you. The skeptic might be inclined to respond that this is more likely to be true for those who have done a lot of living of the wrong sort; the others, especially those with special memories, might need to be persuaded.

Here's one that encourages the recipient to look back over the past fifty-nine years and to think about what he or she has been up to: "Years are made mostly of little days—days made simply of the ordinary business of living, laughing, and loving. One day after another, one small moment at a time, you've made a life worth celebrating. And on your 60th birthday, that's exactly what those who know you are doing." In contrast to the card that suggests the recipient has done "a lot of living," this one is rather low key, suggesting that a retrospective view might lead one to think his or her life has been rather humdrum, but this is not really so. After all, one has been about the ordinary business of living, laughing, and loving, and when you add all of that up, it's worth celebrating.

What are we to make of these milestone cards? To me, they suggest that our birthday card poets are having a little difficulty working up any head of steam over the person turning sixty. The humor of the cards for those turning forty or fifty and the strong emotional appeal of cards for those turning seventy and eighty are both missing. With all due respect to their poetic skills, they seem to be relying on easy cliches—with the past portrayed as a lot of living, laughing, and loving, and the future represented as "just wonderful"—not fantastic, not beyond one's wildest dreams, not the grand climax, and not even "absolutely" wonderful. The cautious wording speaks volumes.

In his poem "Sixty," Stephen Dunn (2000, 21–22) strikes a different note. In his family "the heart goes first / and hardly anyone makes it out of his fifties" (his father died at the age of sixty-two). Family history tells him, therefore, that his "ventricles are stone alleys" and that his heart is a "city with a terrorist / holed up in the mayor's office." So, as he reflects on the fact that he is entering the seventh decade of his life, he isn't like those people who "forget to live as if a great arsenic lobster / could fall on their heads at any moment," but neither does he want to live cautiously, sparingly, and self-protectively, for, after all, "a heart is to be spent."

THE GENERATIVITY VS. STAGNATION CONFLICT

Given the birthday cards' difficulty working up much enthusiasm over the sixties, it may seem odd that I would suggest that this is the decade of *generativity*. When Joan Erikson perceived that an eighth stage was needed, and she and her husband decided it was one of generativity, she was thinking of their own life in their forties: with their children still at home, her husband beginning to come into his own professionally, and her own contributions to his success. Surely, one wants to say, the truly generative years are in the first decade of middle adulthood, not its third and last. But before we rush to judgment, we need a clearer sense of what generativity and its counterpart stagnation are actually about. We begin with definitions.

As far as *Webster's* is concerned, there is no such word as *generativity*, so the words *generate* and *generative* will have to suffice. To *generate* means (1) "to produce (offspring); beget; procreate"; and (2) "to bring into being; cause to be (to *generate* hope)"; and *generative* means (1) "the production of offspring; procreative"; and (2) "having the power of producing or originating" (Agnes 2001, 591). Thus, the first definitions of both words relate specifically to procreation while the second definitions relate to the many and various forms of creativity and productivity.

Webster's notes that *stagnation* is the noun form of the verb *stagnate*, which means "to be or become stagnant." *Stagnant* has three meanings: (1) "not flowing or moving"; (2) "foul from lack of movement (said of water, etc.)"; and (3) "not active, alert, etc.; sluggish (a *stagnant* mind)" (Agnes 2001, 1394). Since Erikson uses the word *stagnation* in reference to humans, the third meaning is most directly relevant, but we may also keep in mind that the first two are metaphorically relevant.

In *Childhood and Society*, Erikson (1950) admits to having made up the word *generativity* and apologizes "for creating a new and not even pleasant term" (231). But he defends the word on the grounds that "neither creativity nor productivity nor any other fashionable term convey what must be conveyed," that "the ability to lose oneself in the meeting of bodies and minds leads to a gradual expansion of ego interests and of libidinal cathexis over that which has thus been generated and accepted as a responsibility" (231). (By "libidinal cathexis" he means to suggest that there is a deep emotional attachment). In *Identity and the Life Cycle*, he adds that the same caveat regarding the words *creativity* and *productivity* is also true of the word *parenthood*, "an all too concrete term which, in quotations from this paper, is often used as a replacement for the seemingly more obscure word 'generativity'" (1959, 97).

Thus, in *Childhood and Society* he states that generativity "is primarily the interest in establishing and guiding the next generation or whatever in a given case may become the absorbing object of a parental kind of responsibility" (1950, 231). In *Identity and the Life Cycle*, he elaborates on this statement, noting that generativity

> is primarily the interest in establishing and guiding the next generation, although there are people who, from misfortune or because of special and genuine gifts in other directions, do not apply this drive to offspring but to other forms of altruistic concern and of creativity, which may absorb their kind of parental responsibility. (1959, 97)

In light of these extensions of the word *generativity* beyond the "all too concrete" word *parenthood*, *Webster's* second meanings of *generate* and *generative*, which emphasize bringing into being and the power of producing or originating, are especially valuable because they challenge the temptation to limit *generativity* to the first meanings of *generate* and *generative*, which emphasize the producing of offspring. This point has particular significance for my proposed location of the generativity vs. stagnation conflict in the seventh decade (the sixties). After all, procreation in one's sixties is relatively uncommon and with possible rare exceptions is exclusive to males.

On the other hand, Erikson's phrase—"a parental kind of responsibility"—suggests that the word *parenthood*, when viewed less concretely and more metaphorically, provides a useful way of emphasizing that generativity applies primarily to those generative intentions and actions that concern the establishing and guiding of the next generation. Thus, in the revised edition of *Childhood and Society*, Erikson (1963) notes that because some persons do not direct the parental drive toward their own offspring, "the concept generativity is meant to include such more popular synonyms as *productivity* and *creativity*, which, however, cannot replace it" (267). I suggest that we keep this broader, more metaphorical understanding of parenthood in mind as we consider his reflections on the generativity vs. stagnation conflict.

These reflections are, however, rather brief. In fact, I have already quoted all of Erikson's comments on generativity in *Childhood and Society* (1950). What remains is his brief, one sentence comment on stagnation. It takes the form of a cautionary note, namely, that when the "enrichment" afforded by participation in generativity fails, a regression "to an obsessive need for pseudo intimacy, punctuated by moments of mutual repulsion, takes place, often with a pervading sense (and objective evidence) of individual stagnation and interpersonal impoverishment" (231).

If generativity were limited to parenthood, this cautionary note would certainly be offensive to married couples who are childless. But when generativity is viewed more broadly, it conveys the various and multiple ways in which the generativity vs. stagnation conflict may manifest itself. Generativity involves an expansion of one's personal interests and emotional attachments to include that which has been generated (conceived, originated, produced, etc.) while stagnation suggests either that nothing has been generated or that, once generated, nothing is being done to insure its survival, growth, or development. That which has been generated is a victim of stagnation, but so is the person who is unable to be truly generative, for when stagnation prevails, there is a self-constriction: no life, no vitality flows out of oneself into that which has been generated.

Erikson (1959) expands on this cautionary note in *Identity and the Life Cycle*. After restating the cautionary note itself, he adds that individuals "who do not develop generativity often begin to indulge themselves as if they were their own one and only child" (97). Then he adds that the "mere fact of having or even wanting children does not of course involve generativity; in fact the majority of young parents seen in child-guidance work suffer, it seems, from the retardation of or inability to develop this stage" (97). He then identifies the primary reasons for this retardation or inability: early childhood impressions, faulty identification with one's own parents, excessive self-love based on a too-strenuously self-made personality, and the lack of some faith or belief in the human species that would make a child "appear to be a welcome trust of the community" (97).

Here, Erikson associates the "pervading sense of stagnation and interpersonal impoverishment" with an inability to expand one's ego boundaries to include one's progeny, and provides explanations for this inability. But, again, if we view these comments within the context of his broader understanding of generativity, these same explanations would apply to the inability to invest *oneself* in the next generation, whatever form this investment might take. Thus, these explanations may provide adults at any stage of life, but especially in their sixties, valuable guidance as to what may be the inhibiting factor or factors in their own difficulty in investing themselves in the next generation (or generations). At this more advanced stage in life, the third and fourth factors—self-love and lack of faith in the species—may have greater explanatory power than the first and second—childhood impressions and faulty parental identifications. And although all four have ethical and religious dimensions, this seems especially true of the latter two.

In the revised edition of *Childhood and Society*, Erikson (1963) adds a new paragraph to the beginning of his discussion of generativity vs. stagnation in which he reminds the reader that the emphasis of this book is on the childhood stages, "otherwise the section on generativity would be of necessity the central one, for this term encompasses the evolutionary development which has made man the teaching and instituting as well as the learning animal" (266). This portrayal of the human species as "the teaching *and* learning animal" leads him to note that the "fashionable insistence on dramatizing the dependence of children on adults often blinds us to the dependence of the older generation on the younger one," for "mature man needs to be needed, and maturity needs guidance as well as encouragement from what has been produced and must be taken care of" (266–67).

This addition to what he had previously written about the parental drive behind generativity suggests another explanation for stagnation, namely, the situation in which an older adult's need to be needed by one or more members of the younger generation is not reciprocated by those who are younger.

This nonreciprocity may, of course, occur at any stage of adulthood, but it may be felt most acutely in one's sixties when one is no longer considered a significant player in the productive enterprise in which one has heretofore been involved. Erikson's emphasis on the older adult's need to be needed by members of the younger generation suggests that this lack of reciprocity is most conducive to stagnation not when it originates from members of one's own generation but from members of the younger generation. Thus, the generativity vs. stagnation conflict is the most self-evidently *intergenerational* of all the conflicts. To invoke Erikson's image of the cogwheel (noted in the introduction), this is the time when the wheel of the one generation is interlocking with the wheel of the other generation. According to *Webster's*, a cogwheel is a wheel with a rim notched into teeth that mesh with those of another wheel to transmit or receive motion, and a cog railway is a railway for a very steep grade with traction supplied by a central cogged rail that meshes with a cogwheel on the engine (Agnes 2001, 284). The operative words here are *mesh* and *motion*. No meshing, no forward motion, and then the species, or that segment of it for which we have particular responsibility, comes to a grinding halt if not a precipitous descent back down the hill from whence it came. Presumably, neither generation wants *this*.

In the revised edition of *Childhood and Society*, Erikson (1963) considers the social institution that safeguards and reinforces generativity and concludes that "one can only say that all institutions codify the ethics of generative succession"

(267). Then he adds a reference to the social institution of monasticism, noting that it is no exception: "Even where philosophical and spiritual tradition suggests the renunciation of the right to procreate or to produce, such early turn to 'ultimate concerns,' wherever instituted in monastic movements, strives to settle at the same time the matter of its relationship to the Care for the creatures of this world and to the Charity which is felt to transcend it" (267–68).

For those having difficulty developing or maintaining generativity due to "the lack of some faith, some 'belief in the species'" (267), they may be helped by the very idea that generativity is a participation in "the Care for the creatures of this world and to the Charity which is felt to transcend it," a conviction to which those who make this early turn to "ultimate concerns" are a living testimony.[1]

Erikson concluded his brief comments on the institutions that safeguard and reinforce generativity with another reference to the fact that *Childhood and Society* is not about adulthood: "If this were a book on adulthood, it would be indispensable and profitable at this point to compare economic and psychological theories (beginning with the strange convergencies and divergencies of Marx and Freud) and to proceed to a discussion of man's relationship to his production as well as to his progeny" (268).

Since Erikson had earlier referred to Karl Marx in his discussion of "the spirit of work" in *Young Man Luther* (1958, 220), we may assume that he would have wanted to explore the issue of one's *alienated* relationship to that which one has produced—not, however, at the expense of neglecting the Freudian emphasis on alienated relationships between parents and their progeny.[2]

THE VIRTUE OF CARE

Erikson's (1963) reference in *Childhood and Society* to the Care for the creatures of the world and the Charity that is felt to transcend it anticipates his assignment of the virtue of care to the generativity vs. stagnation stage (1964a). *Webster's* has five definitions of the word *care*: (1) "a troubled or burdened state of mind; worry; concern (without a *care* in the world)"; (2) "close attention or careful heed (to drive with *care*)"; (3) "a liking or regard (to *care* for another)"; (4) "charge; protection; custody (left in a friend's *care*)"; and (5) "something to watch over or attend to; a responsibility" (Agnes 2001, 221).

Among its suggested synonyms, *Webster's* indicates that *care* suggests "a weighing down of the mind, as by dread, apprehension, or great responsibility"; *con-*

---

1. Erikson was aware that "ultimate concerns" is a phrase that Paul Tillich (1957) introduced in his effort to clarify what faith is and is not (10). Erikson mentions his personal conversations with Tillich in two of his writings, "Womanhood and the Inner Space" (Erikson 1968, 293–94) and his tribute to Tillich in a memorial service in the Harvard University chapel on November 4, 1965 (Erikson 1987g, 727).

2. Erikson was aware of Erich Fromm's writings on Marx and Freud. Fromm's (1962) *Beyond the Chains of Illusion* explores his own attraction to Marx and Freud, their common ground, and the fate of both theories in today's world.

cern suggests "mental uneasiness over someone or something in which one has an affectionate interest"; and *solicitude* implies "thoughtfulness, often excessive apprehension, for the welfare, safety, or comfort of another" (Agnes 2001, 221–22). Antonyms of *care* are *unconcern* and *indifference,* both of which imply a lack of interest or feeling, or apathy (1555, 727). *Apathy* itself has the connotation of an absence of emotion, of being unmoved (64).

In "Human Strength and the Cycle of Generations," Erikson (1964a) states that *care* is "the widening concern for what has been generated by love, necessity, or accident; it overcomes the ambivalences adhering to irreversible obligation" (131). The word *widening* is especially important because it indicates that the concern felt for that which has been generated *expands* with the passage of time. As we will see in a moment, Erikson also believes that this concern is *extensive* in the sense that it carries further and further into the foreseeable and even unforeseeable future.

Erikson's working definition suggests further that care overcomes the ambivalent feelings that adults often experience when they realize that they bear a heavy responsibility for what they have generated, whether they have done so out of love or necessity, or without any conscious intention of doing so. (We may think here of the fact that Erikson himself was accidentally conceived.) He considers this growing care to be relatively unique to the human species. Although other animals instinctively encourage in their young what they are already genetically predisposed for, and some animals can be taught "some tricks and services" by humans, only the human species "can and must extend [its] solicitude over the long, parallel and overlapping childhoods of numerous offspring united in households and communities" (130). As this solicitude is extended through the transmission of the rudiments of hope, will, purpose and competence, adults impart to their children "a particular world image and style of fellowship" (130).

Having emphasized the role of genitality in discussions of the intimacy vs. isolation stage, Erikson now makes a direct association between genitality and generativity, noting that he has "postulated an instinctual and psychosocial stage of 'generativity' beyond that of genitality" (130). To be sure, "parenthood is, for most, the first, and for many, the prime generative encounter, yet the perpetuation of mankind challenges the generative ingenuity of workers and thinkers of many kinds" (130–31). Thus, here again, Erikson insists that generativity is a much more inclusive concept than its association with parenthood suggests, and therefore the virtue of care applies to other generative acts besides parenthood, but especially to those generative acts that contribute to the support and guidance of the next generation. In this regard, teaching plays a major role in generativity. This is because "man *needs* to teach, not only for the sake of those who need to be taught, and not only for the fulfillment of his identity, but because facts are kept alive by being told, logic by being demonstrated, truth by being professed." The teaching passion is not, however, restricted to the teaching profession, for "every mature adult knows the satisfaction of explaining what is dear to him and of being understood by a groping mind" (131).

Teaching, then, is perhaps the most important expression of the virtue of care, and virtually every adult is in one sense or another a teacher. Parents, of course, teach their own children, but the widening of concern that is so central to care is reflected in the fact that adults teach the children of others and often take as much interest in explaining what is dear to them to the offspring of other adults as they do their own.

In the revised edition of *Childhood and Society,* Erikson (1963) said that if this had been a book on adulthood, he would have wanted to discuss "man's relationship to his production as well as to his progeny" (268). In his discussion of the virtue of care, he points out that the ideological polarization that has made Freud the century's theorist of sex and Marx the theorist of work has meant that in his own profession a whole area of the human mind has been left uncharted, namely, "man's love for his works and ideas as well as for his children" (131). Thus, in addition to the need to be needed, adults require the challenge that comes from whatever they have generated and from what now must be nurtured, guarded, preserved, "and eventually transcended" (131). In this regard, he emphasizes that the human species needs to exercise restraint in the face of its capacity not only for "unlimited propagation" but also for an equally unlimited "invention" and "expansion" (132). The virtue of care that has been developed in relation to propagation may serve as a reliable guide in these other respects as well, because it insists on the importance of being able to "care for" and "take care of" that which has been generated.

Erikson's insistence that when he writes about generativity he is not thinking exclusively of parenthood but has in mind a much more inclusive understanding of adult responsibility for the next generation and, by implication, those that follow it suggests that we should not associate the generativity vs. stagnation conflict with the child-rearing years. In fact, one could argue that precisely because adults who are engaged in child-rearing are necessarily centering their attention on their own progeny, they are unable at that time to have the larger perspective that generativity entails. They are developing a rudimentary sense of generativity, but the broader view of generativity and of stagnation is likely to come later. This would also be true, therefore, of the wider and extended concern of the virtue of care. I suggest that the seventh decade of life (the sixties) is the decade in which this conflict and this concern are central.

ERIKSON'S ADDRESSES
AT THE HARVARD MEDICAL SCHOOL

I can think of no better illustration of the generativity vs. stagnation conflict in the seventh decade of life than Erikson himself. In his sixties, Erikson devoted his professional life to the establishment and guidance of the younger generation. His writings in this period reflect his concern to understand the younger generation and convey this understanding to other members of his own generation. It was also the decade in which he was subject to the greatest amount of criticism, most of it issuing from the younger generation itself.[3]

Thus, the explanation for stagnation identified in his later writings—the need of the older adult to be needed by the younger generation and to have this need reciprocated—became especially relevant in his sixties. Its relevance was reflected in his observation that the "fashionable insistence on dramatizing the dependence of children on adults often blinds us to the dependence of the older generation on the younger one" (Erikson 1963, 266). He was sixty-one-years old when these works were published. I believe that the dependence of the older on the younger generation may be greater in this decade than in any other decade before or after. In fact, the fashionable insistence on dramatizing the *physical* dependence of adults on their children in subsequent decades may blind us to the *emotional* dependence that occurs in the seventh decade of life.

Erikson's two addresses at the Harvard Medical School in this decade of his life are illustrative of his concern to be generative at this stage. The first was presented at the very beginning of this decade and the second at its conclusion. The first lecture, "The Golden Rule in the Light of New Insight," was the George W. Gay Lecture on Medical Ethics in 1962. Erikson was born on June 15, 1902, so it was probably delivered a few months before he actually turned sixty, but it wasn't published until 1963, when it appeared in the *Harvard Medical School Alumni Bulletin*. Because the lecture itself was in "very undeveloped form" (Friedman 1999, 340), he continued to work on it, presenting a much-revised version in January, 1963, at the India International Centre in New Delhi. It then became one of the six lectures that comprise his *Insight and Responsibility* (1964b, 217–43).

The second lecture, "On Protest and Affirmation," was presented as an address to the graduating class at the Harvard Medical School in 1972. It was published in the *Harvard Medical School Alumni Bulletin* in the 1972 July–August issue. As it was probably presented before Erikson's birthday on June 15, he would have been sixty-nine years old when he delivered it. It was republished in *A Way of Looking at Things* (Erikson 1987b).

The Golden Rule in the Light of New Insight

"The Golden Rule in the Light of New Insight" begins with the observation that Erikson is a clinician of the psychoanalytic school, and that by means of case

3. Much of this criticism centered around his observation that, at play, girls tend to construct inner spaces (enclosures) while boys construct external spaces, and his suggestion that these tendencies among girls reflect the fact that women have an "inner space" owing to their reproductive organs. His 1965 lecture "On the Potential of Women" (Erikson 1987c), in which he refers to an earlier paper on the subject of women's "inner space" published in *Daedalus*, indicates that he had already been criticized for this view on the grounds that it seems to represent a biological determinism unfavorable to women's success in careers that were previously exclusive to men. Later versions of his views on the subject and efforts to address this and related criticisms are "Womanhood and the Inner Space" (Erikson 1968, 261–94) and "Once More the Inner Space" (Erikson 1975b, 225–47).

histories and life histories "we psychoanalysts have begun to discern certain fateful and certain fruitful patterns of interaction in those most concrete categories (parent and child, man and woman, teacher and pupil) which carry the burden of maintenance from generation to generation" (Erikson 1964b, 220). As a teacher, however, his "base line is the Golden Rule, which advocates that one should do (or not do) to another what one wishes to be (or not be) done by" (220).

He recognizes that systematic students of ethics often express a certain disdain for this "all-too-primitive ancestor of more logical principles," and that George Bernard Shaw found it an easy target: "Don't do to another what you would like to be done by, he warned, because his tastes may differ from yours" (220). Even so, "this rule has marked a mysterious meeting ground between ancient peoples separated by oceans and eras, and has provided a hidden theme in the most memorable sayings of many thinkers" (220).

The Golden Rule has many different versions, he notes, but they basically take one of two forms. Some are stated in the negative, employing the method of warning: "Do *not* as you would *not* be done by." Others are stated in the positive, employing the method of exhortation: "Do as you *would* be done by." The former appeals to one's egotistic prudence; the latter to one's altruistic sympathy (221). Also, some versions reflect greater levels of human maturity than others, with its highest, most unconditional forms expressed in the Upanishad's "He who sees all beings in his own self and his own self in all beings" and the Christian injunction to "love thy neighbor as thyself" (221). Because his own field is the clinical study of the human life cycle, Erikson does not want to argue the "logical merit or spiritual worth" of these various versions, but to distinguish "variations in moral and ethical sensitivity in accordance with stages in the development of human conscience" (221).

Moral Rules, Ethical Ideals, and Ideological Ideas

He notes that moral rules of conduct are based "on a fear of *threats* to be forestalled" and ethical rules are based on ideals "to be striven for with a high degree of rational assent and with a ready consent to a formulated good, a definition of perfection, and some promise of self-realization" (222). Moral rules are developmentally prior to ethical ideals and therefore tend to insinuate themselves into ethical ideals, and this combination produces "malignant forms of righteousness and prejudice which we may call *moralism*" (224). Thus, the Golden Rule "was meant to protect man not only against his enemy's open attacks, but also against his friend's righteousness" (224).

There is, however, a third factor that needs to be considered, "for between the development in childhood of man's *moral* proclivity and that of his *ethical* powers in adulthood, adolescence intervenes when he perceives the universal good in *ideological* terms" (224). The adolescent is capable of an assent to ideals beyond the cognitive capacities of the child. Thus an ethical view is approximated in adolescence, "but it remains susceptible to an alternation of impulsive judgment and odd rationalization" (225). Most troubling is the tendency of the adolescent mind to base its ideals on the repudiation of "outsiders." At its highest and best, the Golden Rule has challenged this exclusivity.

Generativity and Mutuality

Having viewed the Golden Rule from the perspective of stages in the development of human conscience, Erikson next introduces the experiments by Harry Harlow in which monkeys were taken away from their mothers within a few hours after birth, were isolated, and then left with "mothers" made of wire, wood, and terry cloth. The wire contraption gave them food and a sense of physical comfort, and while these laboratory-reared monkeys were physically healthy and and more easily trained in technical know-how than monkeys brought up by real mothers, they eventually became what Harlow called "psychotics," sitting passively and vacantly. Some, when poked, would bite themselves and tear at their own flesh until blood began to flow. As Erikson notes, "They have not learned to experience 'the other,' whether as mother, mate, child—or enemy. Only a tiny minority of the females produced offspring, and only one of them made an attempt to nurse hers" (229).

Although these experiments may suggest that severely disturbed mother-child relationships can "cause" human psychosis, what interests Erikson far more is the fact that, however successful the experiments may be in demonstrating the importance of mother-child relationships, we need a scientific approach toward living beings that is adequate to the study of ongoing life, not of selective extinction: "One can study the nature of things by doing something *to* them, but one can really learn something about the essential nature of living beings only by doing something *with* them or *for* them" (220). This, he suggests, is the principle of clinical science:

> It does not deny that one can learn by dissecting the dead, or that animal or man can be motivated to lend circumscribed parts of themselves to an experimental procedure. But for the study of the carriers of socio-genetic evolution, the chosen unit of observation must be the generation, not the individual, for whether an individual animal or human being has partaken of the stuff of life can only be tested by the kind of observation which includes his ability to transmit life—in some essential form—to the next generation. (229)

Thus, clinical science is fundamentally concerned with *generativity*, with how one generation transmits life "in some essential form" to the next generation. And how is this life transmitted? Basically, through a *mutuality* between the members of the two generations. This mutuality occurs in its most fundamental form in the relationship between the infant and the adult: "While the baby initially smiles at a mere configuration resembling the human face, the adult cannot help smiling back, filled with expectations of a 'recognition' which he needs to secure from the new being as surely as it needs him" (231). Thus, mutuality is "a relationship in which partners depend on each other for the development of their respective strengths" (231).

But what does this mutuality have to do with the Golden Rule? Just this: If the versions of the Golden Rule cited earlier seem to have a tone of either egotistical prudence or altruistic sympathy, perhaps we should "endow the Golden Rule with a principle of mutuality, replacing the reciprocity of both prudence and sympathy" (231). If so, we need to recognize that the earliest form of mutuality between infant and mother "is only a beginning" and that it "leads to more complicated encounters, as both the child and his interaction with a widening circle of persons grow more complicated" (232).

The Principle of Active Choice

If mutuality adds a generational dimension to the developmental process reflected in the movement from moral rules to ethical ideals, one more factor is necessary to express the full meaning of the Golden Rule. Erikson states, "It is implied in the term 'activate,' and I would call it the principle of *active choice*" (232). This active choice is especially reflected in the "commitment to an initiative in love" as expressed in the admonition to "love thy neighbor," but Erikson emphasizes the need to recognize in these words "a psychological verity, namely, that only he who approaches an encounter in a (consciously and unconsciously) active and giving attitude, rather than in a demanding and dependent one, will be able to make of that encounter what it can become" (233).

The Strengthening of One Another

What, then, is Erikson's "understanding" of the Golden Rule? Basically, the Golden Rule expresses a general orientation to life

> which has its center in whatever activity or activities gives man the feeling, as William James put it, of being "most deeply and intensely active and alive." In this, so James promises, each one will find his "real me"; but, I would now add, he will also acquire the experience that *truly worthwhile acts enhance a mutuality between the doer and the other—a mutuality which strengthens the doer even as it strengthens the other*. Thus, the "doer" and the "other" are partners in one deed. (233)[4]

Viewed developmentally, "this means that the doer is activated in whatever strength is *appropriate to his age, stage, and condition*, even as he activates in the other the strength appropriate to *his* age, stage, and condition" (233). Understood in this way, the Golden Rule "would say that it is best to do to another what will strengthen you even as it will strengthen him—that is, what will develop his best potentials even as it develops your own" (233). And this means that the Golden Rule, interpreted here "in the light of new insight," is at the very core of generativity.

Erikson's address continued with an elaboration on his observation that the

---

4. As we saw in chapter 5, Erikson (1968) used the same quotation from William James to express the subjective or personal dimension of the sense of identity (19).

Golden Rule needs to be enacted in ways that are appropriate to one's age, stage, and condition. In contrast to George Bernard Shaw's observation that the problem with the Golden Rule is that the other person may have different tastes from one's own, Erikson's is a more gracious way of saying that this universal principle needs to be adapted to the strengths and limitations of individuals.

He went on to ask whether the parent/child model he has been using to emphasize that mutuality is central to the Golden Rule has "any significant analogies in other situations in which uniqueness depends on a divided function" (233). To illustrate the fact that it does, he discusses the similarities and differences in the paternal and maternal parental roles and observes that the Golden Rule (as expressed above) indicates that the one "enhances the uniqueness of the other" and also implies "that each, to be really unique, depends on a mutuality with an equally unique partner" (236).

Another analogy, he notes, is the professional relationship between the healer and patient. In this case there is "a very real and specific inequality in the relationship of doctor and patient in their roles of knower and known, helper and sufferer, practitioner of life and victim of disease and death" (236). But precisely because of this inequality, "medical people have their own and unique professional oath and strive to live up to a universal ideal of 'the doctor'" (236). He is referring here, of course, to the Hippocratic Oath. To be sure, persons who become doctors have various motivations for striving to live up to this ideal, but all of these motivations may "be reconciled in a Golden Rule amended to include a mutuality of function" (236). Furthermore, each specialty and technique, in its own way, allows the doctor

> to develop as a practitioner, and as a person, even as the patient is cured as a patient, and as a person. For a real cure transcends the transitory state of patient-hood. It is an experience which enables the cured patient to develop and to transmit to home and neighborhood an attitude toward health which is one of the most essential ingredients of an ethical outlook. (236–37)

True, a doctor "can separate his personal, his professional, and his scientific ethics, seeking fulfillment of idiosyncratic needs in personal life, the welfare of others in his profession, and truths independent of personal preference or service in his research" (237). Nonetheless, "there are psychological limits to the multiplicity of values a man can live by, and, in the end, not only the practitioner, but also his patient and his research, depend on a certain unification in him of temperament, intellect, and ethics" (237).

In emphasizing the healer and patient relationship as exemplary of the Golden Rule as seen in the light of human development—that "it is best to do to another what will strengthen you even as it will strengthen him"—Erikson anticipated his later study of Jesus (Erikson 1981) mentioned briefly in chapter 6. In this study, he focused on Jesus' healing of the woman who had suffered from a hemorrhage for twelve years and "had endured much under many physicians, and had spent all that she had; and she was no better, but rather grew worse" (Mark 5:25–26).

In his commentary on this healing, Erikson notes that when the woman touched Jesus, he "felt it as an acute loss of a powerful quantity of something vital" (342). By itself, this statement suggests that this act of healing is not a good illustration of the Golden Rule because what strengthened the woman seems to have weakened Jesus. But Erikson points out that Jesus said to the woman, "Your faith has healed you," and notes that the King James Version says, "My daughter, thy faith hath made thee whole" (v. 34). This rendition "underlines the loving as well as the holistic character of all healing" and acknowledges "the woman's aptitude for trust and her determination to reach [out to] him as an essential counterpart to his capacity to help her" (342). Thus, the healing of the hemorrhaging woman illustrates the centrality of mutuality and active choice in the Golden Rule, for her faith strengthened him in his capacity to strengthen her.

On Protest and Affirmation

Erikson (1987b) begins "On Protest and Affirmation," his address to the graduating class at Harvard Medical School in 1972, with his initial reaction when members of the graduating class requested that he give the customary address preceding their joint affirmation of the Hippocratic Oath. He says he isn't sure if he is expected to talk around this occasion or to speak directly to it. He was aware that some students had met earlier in the day to protest the traditional ceremony of the affirmation of the Hippocratic Oath, so his uncertainty about whether he was expected to talk around this tradition or speak directly to it was more than rhetorical gambit.

He says, however, that he got some help in deciding what to do from attending a recent Harvard Medical School lecture on the history of the Hippocratic Oath by a professor from Johns Hopkins University. After the lecture, "the more professorial types in the audience converged on the speaker to engage him, no doubt, in erudite questions" (699), but a few of the students cornered Erikson. The professor had informed the audience that the Hippocratic Oath had been introduced into this country at the request of medical students. The students had asked Erikson, "Why does one want to take an oath?" Recalling this conversation, Erikson thought, is this a theme for *my* address? Why, indeed, do we want to take an oath, and when? Conversely, why and when do we *not* want to take an oath? (699). He notes that to take an oath means to testify to a joint tradition. On certain occasions, elders like to demand such an oath, and younger people are not adverse to taking them: "But any formula of what is worth testifying for also delineates what one detests and what is worth protesting" (700). Hence the title of his address: "On Protest and Affirmation."

After some remarks about how he resisted an overt identification with his physician father, and how by a circuitous route he became a member of the community headed by Sigmund Freud, one of the greatest doctors of all time, Erikson observes that when he came to this country forty years ago, it was the Harvard Medical School that gave him his first appointment despite the fact that he was not a doctor but a practitioner of Freud's method as applied to work with children. So, he suggests, being asked to testify today rounds things out for him. In the meantime, however, he has also had the experience, during the McCarthy era, of having to refuse to take an oath.[5]

At its best, a prescribed oath is "an occasion for the free and joint affirmation of a strong idea which has become part of a shared identity" (701). The identity in this case is, of course, that of the doctor, and this title "is only an outer confirmation of an inner conversion" for, by virtue of their medical school experience, "none of you will ever *not* be a doctor." In fact, he says, "Wherever you are when, figuratively or really, the question sounds, 'Is there a doctor in the house?' something in you will respond. From here on you are answerable, because what you have learned to do and to be has become part of your identity" (701).

As in his earlier address on the Golden Rule, Erikson notes that our moral rules reach back into childhood, our ideological ideas begin in adolescence, and in early adulthood we are able to formulate our ethical ideals. What, then, does it mean "to confirm ethically that one is a doctor?" To answer this question, we need to ask first, "What is a patient?" and the answer to *this* question is implied in the following story: An old patient enters his doctor's examining room and says, "Doctor, my feet hurt, I have headaches, my bowels are sluggish, my heart pounds. And you know, Doctor, I myself don't feel so good either" (702). Erikson mentions a Jewish version of this story in which the patient says, ". . . the whole of me doesn't feel so good either," then points out that "in both versions, the patient complains that he has lost the connection between the various parts of him. Tell me, he seems to plead, what is wrong with all of my parts—but tell me in such a way that I myself, the whole of me, the middle of me, can feel, 'Yes, I understand, and I will help you help me to handle it'" (702).

This story, he suggests, "tells us a lot about what a doctor is, and what 'medical' really means" (702). Specifically, it supports a linguistic connection between *medical* and *mediation,* as the doctor is one who *mediates* "not only between the patient and his wayward body parts, but also the medicines that upset 'himself' while relieving his symptoms; between the patient, his family, and his community; the patient and numerous specialists and their distant data banks; the patient and an increasing number of health workers and health services" (704).

The critical question, then, is what the patient and the doctor "must be for each other" (703), and Erikson proposes the word *identifiable,* which means to be recognizable as being the very person one claims to be: "Only if the patient feels he is dealing with an identifiable, coherent person-and-method does he

5. He is referring here to the special loyalty oath required of all California state employees during the investigative hearings conducted by the congressional committee headed by Senator Joseph McCarthy in the late 1940s and early 1950s. In his statement explaining why he could not sign it, Erikson (1987e) said that he could not reconcile signing this document and his earlier signing of the contract in which he had declared that he would do his job as a professor to the best of his ability. He felt that signing this new oath would compromise his work with students. Thus, it was a matter of generativity.

become (again) identifiable to himself; and only in being such a person-and-method can the doctor remain identifiable to himself" (703). And this is where, for both doctor and patient, the Hippocratic Oath, the doctor's declaration that he will not knowingly do anything that harms the patient, is vitally important.

Concerning the oath itself, Erikson makes two points. The first is to suggest "a historical attitude which remains aware of the continuity of tradition in the flux of historical change," for a "recourse to tradition always means to acknowledge how much some ancient people knew in their own way of what we only slowly learn to know in ours" (704). The second is to tell the students "that the mere possession of an oath, if ever so debatable in detail, makes you enviable" (704). As the problem of maintaining rather than maiming life becomes a matter of conscience for a mankind gradually recognizing its unity, members of other professions are "becoming aware of the fact that they are working with seemingly innocent forces and insights that cannot only be used for a new way of life but also for many new ways of death, and they are yearning for an oath-like formulation, both manageable and understandable, that would make them again identifiable to themselves" (705).

He concludes by telling the students that, as physicians, "you already have such a tradition" and "you are in the possession of new concrete, interpersonal competencies without which any affirmation and any protest are empty. [Therefore,] whether you wish to *take* any one or the other form of the oath, you *have* it in you" (705).[6]

In this address, as in the Golden Rule address, Erikson presents an argument for the contemporary relevance of an ancient formula expressing an ethical ideal. This, in itself, was a generative act, for generativity involves an awareness of the continuity of generations. But the address was also generative in the sense that he was speaking directly to members of the younger generation, and they were the ones who had invited him to speak to them, thus appealing to his "need to be needed." Furthermore, a conversation with students following a lecture he had previously attended had given him the idea for his topic, and this conversation had occurred when other "more professorial types" were engaging in conversation with the lecturer, who, of course, was one of them.

In his opening comments, Erikson mentioned the fact that he was not a "real" doctor, but the address itself illustrates the principle, or ethical ideal, of *mediation*, in that he sought to mediate between an ancient formulaic professional oath and the realities of a profession that was undergoing massive revolutionary changes; and between the students who had come prepared to affirm the oath and the students who were absent—"some, no doubt, in sincere avoidance of this ceremonial occasion" (699). His *mediatorial* role was also underscored through

---

6. In a section of the address that I did not discuss, Erikson noted that the medical profession was currently undergoing an "identity crisis," but assured his audience that they were not alone. It seems that the Pope had recently "found it necessary to preach against the very term 'identity crisis' as taken too seriously by young priests. He implied that true faith does not permit such a crisis" (703). Needless to say, Erikson disagreed.

his acknowledgment that he had once refused to take an oath and thus understood that the taking of an oath is not a perfunctory act. He therefore not only talked *about* mediation but also modeled it in the address itself, thus providing the students a living image of what he perceived to be the essential meaning of the oath that they were about to affirm.

GENERATIVITY AND ACTIVE CHOICE

In his address on the Golden Rule, Erikson emphasizes that mutuality activates the persons involved; therefore, the principle of active choice is implied in, and is an extension of, the principle of mutuality. In his brief comments on the principle of active choice, he indicates that it gives mutuality an element of initiative (1964b, 232). Only when we approach an encounter in an active and giving attitude, rather than in a demanding and dependent one, will we "be able to make of that encounter what it can become" (233).

As we saw in chapter 3, initiative means to take the first step or move, or to assume responsibility for beginning or originating something, such as new ideas or methods. It also implies thinking and acting without being urged to do so (Agnes 2001, 735). Thus, initiative counters the tendency in the seventh decade of life toward stagnation, which is a state or condition of inactivity, of sluggishness, of not flowing and not moving (Agnes 2001, 1394). For Erikson, it is associated with "interpersonal impoverishment" (1959, 97). Having initiative means that one accepts responsibility for becoming activated and does so in ways that are new and original. There is a difference between being activated and merely keeping busy, for being activated implies that there are external stimuli to one's initiative, such as the need of the younger generation for guidance or to become better established.

In *Childhood and Society* Erikson (1963) warns that generativity cannot develop when individuals "begin to indulge themselves as if they were their own—or one another's—one and only child; and where conditions favor it, early invalidism, physical or psychological, becomes the vehicle of self-concern" (267). This self-indulgence can happen to persons in their sixties, especially as retirement from their jobs occurs or looms and they begin to feel ill used and unappreciated by the younger generation. Why should they be concerned for the younger generation when its members treat them as expendable, as standing in the way of their own advancement, or simply as a nuisance?

But this, it seems, is precisely where the Golden Rule understood in the light of new insight becomes so relevant. As Erikson (1964b) points out in his Golden Rule essay, to feel "active and alive" in William James's sense, one needs to experience *mutuality*—"*a mutuality which strengthens the doer even as it strengthens the other*" (233). And to experience such mutuality, one needs to make an intentional decision to approach encounters with members of the younger generation in an "active and giving attitude, rather than in a demanding and dependent one" (233).

It is rather easy to assume—especially for those of us who are teachers—that we do the guiding and explaining and that the younger generation does the learning. But, as Erikson (1963) notes, "maturity needs guidance as well" (267). Learning how to live the Golden Rule is no exception. Christians, of course, associate the Golden Rule with Jesus' admonition, "'Do to others as you would have them do to you'" (Luke 6:31). But Erikson, who identified himself as a Christian while remaining loyal to the Jewish faith of his childhood, concludes his address on the Golden Rule with the Talmudic version, which he considers an antidote to our tendency to indulge in "some moralizing" when we "speak of ethical subjects" (243). He writes,

> Rabbi Hillel once was asked by an unbeliever to tell the whole of the Torah while he stood on one foot. I do not know whether he meant to answer the request or to remark on its condition when he said: "What is hateful to yourself, do not do to your fellow man. That is the whole of the Torah and the rest is but commentary." At any rate, he did not add: "Act accordingly." He said: "Go and learn it." (243)

Many in their sixties may not be able to stand on one foot, and many more would not take kindly to the request that they do so. But they are not too old or to stagnant to learn, especially when it has to do with an old truth that is always open to new insight.

THE CARING SELF

As we have seen, Erikson suggests that *care* is "the widening concern for what has been generated by love, necessity, or accident; it overcomes ambivalences adhering to irreversible obligation" (1964a,131). In the earliest formulations of the deadly sins, one that appeared on every list was *acedia*, a Greek word meaning "not caring." It was reflected in malaise, lassitude, laxness, and apathy. Later, it was translated "sloth," and came to be viewed as laziness and idleness, and its original meaning of "not caring" was more or less lost (see Capps 2000, 58–63; and Capps 2001, 107–17). In contemporary society, where many of us feel that we are overworked and are feeling stressed out and fatigued, it may be rather difficult to get overly exercised about the sinfulness of "sloth." What's so wrong, after all, with spending a few hours or even a day in laziness or idleness?

"Not caring" is a different matter. After all, working hard and caring about what one is doing are not necessarily synonymous. Oftentimes, we feel that the two are actually antithetical to one another. What does it mean, therefore, to be a caring self?

In May, 1973, when he was seventy years old, Erikson gave the National Endowment for the Humanities Jefferson Lectures in Washington, D.C. They were subsequently expanded into a book titled *Dimensions of a New Identity* (Erikson, 1974). In the concluding paragraphs of the book he noted that in youth "you find out what you *care to do* and who you *care to be*," in young adulthood "you learn whom you *care to be with*," and in adulthood "you learn to know what and whom you can *take care of*" (124). He suggests that this learning to know what and whom you can take care of is expressed in the Hindu principle of "the maintenance of the world," and adds that this principle is associated with "the middle period of the life cycle when existence permits you and demands you to consider death as peripheral and to the balance its certainty with the only happiness that is lasting: to increase, by whatever is yours to give, the good will and the higher order in your sector of the world" (124).

The sixties are that decade in life when it is especially easy to succumb to apathy, to a state of not caring. For most of us, retirement from our occupations and professions is either happening or looming, and with retirements there may be a loss of interest in earlier investments and engagements, and physical and emotional disengagement from the persons with whom we have associated on a daily basis. There may also be plans to relocate and to leave the neighborhoods in which we have lived for many years.

We may, under such circumstances, feel that we have to adopt an attitude of not caring as a means of coping with these changes. We may even begin to resort to a feature of the "identity vs. identity confusion" conflict, namely, "a sharp and intolerant readiness to discard and disavow people" in acts of *repudiation* which are "often snobbish, fitful, perverted, or simply thoughtless" (Erikson 1958, 42). When such repudiation occurs among sixty-year-olds, we may surmise that it is often a defense against the growing awareness that one's need to be needed is not being reciprocated by members of the younger generation. Nonreciprocity feeds repudiation.

Erikson's reflections on care, however, conclude with the observation that "there is a new greeting around these days which, used casually, seems to suggest not much more than that we should be careful, or take care of ourselves." He hopes, however, "that it could come to mean more" and therefore ends the final lecture with this very greeting: "TAKE CARE" (125). Simply by capitalizing it, he seems to make it mean more than it usually means, but he could have added that a decade earlier he had referred to "the Care for the creatures of this world and to the Charity which is felt to transcend it" (Erikson 1963, 267–68). Certainly, this makes the greeting—"Take Care"—seem more like a benediction, as though he viewed the lectures themselves as personal expressions of generativity.

Earlier in the Jefferson lectures, he mentioned that Thomas Jefferson had put together a small book consisting of a selection of Jesus' sayings from the Gospels which were, in Jefferson's own words, "diamonds in a dunghill" (45). Erikson applauded Jefferson's selections, noting that his own theological friends have informed him that Jefferson's selections "stand up well under modern Bible research," that is, as being the authentic words of Jesus himself. But he also noted that Jefferson's omission of "all references to Jesus' healing mission" (47) was unfortunate. After all, the healing stories reflect the importance that Jesus himself placed on "the Care for the creatures of this world and to the Charity which is felt to transcend it" (267–68).

On the other hand, Jefferson included Jesus' allusion to "the birds of the air" and "the lilies of the field," and assurance that if "your heavenly Father feeds them" and "clothes them" will he not also feed and clothe you? (Matt. 6:26–30). Are not these sayings also an affirmation of "the Care for the creatures of this world and to the Charity which is felt to transcend it"? And is not Jesus' assurance that our heavenly Father will feed and clothe us a way of saying that the new greeting—"Take care"—means much more than it may seem, for it suggests that we are able to take care because we know that, in an ultimate sense, we, too, are being taken care of.

PART FOUR
THE OLDER-ADULT
DECADES

Chapter 8

The Eighth Decade:
The Wise Self

People disagree a lot on when we cross the divide between middle and older adulthood, but milestone birthday cards provide some pretty compelling evidence that it happens when we turn seventy. For example, you can send a card to someone who is turning forty or fifty that ascribes to the recipient the physical characteristics that are popularly assumed to be signs of old age: drooling, inability to bend down and tie your shoes, unable to tolerate loud music, uncontrollable flatulence, and so forth. But for someone turning seventy, you can't find a card that jokes about the tell-tale signs of aging. After all, there's always the chance that one or more of them is true.

To be sure, cards for persons turning sixty also tend to avoid references to these signs of aging, but the need to say that the recipient looks and acts *younger* than his or her chronological age begins at seventy, not sixty. Also, the seventies are the first decade that cards make a big point of the recipients' "special memories," life's "wonderful moments," their achievements in life, and the inspiration that they have been to others. Although persons turning sixty are being told that they've had a lot of love and laughter in the course of their lives, they are also being assured that their best years are ahead of them. In contrast, those turning seventy are being encouraged to consider—and be proud of the fact—that they have done so much for so many appreciative others.

Thus in a single decade one has gone from being a forward-looking person whose best years lie ahead to being one who has taken a ninety-degree turn and is now looking with fondness on the past. The implicit message is that you are "over the hill" and not much will be expected of you from this time on. A birthday card that makes this point in a rather blunt manner is one with a photo of a football referee wearing a striped cap and shirt and large eyeglasses. He is blowing his whistle. On the inside it says simply, "Game over; you're old." It doesn't specify the recipient's age, but because the referee appears to be seventy or older, it is probably meant for someone who is roughly his own age. Perhaps the only person who would dare send this card to a relative or friend would be someone who is as old or older.

I find this birthday card a rather refreshing departure from those that emphasize the recipient's memories and life's accomplishments, but anyone who is entering the eighth decade of life is likely to question its association of "You're old" with "game over." In fact, the following, rather dubious poem of my own, inspired by a two-line poem by Robert Frost issues a strong objection.

The Span of Life

The old dog barks backward without getting up.
I can remember when he was a pup.
                              (Frost 1975, 308)

Old Dog Learns New Trick

The old dog barks backward through his butt.
Couldn't do *that* as a frisky young mutt.

Game over? Not this Rover!

No doubt, our contemporary poets would give us a somewhat more complex view of the prospect of turning seventy, but I haven't had much luck in finding poems on the subject. I'm sure that they exist, but the fact that I have had trouble locating any is rather telling in itself. Since poems on turning "the big number," as Billy Collins puts it, are usually written about oneself, there may simply be some reticence in writing about the turn to seventy. Poets may even feel that by announcing the fact that they have turned seventy, their younger readers will decide that they are "over the hill." You can write poems about other people in their seventies and older, and readers will like them, but a poem about oneself may be a very different story.

On the other hand, the following poem by William Stafford (1987, 55) appeared in a book of his poems published when he was seventy-three-years old. Because another book of his poems (Stafford 1982) was published five years earlier, I assume that this poem was written at about the time he was turning seventy:

Waiting in Line

You the very old. I have come
to the edge of your country and looked across,
how your eyes warily look into mine
when we pass, how you hesitate when
we approach a door. Sometimes
I understand how steep your hills
are, and your way of seeing the madness
around you, the careless waste of the calendar,
the rush of people on buses. I have
studied how you carry packages,
balancing them better, giving them attention.
I have glimpsed from within the gray-eyed look
at those who push, and occasionally even I
can achieve your beautiful bleak perspective
on the loud, the inattentive, shoving boors
jostling past you toward their doom.

With you, from the pavement I have watched
the nation of the young, like jungle birds
that scream as they pass, or gyrate on playgrounds,
their frenzied bodies jittering with the disease
of youth. Knowledge can cure them. But
not all at once. It will take time.

There have been evenings when the light
has turned everything silver, and like you
I have stopped at a corner and suddenly
staggered with the grace of it all: to have
inherited all this, or even the bereavement
of it and finally being cheated!—the chance
to stand on a corner and tell it goodby!

Every day, every evening, every
abject step or stumble has become heroic—

You others, we the very old have a country.
A passport costs everything there is.

Some persons in their seventies—or even eighties—might object to being referred to as "the very old," and they might try to assure Stafford that merely because he has turned seventy, he is not "very old." On the other hand, the poem suggests that he has entered the country of the old and left the nation of the young behind, and if the passport costs everything that one has, he is certainly in no position to try to buy his way back into the nation from whence he has come. Perhaps he had a premonition, aided by his knowledge of the fact that he suffered from myocardial arrhythmia, that he would not make it out of his seventies. He died at the age of seventy-nine, thus pretty much in step with the psalmist's observation that "The days of our life are seventy years / or perhaps eighty, if we are strong" (Ps. 90:10). In any event, there is a time when one begins to identify with the old, and for Stafford, this time has come.

Assuming, then, that the eighth decade is the first decade in older adulthood, let's see what we can make of it by considering it to be the decade in which the integrity vs. despair and disgust conflict is central. Because Erikson himself places this conflict in "old age," there is a sense in which my relocation of this particular dynamic conflict is no relocation at all. The difference, however, lies in the fact that I consider it to be central in the eighth decade and do not consider it to be central in the ninth and tenth. I believe that this dynamic conflict is superseded by other conflicts in these subsequent decades and, as noted in the introduction, I will present these conflicts in the chapters that follow.

THE INTEGRITY VS. DESPAIR AND DISGUST CONFLICT

Webster's has three definitions of *integrity*: (1) "the quality or state of being complete; unbroken condition; wholeness; entirety"; (2) "the quality or state of being unimpaired; perfect condition; soundness"; and (3) "the quality or state of being of sound moral principle; uprightness, honesty, sincerity" (Agnes 2001, 742). The words that seem especially central to these definitions are *complete, unimpaired, wholeness,* and *soundness.* These definitions also indicate that *integrity* is both a quality and a state. A *quality* is a characteristic "that constitutes the basic nature of a thing or is one of its distinguishing features" (1173). A *state* is "a set of circumstances or attributes characterizing a person or thing at a given time; a way or form of being" (1399).

As a particular quality, integrity would appear to be a characteristic that constitutes the basic nature of a person. As a state, it might be a characteristic of a person at a given time and therefore *not* characteristic of that person if circumstances changed. *Integrity,* however, implies that it is more "a way or form of being," so it tends to be relatively immune to changing circumstances. We expect that the integrity of a person will survive minor changes in circumstances, and we assume that there must have been a dramatic, even tumultuous change in circumstances when a person's integrity is compromised or lost, leading us to conclude that, in some very important respect, the person is no longer the same person. In other words, there has also been a loss of *personal identity.*

Erikson's use of the word *integrity* reflects these understandings. In his opening paragraph on the integrity vs. despair and disgust conflict in *Identity and the Life Cycle* (1959), he emphasizes that integrity represents the culmination of all the preceding stages. Thus, it represents the very *wholeness* of life. More specifically, however, it reflects the individual's attentiveness to the responsibilities that accrue to the person who has been or become generative. Thus,

> Only he who in some way has taken care of things and people and has adapted himself to the triumphs and disappointments to being, by necessity,

the originator of others and the generator of things and ideas—only he may gradually grow the fruit of these seven stages. I know no better word for it than ego integrity. (98)

Then, apparently dissatisfied with dictionary definitions of the word *integrity,* he adds, "Lacking a clear definition, I shall point to a few attributes of this state of mind" (98). That he considers it a "state of mind" suggests that it is "a way or form of being" (Agnes 2001, 1399). But of what does it consist?

First, it "is the acceptance of one's own and only life cycle and of the people who have become significant to it as something that had to be and that, by necessity, permitted of no substitutions" (1959, 98). Thus, it means "a new and different love of one's parents, "free of the wish that they should have been different, and an acceptance of the fact that one's life is one's own responsibility" (98). The key word here is *acceptance. Acceptance* may suggest a sense of resignation (as when a person accepts defeat), but it may also mean approval or a favorable reception (as when a student accepts a grade that was higher than expected) (Agnes 2001, 8). Thus, acceptance of "one's own and only life cycle" could range from feeling that although one was dealt a bad hand it could have been much worse to believing that one has truly been blessed.

Second, it "is a sense of comradeship with men and women of distant times and of different pursuits, who have created orders and objects and sayings conveying human dignity and love" (98). A *comrade* is "a friend [or] close companion," or "a person who shares interests and activities in common with others" (Agnes 2001, 300). Thus Erikson suggests that integrity involves friendship or companionship with persons who lived many years ago but whose lives reflect the values that we hold dear. The fact that he explicitly mentions "sayings" recalls our discussion in chapter 7 of the Golden Rule and the Hippocratic Oath. But this "sense of comradeship" with the creators of ancient sayings is especially apparent in "The Galilean Sayings and the Sense of 'I'" (Erikson 1981), also mentioned in chapter 7. In this article, published when he was in his late seventies, Erikson relates some of Jesus' sayings to the stages of the life cycle, thereby implying that these sayings express the values implicit in his life-cycle model, while the model sheds "new light" on these sayings. Thus, he has a sense of comradeship with Jesus because their views are compatible even though they lived in different times and engaged in different pursuits.

He also feels a particular comradeship with those who have created orders—especially structures of meaning—because this was also what he has tried to do. In *Toys and Reasons* (1977), published when he was seventy-five years old, he refers to his penchant for creating charts depicting the stages of life and asks, "Have my students not long suspected that all these neat listings are my own ceremonial reassurances?" (116). He added that there is a deep human need "for a world image linking everyday life with some universal vision" (117). If young students can afford to be a bit suspicious of his "ceremonial reassurances" that such an order of life actually exists, a person in the eighth stage of life has grounds for believing it to be true—namely, the experiences of a lifetime.

Third, this state of mind is one in which the possessor of integrity, "although aware of the relativity of all the various life styles which have given meaning to human striving," is "ready to defend his own life style against all physical and economic threats" (1959, 98). This possessor of integrity knows "that an individual life is the accidental coincidence of but one life cycle with but one segment of history," but because this *is* the case, "for him all human integrity stands and falls with the one style of integrity of which he partakes" (98). Thus, if the second attribute of this state of mind emphasizes the connection between one's own life and those of men and women of long ago, the third affirms the essential validity of one's own life style and does not treat some historical form or expression of integrity as the norm against which it is to be evaluated and judged. A life of integrity is possible in every generation, and by claiming the integrity of the style of life that one has lived, one implicitly affirms the integrity of the lives of our ancestors, however different they were from ours.

To this point in Erikson's discussion, the development of this state of mind seems rather straightforward. One *can* be a "possessor of integrity," and others are able to recognize those individuals who possess it because it reflects the very qualities of integrity, such as wholeness and soundness. But integrity does not live in an ivory tower. It has to contend with *despair* and *disgust.*

Webster's defines *despair* as "to be without hope" or "a loss of hope," and *disgust* as "a sickening distaste or dislike; deep aversion; repugnance" (Agnes 2001, 391, 412). Erikson understands *despair* somewhat differently, but practically speaking it comes down to the same thing—"to be without hope." Drawing on his understanding of *integrity* as "the acceptance of one's own and only life cycle," he suggests that *despair* is the state of mind in which such acceptance is not forthcoming. *Despair* "expresses the feeling that time is short, too short for the attempt to start another life and to try out alternate roads to integrity" (98). If it is already too late there is no reason to hope, for hope is based on the fact that there is still time.[1]

Erikson would not disagree with *Webster's* definition of *disgust,* but he wants to make the point that despair and disgust are related. He observes that despair "is often hidden behind a show of disgust, a misanthropy, or a chronic contemptuous

---

1. In a sermon titled "Listening to the Parables of Jesus," Paul Ricoeur (1978) refers to Joachim Jeremias's phrase "it may be too late" for the parables in Matt. 24:36–25:13 (for example, the parable of the Ten Bridesmaids). He notes that the idea that "it may be too late" is "paradoxical because it runs counter to actual experience where there will always be another chance" (244). In *Psychology for Screenwriters,* William Indick (2004) uses Erikson's integrity vs. despair and disgust conflict as an interpretive lens for films such as *About Schmidt, My Life,* and *Ikiru,* in which "characters are forced to reappraise the meaning of their lives when they realize that they only have a short amount of time to change the final acts of their life stories. The motivation to change is real and believable, and the viewer is willing to follow these driven characters through their inspiring journeys of self-redemption" (103). These films appear to affirm the view that it is never too late to be a "possessor of integrity."

displeasure with particular institutions and particular people—a disgust and a displeasure which (where not allied with constructive ideas and a life of cooperation) only signify the individual's contempt of himself" (98).

"Contempt" is a strong word, because it means that one views the object of this attitude and feeling as someone to be looked down upon, as worthless or despicable (Agnes 2001, 314). On the other hand, the very fact that one has such feelings about oneself also means that a part of oneself assumes the right to this more superior attitude, so, in this sense, integrity still has a chance, but only if the superior self can find a way to embrace the inferior self and love it as its own. For integrity is a state of mind that is not fundamentally divided or at odds with itself, a sense of equanimity based on an acceptance of one's life, not in resignation but in fundamental approval.

In locating the integrity vs. despair and disgust conflict in the final stage of life, Erikson intends the very word *integrity* to support his representation of human life as a *cycle*. In his own citation of *Webster's* in the original version of *Childhood and Society* (1950) he notes that

> Webster's Dictionary is kind enough to help us complete this outline [of the eight stages] in a circular fashion. Trust (the first of our ego values) is here defined as "the assured reliance on another's integrity," the last of our values. I suspect that Webster had business in mind rather than babies, credit rather than faith. But the formulation stands. (233)

He does not say what sort of "faith" he has in mind, but I think that his observation in *Identity and the Life Cycle* (1959) that generativity requires "some faith, some 'belief in the species,' which would make a child appear to be a welcome trust of the community" (97) is relevant. If so, what integrity adds to this idea is suggested in the sentence that follows his declaration that the formulation stands: "And it seems possible to further paraphrase the relation of adult integrity and infantile trust by saying that healthy children will not fear life if their parents have integrity enough not to fear death" (233).

In the revised edition of *Childhood and Society*, Erikson (1963) proposes that the institutional safeguard of integrity is all of the previous institutional and cultural safeguards, but especially as these are reflected in cultural "image bearers"— those persons who are worthy of followers precisely because their lives reflect and represent the integrity of life (269). These would appear to be the contemporary counterparts of the previously mentioned "men and women of distant times and different pursuits, who have created orders and objects and sayings conveying human dignity and love" (98).

I would also assume that these "image bearers" need not be famous persons or celebrities. When I was a boy, I read Nathaniel Hawthorne's (1946) "The Great Stone Face," the story of a young boy who grew up in a town not far from a mountain with a rock formation that resembled a human face: "It was a work of Nature in her mood of majestic playfulness, formed on the perpendicular side of a mountain by some immense rocks, which had been thrown together in such a position as, when viewed at a proper distance, precisely to resemble the features of the human countenance" (292).

As the story begins, a little boy named Ernest is sitting with his mother at the door of their cottage, talking about the Great Stone Face. Ernest says to his mother that he wishes that it could speak, for it looks so very kindly that its voice must be a pleasant one. He adds, "If I were to see a man with such a face, I should love him dearly" (293). She tells him that there is an old prophecy that, at some future day, a child would be born somewhere in the general vicinity of the mountain who is destined to become the greatest and noblest personage of his time, "and whose countenance, in manhood, should bear an exact resemblance to the Great Stone Face" (293). She adds that some people, both young and old, had an enduring faith in this old prophecy, while others had watched and waited for so long that they had concluded the prophecy was nothing but an idle tale.

Ernest never forgets the story that his mother told him. He grows up to be a mild, quiet, unobtrusive boy, who works in the fields by day. When work was done, he would gaze at the Great Stone Face for hours, "until he began to imagine that those vast features recognized him, and gave him a smile of kindness and encouragement, responsive to his own look of veneration" (294). Because he did not receive any formal schooling, the Great Stone Face was his only teacher.

When he is still a boy, a rumor spreads that a very rich merchant named Mr. Gathergold is the prophesied one, but when he comes to town, it is clear that he is not the man. Still, Ernest hopes. Years go by, and when he is a young man, Ernest hears rumors that an old military man, General Blood-and-Thunder, is the prophesied one, but when he comes to town it is equally clear that he is not the man either. Then, when Ernest is middle-aged, a politician whom many were touting for President, a man whose nickname is Old Stony Phiz, returns to the region of his childhood. Because he was nicknamed for the Great Stone Face, the townspeople are certain that this is the man they had been waiting for all these years. Ernest wants to believe it, but, again, his hopes go unfulfilled.

Then, when Ernest is old, a poet who had heard of Ernest comes to town and asks Ernest if he would give him a night's lodging. Ernest replies, "Willingly," and adds that it seems to him that the Great Stone Face had never looked so hospitably at a stranger. Ernest, who had long been a lover of the poet's words, begins to feel that this is the man, especially as they discourse together throughout the afternoon. But something is missing, and Ernest's countenance begins to fall. Sensing his sadness, the poet asks him why he is sad, and Ernest tells him that when he had read his poems, he hoped that the prophecy would be fulfilled in him. The poet replies, "It's true that you can hear in my poems the far-off echo of a heavenly song. But my life, dear Ernest, has not corresponded with my thought" (309). He went on to note that he lacks "faith in the grandeur, the beauty, and the goodness, which my own works are said to have made more evident in nature and in human life" (309–310). He spoke sadly, and his eyes were dim with tears, as were those of Ernest himself.

At sunset, as had long been his frequent custom, Ernest was to discourse to his neighbors in the open air. He and the poet, arm in arm, and still talking together as they went along, proceed to the spot. Ernest begins to speak, "giving to the people of what was in his heart and mind," and "his words had power, because they accorded with his thought; and his thoughts had reality and depth, because they harmonized with the life he had always lived" (310). As the poet listened, he felt that the being and character of Ernest "were a nobler strain of poetry than he had ever written." His eyes glistened with tears as he "gazed reverentially at the venerable man" (310). At a distance, the Great Stone Face appeared in the golden light of the setting sun. With the mists around it, it resembled the white hairs around the brow of Ernest, and "its look of grand beneficence seemed to embrace the world" (311).

At that moment, Ernest's own face "assumed a grandeur of expression," and it was "so imbued with benevolence, that the poet, by an irresistible impulse, threw his arms aloft and shouted—'Behold! Behold! Ernest is himself the likeness of the Great Stone Face!'" (311). Then all the people looked, and they saw that what the deep-sighted poet said was true. The prophecy had been fulfilled before their very eyes. But when Ernest finished what he had to say, he took the poet's arm, and walked slowly homeward, "still hoping that some wiser and better man than himself would by and by appear, bearing a resemblance to the Great Stone Face" (311).

A sentimental story perhaps. But it makes the point that Ernest, having lived his life in the presence of the Great Stone Face, had been so shaped by its presence that he had become its living representation. He had become the very possessor of the integrity symbolized by the rock formation that had formed and informed his life and had inspired the townspeople's own collective wisdom.

THE VIRTUE OF WISDOM

For Erikson, *wisdom* is the virtue of the integrity vs. despair and disgust stage of the life cycle. *Webster's* has essentially three definitions of wisdom: (1) "the quality of being wise; power of judging rightly and following the soundest course of action, based on knowledge, experience, understanding, etc; good judgment; sagacity"; (2) "learning, knowledge, erudition (the *wisdom* of the ages)"; and (3) "a wise plan or course of action" (Agnes 2001, 1643). The word that especially stands out here is judgment, especially good judgment, and the idea is that this good judgment is employed in deciding on a course of action deemed to be sound because it reflects understanding of the situation based on experience and knowledge. Wisdom is therefore not equated with esoteric knowledge or abstract theorizing. Rather, it is practical, sensible, and capable of explaining why it recommends *this* over *that* course of action.

In "Human Strength and the Cycle of Generations," Erikson (1964a) is so concerned to link *wisdom* to the final stage of life that his working definition seems, at first glance, to have little in common with these dictionary definitions.

He states that wisdom is "detached concern with life itself, in the face of death itself" (133). On the other hand, when this definition is viewed in the context of his discussion of the role that wisdom plays as the culminating human strength or virtue of the life cycle, its compatibility with the definitions that *Webster's* offers becomes evident.

He begins this discussion by noting that, unlike the civilizations of the East, our Western civilization does not have a concept of "the whole of life" (132). Western psychology has tended to avoid "looking at the range of the whole cycle" of life but instead has merely reflected the Western "world-image" itself: "As our world-image is a one-way street to never-ending progress interrupted only by small and big catastrophes, our lives are to be one-way streets to success—and sudden oblivion" (132). Erikson wants to challenge this "one-way street" view of human life, and does so by employing the phrase "life cycle."

He notes, however, that when he speaks of a cycle of life, he means "two cycles in one: the cycle of one generation concluding itself in the next, and the cycle of individual life coming to a conclusion" (132–33). This means that the cycle "turns back on its beginnings, so that the very old become again like children" (133), and this raises the question of "whether the return is to a childlikeness seasoned with wisdom—or to a finite childishness" (133). Which one of these occurs is

> not only important within the cycle of individual life, but also within that of generations, for it can only weaken the vital fiber of the younger generation if the evidence of daily living verifies man's prolonged last phase as a sanctioned period of childishness. Any span of the cycle that is lived without vigorous meaning, at the beginning, in the middle, or at the end, endangers the sense of life and the meaning of death in all whose life stages are intertwined. (133)

The "vigorous meaning" that is required of the person in the last stage of life is largely determined by how one responds to the "ultimate test" of one's individuality, namely, "man's existence at the entrance to that valley which he must cross alone" (133).

Erikson says that he is "not ready to discuss the psychology of 'ultimate concern'," but as he comes to the conclusion of his "outline" of the human strengths, he

> cannot help feeling that the order depicted suggests an existential complementarity of the great Nothingness and the actuality of the cycle of generations. For if there is any responsibility in the cycle of life it must be that one generation owes to the next that strength by which it can come to face ultimate concerns in its own way—unmarred by debilitating poverty or by the neurotic concerns caused by emotional exploitation. (133)

That the next generation has received this "strength" from the preceding generation is evident in its own capacity to find "the wisdom of the ages in the form of its own wisdom" (133).

Although readers of this book may be pleased that Erikson associates the wisdom of this stage with "ultimate concerns," they may also be disconcerted by his suggestion that there is a complementarity between "the great Nothingness" and the actuality of the cycle of generations. If his intention is to affirm that there is a necessary interrelationship or correspondence between the ultimate order of all things and the order of the cycle of generations, why would he refer to the former as "the great Nothingness"? The epilogue of *Young Man Luther* (Erikson 1958) provides an explanation. Here, Erikson proposes that our image of God as commanding voice of conscience may be traced to our early childhood experience of the voice of our fathers; that our image of God as an affirming face, graciously inclined, may be traced to our infancy experience of the face of our mothers; and that our sense of God as "pure nothing" may be traced to the period when we take form in our mother's womb. Invoking St. Paul's image of the mirror in which we see darkly, but then face to face (1 Cor. 13:12), he writes,

> Finally, the glass shows the pure self itself, the unborn core of creation, the— as it were, preparental—center where God is pure nothing: *ein lauter Nichts,* in the words of [the German mystic] Angelus Silesius. God is so designated in many ways in Eastern mysticism. This pure self is the self no longer sick with a conflict between right and wrong [the voice of conscience], not dependent on providers [the face graciously inclined], and not dependent on guides to reason and reality. (264)

In the darkness of the womb, there are no images, yet one is enveloped in "the Care for the creatures of this world" and "the Charity that is felt to transcend it" (Erikson 1963, 267–68). Thus, even as we possess a "self" that preexists and survives our "images" of our selves, this may also be said of the selfhood of God. The God who is perceived as "the great Nothingness" may be understood as the ground of being (Tillich 1952, 160).[2]

Erikson concludes his discussion of the virtue of wisdom with the observation that the human strength of the old "takes the form of wisdom in all of its connotations from ripened 'wits' to accumulated knowledge and matured judgment. It is the essence of knowledge freed from temporal relativity" (1964a, 133). Thus, wisdom, a detached concern with life itself in the face of death itself, "maintains and conveys the integrity of experience, in spite of the decline of bodily and mental functions" (133). He acknowledges that

---

2. As Tillich notes, "In terms like ultimate, unconditional, infinite, absolute, the difference between subjectivity and objectivity is overcome. The ultimate of the act of faith and the ultimate that is meant in the act of faith are one and the same. This is symbolically expressed by the mystics when they say that their knowledge of God is the knowledge God has of himself; and it is expressed by Paul when he says (1 Cor. 13) that he will know as he is known, namely, by God. God never can be object without being at the same time subject" (11). When Erikson says that he is not ready to discuss the psychology of ultimate concern, he seems to have in mind the experiences of ultimacy that occur in purest form at the very beginning (the womb) and ending (the oblivion of death) of the life cycle, when the difference between subjectivity and objectivity is overcome.

potency, performance, and adaptability decline; but if vigor of mind combines with the gift of responsible renunciation, some old people can envisage human problems in their entirety (which is what 'integrity' means) and can represent to the coming generation a living example of the 'closure' of a style of life. Only such integrity can balance the despair of the knowledge that a limited life is coming to a conscious conclusion, only such wholeness can transcend the petty disgust of feeling finished and passed by, and the despair of facing the period of relative helplessness which marks the end as it marked the beginning. (134)

Erikson concludes his reflections on wisdom with the observation that there are some persons who seem to be especially gifted as representatives of wisdom: there are the leaders and thinkers "who round out long productive lives in positions in which wisdom is of the essence and is of service," and there are those "who feel verified in numerous and vigorous progeny" (134). But, eventually, they, too, will join the very old "who are reduced to a narrow space-time, in which only a few things, in their self-contained form, offer a last but firm whisper of confirmation" (134).

VITAL INVOLVEMENT IN OLD AGE

So far, our discussion of the integrity vs. despair and disgust conflict and the virtue of wisdom has been rather theoretical. As we saw, however, wisdom itself reflects soundness of judgment regarding a course of action. So I now want to turn to the research study of older adults in which both Erik and Joan Erikson were involved when they were in their late seventies. Helen O. Kivnick, an associate professor at the California School of Professional Psychology in Berkeley and a practicing clinical psychologist, was the primary researcher. The results of this study are presented in *Vital Involvement in Old Age* (Erikson, Erikson, & Kivnick 1986).

The subjects of the study were the parents of children who were in their early teens when they were the research subjects of the Guidance Study Project of the Institute of Human Development of the University of California at Berkeley initiated in 1929. There were 248 early teenagers in the original study. Erikson had been a member of the research team in the 1940s, the same period in which he formulated his life-cycle model.

Funding in 1981 from the National Institute of Mental Health under the auspices of the Rehabilitation Research and Training Center on Aging at the University of Pennsylvania made it possible to study some of the parents of the Guidance Study teenagers. The children were in their fifties or older, and the twenty-nine parents ranged from seventy-five to ninety-five years of age.

The research design involved two interviews two hours each in length conducted in the informants' own places of residence. The Eriksons were living in Tiburon, California, at the time. They participated in all of the interviews, and their very presence enabled the subjects of the study to feel that they would be treated with respect.

Fourteen of the twenty-nine subjects (or informants) lived in the homes where they lived when their children were growing up; five lived in fairly luxurious retirement communities; five widows lived in small apartments, and one of the five shared the apartment with her widowed sister; one couple lived in a government-subsidized partial-care facility; one woman lived alone in a modest retirement center apartment; one woman lived in her daughter's home; and one man lived alone in a small cabin. Fourteen were single women; five were single men; and there were five couples. Thus, nineteen of the twenty-nine informants were women.

Because the participants were between the ages of seventy-five and ninety-five, the assumption was that they were in the integrity vs. despair and disgust life-stage. The major part of the book, however, which focuses on "the voices of our informants," places their present experiences and insights within the framework of all the life-cycle stages, the point being that when persons are in the older adult period of their life, they try to reconcile the tensions of the earlier stages. The following provides a very general summary of the study by focusing on what counted as evidence of integrity, what experiences and thoughts were evidence of or grounds for despair, and what strategies were employed to maintain integrity over despair.

Evidence of Integrity

I was able to identify six indications that the informants were, in fact, experiencing or developing a sense of integrity. The first was reflected in the fact that they were seeking and receiving guidance from someone held in very high esteem. These esteemed persons may be someone for whom they had the highest regard at an earlier stage of life, such as a grandparent or parent, or someone whom they admired a great deal, such as a celebrity, a neighbor, or a Good Samaritan whom the informant met at a seniors' center.

The second was that they had an increased concern for the world and its multifarious inhabitants. They were more tolerant, patient, open-minded, understanding, compassionate, and less critical, and they were able to see "both sides" of an issue. An awareness that they may be becoming "more set in their ways" was not inconsistent with this greater tolerance, for insistence on their own preferred way of doing things could enable them to be more tolerant of other people when *they* insisted on doing things *their* way.

Third, they were developing a philosophy of aging, one that included a determination to continue to grow and not allow themselves to stagnate, energetic commitment to a positive daily routine, remaining actively involved with other persons, acting on their own need to be needed, and maintaining a sense of humor, especially concerning themselves.

Fourth, there was an appreciative turn toward religion, a turn that might manifest itself in the recollection of engagement in religious observances as a child, in actual church attendance, or in affirmation of the importance of the ritualized community that churches and synagogues represent.

Fifth, they were able to acknowledge and accept their past choices. This would involve accepting the fact that earlier decisions could not be altered now, but it would also mean ascribing new meaning to earlier experiences that were painful, seeing them from a larger and generally more positive perspective.

Sixth, they integrated legitimate feelings of cynicism and hopelessness into a more accepting and hopeful perspective.

Of course, not all of the twenty-nine informants reflected these tendencies, but those whose lives seemed to express a more pronounced sense of integrity were exhibiting more of these tendencies than the others.

Grounds for Despair

The informants also brought up issues that were grounds for despair. I identified six of these as well. First, they were feeling the loss of those their own age who were leaving the community in which they had spent much of their lives together. This was especially the case of the fourteen informants who were still living in their own homes.

Second, they were experiencing largely involuntary thoughts about dying, and they were not feeling well, were feeling depressed, or were feeling "somehow let down."

Third, they were keenly aware of the fact that necessary thinking about the future was taking place in the context of the recognition of the fact that death may not be very far off.

Fourth, they perceived that the future of the world is not very hopeful, together with the realization that there wasn't much that they could do about it.

Fifth, they ruminated over their earlier powerlessness to save a loved one from dying and what they could have done differently about it.

Sixth, they felt obligated to provide material assistance to family members when these family members should be capable of taking care of their own affairs.

As with the signs and indications of a sense of integrity, not all of the twenty-nine informants were having these experiences, feelings, and perceptions. But the more of these that they confessed to, the more they seemed to be experiencing a sense of despair.

Strategies for Maintaining Integrity Over Despair

Finally, the informants adopted certain strategies to maintain integrity over despair. The following four are especially noteworthy:

First, they took a viable future for granted by involving themselves in activities that assumed that they have several or many productive years ahead.

Second, they took an interest in their grandchildren as representative of a future that extends not only beyond their own future but also that of their own children.

Third, they began to emulate an older person, especially a family member, who exemplified mental vigor and emotional strength when that person was the informant's current age.

Fourth, they would "revise" the past by minimizing or even seeming to ignore the painful experiences or questionable decisions in earlier stages of life. It was evident that some of their informants were engaging in this strategy because the researchers had access to the extensive files that the Guidance Study Project had collected several decades earlier.

This last strategy might be considered a form of denial or self-deception, but psychotherapists Ben Furman and Tapani Ahola (1992) make the following observation in their book *Solution Talk*:

> Our history is an integral part of ourselves. As long as we think of the past as a source of our problems, we set up, in a sense, an adversarial relationship within ourselves. The past, very humanly, responds negatively to criticism and blaming but favorably to respect and stroking. The past prefers to be seen as a resource, a store of memories, good and bad, and a source of wisdom emanating from life experience. (18)

Their use of the word "wisdom" is significant in itself, but it also invites us to see all four strategies as a form of wisdom. In fact, these strategies reflect many of the key characteristics that Erikson identifies in his discussion of wisdom as a human strength. No doubt, a more intentional effort to exemplify these characteristics of wisdom would produce other strategies for enhancing the sense of integrity and reducing the sense of despair, but these four rather clearly indicate that the informants were attempting to see their lives in a holistic way by maintaining both a future orientation and appreciation for the past.

Vital Involvement in Old Age is filled with incidents that illustrate the continuing influence of earlier stage dynamics on the informants in their older adult years, but there are no actual "cases." To illustrate how the integrity vs. despair and disgust conflict plays a central role in the lives of persons who are in their eighth decade of life, I will draw on a case presented by Sharon R. Kaufman (1986) in her book *The Ageless Self*.

BEN: "I TRIED TO AVOID COMPLICATIONS"

Kaufman's book is based on research that she conducted for her doctoral dissertation at the University of California at San Francisco and Berkeley. She conducted interviews with sixty persons ranging in age from seventy to ninety-seven, and then chose six, four women and two men, as the basis for her book. The two men and one of the women were in their seventies; the other three women were in their eighties. The most extensively reported of the three people in their seventies is a man named Ben, born in 1904, who was seventy-four-years old when he was interviewed.

The Dichotomy of Self

Kaufman suggests that one of the major themes in Ben's life story is the dichotomy of self. For most of his seventy-four years he has been fighting a battle within himself between his sober, steady, responsible side and his carefree, happy, romantic side. He sees much of his life experience in terms of the struggle between these two selves. He said to Kaufman, "I *look* in the mirror and I see my father, a very serious guy. My normal, deadpan expression is what my father had, which was a no-nonsense guy who had a big burden on his shoulders. And that's the kind of face I show to the world" (48). "But," he added, "I don't *feel* that way. I feel carefree and happy. . . . I could easily slide or slip into a romantic adventure" (48).

Ben was raised in a small town in the Midwest. His father was a factory worker who labored long hours most of his life. He had no worker's compensation and lived in constant fear of potential accidents at the factory or a debilitating illness. Ben remembers his father as a nervous man who was greatly burdened by financial worries. There were six children in the family, and his father felt responsible for providing them all a college education. It was not until Ben was an adult himself that he realized how precarious the family's financial situation was. He never felt that he lacked anything as a child, but he remembers his mother as similar to his father because she was constantly worried over how to provide for the children and make sure that they received an education.

Throughout childhood Ben worried that he would not amount to anything. His reflections on his youth focus mainly on his education, his desire to do well in school, and his worries that he would be "found out to be stupid" (50). When he was fourteen, his parents, wanting him to become a priest, sent him to a nearby boarding school operated by a Catholic order. At twenty, he left the order and returned home because he didn't want to devote his life to service, but he continued to express his sober and serious side through the choices he made in terms of his career and marriage.

Soon, he left home to attend college, then moved to a larger Midwestern city at the age of twenty-four when he got his first teaching job. He taught high school mathematics for ten years prior to World War II, when he was drafted into the army. While in military service, he realized that there were many men who were not as smart as he was but were making a lot more money. So when he left the military, he decided not to return to teaching, which he had found rather boring, and moved to the East Coast where he was offered a job as a writer in a large corporation. He stayed with this job for thirty years.

At some point he met a stockbroker, and through him was able to make as much money in the market as he made from his job. The money he made in the stock market gave him "freedom to pursue all my dreams" (53), which he described as travel, excitement, and adventure, but he never actually used his economic freedom to realize his fantasies. During all the years that he was a bureaucrat for a single company, he was "bored out of [his] skull," and said that he "stayed there twenty years too long" (51).

The primary reason he gives for not leaving his job or taking advantage of his success in the stock market was that he needed to focus on his wife's care. They had married when he was in his mid-thirties, and during the second half of their marriage she was bedridden by a seriously debilitating illness, the fate that his father had feared for himself. She had died a few months before Ben talked with Kaufman. He had little to say about their marriage that was positive. He felt that his wife should have married her mother because she was closer to her mother than to him, and mentioned that they were "too dumb to go to a marriage counselor" (50).

But unsatisfactory though it was, he accepted the relationship: "You don't walk out on something just because it's difficult" (50). When she became ill, he felt responsible both for maintaining his marriage and for providing her with all the comforts he could manage. He hired people to take care of her, but he spent a great deal of time with her himself, even though he was frustrated by such a limiting existence. As Kaufman puts it, "He chose the loyal, moral response to this situation, and placed devotion to his wife above the gratification of personal desires" (50).

Financial Security, Religion, and Disengagement

Ben spoke frequently about what he wishes he could have done with his life. He mentioned that he "would have longed to have been a stockbroker, or a real estate speculator, or a traveler" but that he "wasn't adventurous enough to quit [his] job" (51). Later he said, "I would have given a lot to have been a successful fiction writer. But to write an exciting story you have to experience some things. But my experience—there are no high points, no dramas in it. It's all slow, enduring patience" (51). He also mentioned being inhibited by the prospect of competing with other writers: "If I didn't read what others were writing, I might be dumb enough to think I could sell something. But as I would read something I'd think, this guy is wonderful. Why should I dream about competing with him? I mean, I was third, fourth, fifth echelon down, and the only people who were selling were the top echelons" (54). As Kaufman notes, "He measures success by writing by the amount of money made in selling the product" and "wrote stories with the idea of selling them. When he realized his stories would not sell, he gave up" (54). Thus, a major theme in his life was the priority he placed on financial security.

Religion was another life theme. When Kaufman asked him to tell about his childhood, he said, "We were brought up in an Irish Catholic family a few blocks away from the parochial school I attended. My mother was a very pious, a very good woman. Worried a lot about bringing up the children the proper way. Both my parents were very proud of my oldest brother who became a priest, and one of my sisters became a nun" (54–55). He added, "They tried very hard to make a priest out of me, but I was the one who was sort of the black sheep. A good boy, but I didn't take to the priesthood idea, and what else compares with that?" (55).

Abandoning studies toward the priesthood was probably the most difficult decision of his life. His primary explanation for why he "lost my vocation before very long" was his dissatisfaction with the minimum amount of education he would receive as a member of the order: "I was an intellectual, or thought so at the time, and that's what drove me out of the order. Had they given me ten years of schooling at the time I wanted it, I would have been a member yet" (55). He felt he had let his parents down, and, Kaufman notes, "the religiously based self-concept of youth has contributed greatly to the somber side of his identity" (55).

Moreover, he could leave the order, but this did not resolve "the dilemma of whether or not to dedicate his life to spiritual goals" (55). In his life story, "religious activities do not emerge as a primary concern of Ben's middle years," but now, "as he speaks of the present and future, his ambivalence over whether or not to serve some higher purpose manifests itself in a major preoccupation— the need to be generous" (55–56). His personal ideals are the Christian saints whose lives were guided by unequivocal altruism, and he discusses at great length their charity and compassion in the face of utter poverty. He is especially impressed by Mother Theresa. No one he has known personally impresses him as much as she does.

When asked to identify his own best character trait, he replied, "Generosity. Anybody who wants anything that I can give them, including just little things like transportation and time, I do it without question" (56). But as he talked further, it was clear that he had another view of himself: "I don't have this self-giving that other people do. Some of my friends will go visit people in hospitals. I admire that tremendously. That's what I should do, but I'm not generous. I've thought to myself often, that's a great way to end one's life—doing things for other people. That's what I should do, but I'm not going to do that, I know it" (56).

He also said that he could have been generous with his money, but he "has always been too frightened of the economic future to be generous. Lots of causes have come up for which I gave a dollar, when I could have given a hundred" (56–57). On the other hand, he said, "I don't do things personally for people, but the money I have I am already dispensing to friends and relatives" (57). Here, Kaufman notes, he seems to contradict his assessment of himself as not a very generous person, but she believes that "his priorities of giving money rather than time and energy are clearly ordered now, for he says of an acquaintance who talks incessantly, 'I haven't got the generosity to listen to him by the hour. I would rather give him $1,000 than listen to him for 1,000 hours'" (57). Of course, he does not say that he actually gives the other man $1,000. But, in any event, he certainly considers generosity a central characteristic of what it means to be a religious person.

Also, according to Kaufman, religion gives him "an optimistic outlook on life and enables him to deal positively with the difficult experiences he has had to face" (57). He believes that his religious beliefs have enabled him to weather successfully the "tragedy" of his wife's illness and the "perpetual crisis" of his life the last few years. As he said of religion, "I haven't seen anything else to compare with it. And the friends I have [who are not religious] are far less happy than I am with their world outlook and their look to the future" (57). He added, "I consider life a big gift. And the next life an even greater one. So, I don't regret. I'm very grateful" (57). He also feels that his religious faith will become even more meaningful as he grows older: "My whole quest is to learn more about what does the Supreme Being ask of me for the balance of my life? I will probably start to read more, more conscientiously about religion, because it's the only lasting thing, the only stable thing" (57). The fact that he emphasizes reading more conscientiously about religion may reflect his feeling that he would have remained in the order if his intellectual interests had been recognized and encouraged. Kaufman concludes that Ben's "faith has kept him from being bitter about his empty marriage and sad, limited domestic situation. Apparently his faith has a positive effect, because his eyes are full of life and he always smiles. He does not look like a man heavily burdened. On the contrary, he *looks* like the 'carefree,' 'happy' person he feels he is inside" (57–58).

On the other hand, Kaufman identifies another major theme in Ben's life, the theme of disengagement. His life seems monotonous, with, as he says, "no high points," just "slow enduring patience," and the reason for this is that disengagement runs through it. As Kaufman observes, "We see his disengagement in the way Ben describes entering into—and avoiding—relationships" (58). When she asked him how he would divide his life into chapters, he said that he would proceed chronologically and "then have to add chapters on the emotional states" (59). Thus, "for Ben, emotional states, indeed, human relations are perceived as something added to life; they do not seem to be an integral part of it" (59).

He seems to have no close personal friends, and when asked to whom he feels closest to at present, he mentioned a brother and a sister, neither of whom lives close by. Both, however, came to his assistance when his household needed reorganizing after his wife died. He summarizes his lifelong attitudes toward all relationships this way: "I tried to avoid complications. I take the easy way out—in personal relationships and other things. Rather than blasting away arguing with somebody about the way it should be, I would rather skip it" (59). His marriage produced no children. At the time, he had "no particular ambition to have children," and he is now glad for this: "I don't think I would have been a good parent. Much too nervous and worried—like my own parents. I guess that had something to do with it. It would have been a difficult adjustment for me" (59). As he does not expect to make new friends, he anticipates the time when he will "be narrowed down to the time when [he] will be alone" (60).

When asked to describe his daily routine, it was evident Ben spent most of his days alone. He attended Mass every day, and sometimes he would eat breakfast at a cafeteria where he would meet "a couple of people" that he knows (60), but the rest of the day would be spent swimming by himself at the 'Y,' reading in the afternoon, going to a movie by himself because he'd "rather not fuss around calling someone," and reading again until midnight. The only variation in his daily routine was the occasional dentist or doctor's appointment. He predicted that the rest of his life would be much the same: "Unless somebody comes along and fires me up with a new enthusiasm, I guess it's going to continue pretty much the way it is now" (60–61). He could imagine that such a person might get him "tremendously interested" in becoming a great poker player, a great traveler, a great golfer, a great hospital visitor, but he himself felt "none of that" (61). On the other hand, he believes that most people "have led lives even more fearful and timid and unexciting" than he has (61).

As further evidence of his disengagement and detachment, Kaufman notes that Ben does not really "live" in his own house, which Kaufman describes as extremely drab and depressing. He and his wife had moved to California when he retired because his wife's mother felt she could take better care of her daughter. So they moved into her house, and he remained there after both women died. While they were alive, he spent most of his time in a room upstairs, an overcrowded room with his bed, desk, typewriter, TV set, radio, and books. At the time of Kaufman's visits, he had not yet "moved into" the rest of the quite sizable house. The furniture belonged to his wife's mother, and his own furniture remained in storage. "He clearly prefers to reside in the only space he felt comfortable in during the preceding years," Kaufman notes (62).

How Old Do You Feel?

Kaufman asked Ben if he felt as though he were seventy-four-years old. Like all the other persons in her study who were asked if they identify with their chronological age, Ben said no. Rather, he said, "I feel the same as I did when I was much younger. And as a matter of fact, I have a strong desire since my wife died to relive my college days" (155). These years stand out "as the closest he was able to come to his 'carefree,' 'romantic' self. His arrival in the college town in his early twenties symbolized both his break away from the small town where he was raised and forced into a religious mold that he did not fit" (156). He recalled those days: "What a thrill it was to be there, and see four streetcar tracks, and all the excitement. I got a little Chevy coupe, and I started to date girls. And I enjoyed life as a single person" (156). He knows, of course, that he cannot relive his college days, and although he thinks about it, he has no real intention of trying to "get going with a younger person," because "that would be unfair to the younger person and make a fool out of myself" (156). But he does not really identify with his chronological age either. He is healthy and has no physical ailments.

When Kaufman asked him if, when he was growing up, he had any expectations of what being old would be like, he responded that he thought of old people as infirm, sick, in fear of abject poverty and dependency: "His fears of catastrophic illness and destitution, formed by his image of his father and his early family life, have largely shaped his conception of the aging process" (157). But his picture of aging is not completely negative. His religion especially provides a source of hope and solace as he anticipates the next twenty years of his life: "If I didn't have that final resource, life would look very bleak to me. I don't see how people can get along, why they aren't driven to great sadness by the fact that people are going to desert them. I would call on my religious aids, on the parish priest, and I would expect him to reinforce my hopes about the next life" (157). Kaufman also notes that the disengagement theme is actually a positive resource as Ben considers the aging process. He views "desertion" as an inevitable fact of aging and believes that there will be few visitors when he faces the end of his life. But disengagement has been a major theme of his life, having defined its very style, so although it is "ultimately pessimistic, it provides an explanation of old age and *a connection with his sense of himself at other times in his life*" (158, emphasis added).

Ben's State of Mind

Kaufman does not use the language of integrity vs. despair and disgust to describe Ben's state of mind at the time she conducted her interviews. But the dichotomy-of-self theme with which she begins her discussion suggests that he is conflicted about his life, especially about the decisions he had made and how he responded to circumstances over which he seemed to have no control. Does the integrity vs. despair and disgust formulation shed light on this conflict? I believe that it does. As we consider his state of mind, let's remember that integrity is an acceptance of one's life as what it had to be and could not have been other than it was; a sense of one's participation in the succession of generations; and a maturity of life that reflects the positive tendencies of the earlier stages, now integrated into a congruent whole. In contrast, despair involves a fear of death due largely to the inability to accept the life that one has lived and the feeling that it's too late to begin another life or try out alternate roads to integrity; it hides behind a show of disgust, misanthropy, and contempt for others and institutions and reflects a self-contempt because one lacks any sense of comradeship with those whose lives mirror human dignity and love.

Ben's general state of mind manifested both sides of this conflict. Concerning integrity, he recognized that he had needed to emphasize his sober, serious, and responsible self in light of his wife's tragic illness, but it was a rather resigned and reluctant acceptance, for he felt that he should have given the self that craved excitement and adventure a chance to express itself as well. He does not have any real sense of participating in the succession of generations, as he does not have any children of his own, nor is he in any contact with members of the younger generation, except, of course, Sharon Kaufman herself. On the other hand, his religion provides him with the conviction that he is connected to people of faith throughout the ages and that he will have a life after this life is over, one infinitely better than the life he has had.

As for the maturity of life that reflects the strengths acquired and developed in earlier stages of life, Ben tends to discount his possession of personal and ethical strengths, viewing himself as inferior to the great Christian saints and the top echelon of writers of fiction. But Kaufman notes his moral commitment to his wife's care, his cheerful disposition, his newly discovered understanding of how he can fulfill his desire to be generous to others, and he speaks of his gratitude for life itself. All these are evidence of a man who developed a personal and ethical maturity over the years.

On the other hand, he doesn't experience much personal satisfaction concerning these strengths because, to him, they carried a heavy price tag, the fact that they were the consequence of a timid life, one in which he was inhibited from allowing his more creative, adventurous self to develop. In the chart in *Vital Involvement in Old Age* (Erikson, Erikson, & Kivnik 1986) mentioned in chapter 3, *inhibition* is the malignant tendency of the initiative vs. guilt conflict (45). In fact, this was the decade (his twenties) in which Ben experienced the emergence of his carefree, adventurous self, but he then left this self behind as he moved into a safe but boring job in which he remained the rest of his working life.

We might conclude that he is despairing over the fact that it is now too late to begin another life, but he seems more disappointed than despairing. He knows that if he had tried to give greater prominence to his adventurous self, he may not have been successful and may have jeopardized all that he had achieved through "slow, patient endurance" (Kaufman 1986, 58). In chapter 3, I referred to William James's (1992) observation that a person may make a fateful decision between two careers and from then on be committed to the chosen career while the other career "which once lay so near, ceases to be reckoned among his possibilities. At first, he may sometimes doubt whether the self he murdered in that decisive hour might not have been the better of the two; but with the years such questions themselves expire, and the old alternative *ego*, once so vivid, fades into something less substantial than a dream" (626). James may exaggerate the degree to which the old, alternative ego fades away, for it is clearly on Ben's mind as he talks with Sharon Kaufman about his choices in life. Yet, as she points out, he seems reluctant, even now, to try out the alternative path that he has the time and resources to pursue and refers to them as "fantasies" (53). He recognizes this inhibition in himself and entertains another fantasy that someone may come along—like the stockbroker years ago—and appeal to his adventurous self. Failing that, he does not anticipate that anything will change in the priorities that he has given to the two selves that continue to occupy his mind and spirit.

As for the despair that manifests itself in disgust, either for other persons and institutions or for oneself, Kaufman astutely observes that Ben's habit of disengagement is a valuable, if unexpected, resource as he anticipates the next twenty years of his life. Not having expected much from anyone or any social institution (other than the church), he is remarkably devoid of disgust. Any self-contempt due to a lack of comradeship with those whose lives and achievements mirror human dignity and love is neutralized by the fact that although he cannot claim to be a Mother Theresa, he seems to have some identification with her by virtue of the fact that they belong to the same religious faith. Although he feels that he is unable or unwilling to give generously of *himself,* he is becoming less reluctant to part with his resources now that he knows that they are no longer needed for his wife's care. In addition, even though he did not become a priest, his lifestyle might be compared to that of a solitary monk, as he confines himself to his room and does not allow himself the full run of the house. This may simply be a matter of habit, but it *might* be viewed as a reflection of his sense of integrity, the integrity that his religion, together with his disengagement, have enabled him to develop following his release from responsibilities that weighed him down prior to his wife's death.

Ben's disengagement, together with his religion, may also be serving the development of the virtue of wisdom, a "detached concern with life itself, in the face of death itself" (Erikson 1964a, 133). He possesses the necessary resources, through his religious faith and his reading, to be a person of wisdom, and his thoughtful, if sometimes disparaging comments about himself in his conversation with Sharon Kaufman suggest that he is capable of thinking wisely about life and death. What seems lacking, however, is the generativity that is a vital part of wisdom. As Erikson points out, wisdom "responds to the need of the on-coming generation for an integrated heritage" and "some old people can envisage human problems in their entirety (which is what 'integrity' means) and can represent to the coming generation a living example of the 'closure' of a style of life" (1986, 133–34). Lacking children of his own and any apparent contact with persons of the younger generation, Ben seems to lack opportunities to be a generative person. He said to Kaufman, "My whole quest is to learn more about what does the Supreme Being ask of me for the balance of my life" (57). This, it would seem, is a generativity question. Perhaps the answer to this question will be forthcoming.

The fact that Sharon Kaufman chose Ben's story for her book from among the sixty indicates the effect that he might have on persons of younger generations. He is no Mother Theresa, yet he communicates through his words and physical appearance the image of an older man who assumed his moral responsibilities in life, an image that his tendency to be self-deprecating actually enhances, for a self-congratulatory self-presentation would probably have put Kaufman off. No doubt, his honesty about himself and the fact that "his eyes are full of life and he always smiles" (58) gave Kaufman the sense of a man who is perhaps wiser than he knows.

At seventy-four, Ben has a few more years before he moves to the next decade of his life. We may expect that he will continue to experience the conflict between integrity and despair. Hopefully, he will come to greater peace concerning his conflicting selves and move from a resigned to a more favorable "acceptance of his one and only life cycle as something that had to be and that, by necessity, permitted of no substitutions" (Erikson 1950, 232). And although he recognizes that he is no Christian saint and will not be spoken of in the same breath with Mother Theresa, perhaps he will begin to perceive that he, too, has exhibited "the gift of responsible renunciation" (1964, 134).

THE WISE SELF

When Erikson's wife Joan was eighty-five-years old, her book *Wisdom and the Senses* (1988) was published. It began with a reference to William James's essay "On Vital Reserves" (1922) which claims, according to Joan Erikson, that "we are all using only a very small portion of the energy and attention of which we are capable" (17; see also James 1907). She believes that this problem and its challenges still exist, perhaps more urgently than before, and she wants to consider what the reasons may be for our lethargy and dullness compared to what our potentials promise. She argues that the basic problem lies with the fact that, over time, we lose the keenness of our senses—sight, hearing, taste, smell, and touch—due to the uses, strains, and misuse to which they are subject in the course of our lives, and that the way for older persons to stay mentally and emotionally alive is through the stimulation of their senses (44).

In the concluding chapter, Joan Erikson notes that although the earlier chapters have made the case that "the senses offer an experiential source of wisdom," the question that remains is "where among the principles of social order does wisdom find its place and play its role?" (156). More specifically, "How does the wisdom of the serenely quiet, enlightened old ones seep into the social fabric?" (157). She suggests that the life cycle itself acts as a "quiet transmitter of values that are never put into word or form, but suddenly emerge in serene old men and women," but she contends that the arts, which require the use of our sense perceptions, provide more visible and tangible evidence of the wisdom of the old. This is because "the arts are honored and acclaimed as a universal, perhaps the only universal language, each true form representing the highest and deepest expression of one of the senses in cooperation with the others" (157).

In *Old Masters: Great Artists in Old Age* (2000), Thomas Dormandy argues that some of the greatest artists in history painted their best works when they were in their seventies or older. Seeking to understand why this was so, Dormandy considers a variety of explanations but finally focuses on the fact that art historians have often noted that artists' late work seems "prophetic" of the art of a later period. He suggests, however, that it is not so much that old painters were developing new styles, techniques, or themes, but that they exercised the freedom to "jettison rules and paint the style that best suited their purpose" (294). If younger painters responded to their predecessors' "sense of liberation" by adopting their manner and mannerisms, the results were often poor, but when they learned that the "sense of liberation" was itself the point, and began to discover their own personal style and "their own path to freedom," their work would come alive.[3]

We do not ordinarily associate older adults—persons in their seventies or older—with the "sense of liberation," but if we did, I am certain that we would begin to recognize that the wisdom that we ceremoniously (and perhaps even patronizingly) attribute to the old has very much to do with their sense of liberation and freedom from the "rules" that they were expected or required to follow in earlier decades. In this sense, wisdom is not necessarily reflected in the fact that one has more years of experience than those who are younger but that one's perspectives on the world and on human relationships reflect an inner sense of liberation from the rules, roles, and rituals of the past. Perhaps it is this very sense of liberation that enables one to begin using one's "vital reserves" as one has never used them before.

3. A painter who captured the imagination of millions of Americans in the 1940s and 1950s was Anna Mary Robertson Moses, otherwise known as Grandma Moses, who was born in 1860 and died in 1961. Her career as an artist began in the late 1930s, when arthritis made it difficult for her to do needlework, and her daughter suggested that she might take up painting instead. In her study of Grandma Moses' life and art, Karal Ann Marling asks: "Was she a Sunday painter? A primitive? A folk artist? A force of nature? An American phenomenon? Was she cherished for her wit, her beautiful old face? Does it matter? 'I look back on my life like a good day's work,' she wrote toward the end of that life and those long years of painting the pages of her story. 'It was done and I feel satisfied with it. I was happy and contented. I knew nothing better and made the best out of what life offered. And life is what we make it, always has been, always will be'" (258–59). These, I believe, are the words of a very wise person.

Chapter 9

The Ninth Decade:
The Graceful Self

If contemporary birthday cards emphasize the memories and achievements of the person turning seventy, they see no reason to change course with the person turning eighty, but in addition to mentioning the wonderful memories and great achievements of the new eighty-year-old, there's a tendency to mention what a great person the recipient of the card has become. Here's a typical card for the new eighty-year-old: "For you this is probably just another birthday, but it's so much more than that. It's the day you were born, and all the years that have come and gone and made you the incredible person you are—someone whose life is a real inspiration to the many lives you've touched along the way."

Some new eighty-year-olds might find this card a bit patronizing, as it brings attention to the fact that its recipient has chalked up an awful lot of birthdays, so many in fact that even entering a new decade may not seem like a big deal. In addition, it reminds the receiver that this is the day he or she was born, as if one needed to be reminded of one of the few facts that is indelibly fixed in one's admittedly unreliable mind. Furthermore, it suggests that it is one's birth date plus the years that have "come and gone" that have made one "the incredible person" one is, implying that all one needs to do to become an "incredible person" is to get yourself born and then amass an incredible number of years. To be sure, the card may redeem itself when it says the recipient has led a life that is an inspiration to "the many other lives you've touched along the way," but by this time, the damage, it seems to me, has already been done.

Then there's this card: "It's your 80th Birthday! A day to celebrate and enjoy yourself. . . . So go ahead—party like two 40-year-olds!" This seems a lot better than the previous one until the receiver recalls the cards for persons turning forty. As noted in chapter 5, the turning-forty cards emphasize that the recipient is getting older and to underscore this fact, they attribute to the forty-year-old some of the signs of aging that may begin to occur when a person is an older adult. They also suggest that something pretty awful has just happened: "Inside every 40-year-old person is a 39-year-old person wondering what in the world just happened!" If one knows what has been said about the new forty-year-old, it isn't especially pleasant to think of oneself as not just one but *two* of them. It would have been a lot better if the card had said, "So go ahead—party like four 21-year-olds!" In that case, the idea of partying would at least have had some credibility.

On the other hand, there is a sense in which this association of the eighty-year-old and the forty-year-old makes sense. In chapter 5 I mentioned Daniel J. Levinson's (1978) view that becoming forty marks a major turning point in life, one that sometimes assumes crisis proportions due, in part, to knowing that one is as old as one is young. I also noted that this may be the point in life that one experiences a "conversion" (even if it is not named or claimed as such) that reflects one's desire to take major steps toward the integration of the four polarities of young/old, destruction/creation, attachment/separateness, and masculine/feminine (191–244).

Becoming eighty may represent another major turning point in life, one that may also warrant the term *conversion*. Consider the two biblical texts that refer to the overall span of human life. Gen. 6:3 states, "Then the LORD said, 'My spirit shall not abide in mortals forever, for they are flesh; their days shall be one hundred twenty years,'" and Ps. 90:10a says, "The days of our life are seventy years, or perhaps eighty, if we are strong." If the former envisions a 120-year life span, it may be divided into three equal parts of forty years; and if the latter envisions an 80-year life span, it is divisible into two equal parts of forty years.

The oldest documented person to date is a woman, Jeanne Calment, who lived to age 117 (Cole 2005). Thus, the 120-year life span in Genesis has held true. It seems plausible, therefore, to suggest that there are two critical junctures in the life span, the first at age forty and the second at age eighty. Levinson calls the first the "mid-life transition." I would call the second the "end-life transition." If the identity vs. identity confusion conflict is associated with the former, what is the conflict associated with the latter? I suggest that it is the conflict of release vs. control.

THE RELEASE VS. CONTROL CONFLICT

According to *Webster's, release* has many meanings, the most relevant being (1) "to set free, as from confinement, duty, work, etc."; (2) "to let go or let loose (to *release* an arrow)"; (3) "to grant freedom from a tax, penalty, obligation"; (4) "to give up or surrender to someone else a claim, right, etc."; (5) "relief from pain, cares, etc."; (6) "relief from emotional tension through a spontaneous, uninhibited expression of an emotion"; and (7) "the act of letting loose something caught, held in position, etc." (Agnes 2001, 1210). There is also the idea of *released time,* which means being freed from one's regular duties in order to pursue other tasks or activities (1210). It may also refer to a capsule whose medicinal effect is sustained over a relatively long period of time.

There is an interesting dynamic in the meanings that concern granting freedom from a tax, penalty, or obligation, and giving up or surrendering a claim. If these happen to concern two individuals, the act of the first person releases the second person from having to make good on an obligation, but it also releases the first person from having to persuade or coerce the other to do so. I think that Jesus has something like this second form of release in mind when he advises his listeners, "If anyone takes away your goods, do not ask for them again" (Luke 6:30b).

Billy Collins (2002) tells in the following poem about how he trapped a threatened sparrow and then released it to safety (115–16):

Christmas Sparrow

The first thing I heard this morning
was a rapid, flapping sound, soft, insistent—

wings against glass as it turned out
downstairs when I saw the small bird
rioting in the frame of a high window,
trying to hurl itself through
the enigma of glass into the spacious light.

Then a noise in the throat of the cat
who was hunkered on the rug
told me how the bird had gotten inside,
carried in the cold night
through the flap of a basement door,
and later released from the soft grip of teeth.

On a chair, I trapped its pulsations
in a shirt and got it to the door,
so weightless it seemed
to have vanished into the nest of cloth.

But outside, when I uncupped my hands,
it burst into its element,

dipping over the dormant garden
in a spasm of wing beats
then disappeared over a row of tall hemlocks.

For the rest of the day,
I could feel its wild thrumming
against my palms as I wondered about
the hours it must have spent
pent in the shadows of that room,
hidden in the spiky branches
of our decorated tree, breathing there
among the metallic angels, ceramic apples, stars of yarn,
its eyes open, like mine as I lie in bed tonight
picturing this rare, lucky sparrow
tucked into a holly bush now,
a light snow tumbling through the windless dark.

Collins uses the word "released" in reference to the cat having let the bird escape from its teeth, but the true release occurred when he carried the sparrow outside and let it go. And now, as he reflects on the sparrow's good luck, he seems to feel a similar release from knowing that the bird is outside the house and safe from harm.

William Stafford (1998b) conveys another kind of release in the following poem (236):

Old Blue

Some day I'll crank up that Corvette, let it
mumble those marvelous oil-swimming gears
and speak its authority. I'll rock its big wheels
till they roll free onto the drive. Nobody can
stop us then: loaded with everything, we'll pick up
momentum for the hill north of town. Mona,
you didn't value me and it's too late now.
Steve, remember your refusal to go along on
those deals when you all opposed me?—you had
your chance. Goodbye, you squealers and grubbies;
goodbye, old house that begins to leak, neighbors
gone stodgy, days that lean casually grunting
and snoring together. For anyone who ever needs
the person they slighted, this is my address: "Gone."

This poem has a certain edge to it: the speaker relishes the thought that his release will catch those who have mistreated him by surprise. He also likes the thought that if they should ever need him, if only to oppose or belittle him, they won't know where to find him.

Many more poems than these could be presented to convey the full range of meanings of the word *release*, but these should suffice to show that *release* is a word with many nuances, all suggesting in one way or another that it stands in opposition to *control*. According to *Webster's*, *control* means (1) "to exercise authority over; direct; command"; (2) "to operate or regulate (this knob *controls* the volume of sound)"; and (3) "to hold back; curb; restrain (*control* your grief)" (Agnes 2001, 317).

These definitions suggest that control can be imposed by others and that they can claim the right to do so, but it can also be self-imposed, as when we make an effort to restrain our emotions. The same is true of release. Others may decide not to impose taxes, penalties, obligations, and so forth that they have a right to impose. On the other hand, we can release ourselves from a self-imposed restriction, as when we express an emotion in a spontaneous, uninhibited manner. Thus, release and control may apply to our relations with others, but they may also apply to our relations with ourselves.

A definition of *release* that may have particular relevance for persons in the ninth decade of life (the eighties) is "relief from pain and cares," and it has its corollary in the definition of *control* as regulative, especially in the sense of medicinal substances and medical treatments that regulate physical pain. Thus, release and control may also apply to one's relationship to one's body.

These definitions suggest that one needs a ratio of release and control that favors release, the positive tendency of this dynamic conflict, but this does not mean that all control is to be avoided, challenged, or condemned.

THE VIRTUE OF GRACEFULNESS

I suggest that gracefulness is the human strength that assumes an important role in the ninth decade (the eighties) of life. Following the three preceding virtues of care, love, and wisdom, this virtue may not seem very impressive, especially if viewed in the light of Erikson's emphasis in his addresses at Harvard Medical School on ethical ideals. Gracefulness would probably not be rated very highly by ethicists as an ethical ideal, and it may not even be placed high in their lists of exemplary moral behavior. Even so, I believe it has its own intrinsic worthiness and is also a worthy successor to wisdom.

Webster's defines *graceful* as "having grace or beauty of form, composition, movement, or expression; elegant" (Agnes 2001, 615). This definition immediately clues us in to why *gracefulness* would not be ranked very high as a virtue. Virtues are usually considered to be expressions of ethical ideals, but this definition suggests that it is an aesthetic ideal. The word *graceful* makes us think of ballet dancers or of gazelles, those "small, swift, graceful antelopes with spirally twisted, backward pointing horns and large, lustrous eyes" (Agnes 2001, 589). Who can resist the beauty of a gracefully moving form with large lustrous eyes? This sight will certainly cause any human male, whatever his age, to overlook the horns. To me, the very fact that *graceful* is an aesthetic ideal makes *gracefulness* a worthy addition to the preceding eight virtues.

But there is also the fact that the word *gracefulness* contains the word *grace,* a word that is very dear to the hearts of most persons who profess the Christian faith. The word, in fact, is such a familiar one that it may seem unnecessary to cite its dictionary definitions. But these definitions remind us of its multiplicity of meanings. They include: (1) "beauty or charm of form, composition, movement, or expression"; (2) "a sense of what is right and proper; decency"; (3) "thoughtfulness toward others"; (4) "goodwill, favor"; (5) "mercy, clemency"; (6) "a period of time granted beyond the date set for the performance of an act or payment of an obligation; favor shown by granting such a delay"; (7) "a short prayer in which blessing is asked, or thanks are given, for a meal"; and (8) several theological meanings of the word *grace*, including (a) "the unmerited love and favor of God toward mankind"; (b) "divine influence acting in a person to make the person pure, morally strong, etc."; (c) "the condition of a person brought to God's favor through this influence"; and (d) "a special virtue, gift, or help given to a person by God" (Agnes 2001, 614–15).

These definitions of the word *grace* include the idea of beauty of form, composition, movement, or expression, but they add several that relate to interactions between persons, ranging from having a sense of what is right and proper to allowing another person more time to fulfill a commitment. In the academic world, we call these "extensions." Thus, even before God comes into the picture, there are several ways in which grace manifests itself in the manner in which we relate to one another. When we get to the theological definitions, we come upon the idea that this is how God relates to us.

For our purposes here, I would like to retain the aesthetic meaning of *gracefulness* because it has metaphorical importance even for those of us who could hardly claim to be physically graceful, and it suggests that there can be a certain beauty in the way we relate to one another with simple, everyday thoughtfulness. Because they may not involve acts of charity or efforts to confront the injustices in this world, these acts are unlikely to attract the attention of ethicists, but hardly anyone would argue against the view that they make our lives seem better and the world more hospitable.

How does the virtue of gracefulness relate to the release vs. control conflict? The most obvious connection is the definition of *release* as the granting of freedom from a tax, penalty, or obligation and the definition of *grace* as a period of time granted beyond the time set for the performance of an act or payment of an obligation. Granting a grace period for meeting an obligation does not go so far as to release a person from the obligation altogether, but these two definitions reflect the desire of the person who grants it to make a thoughtful gesture that is likely to produce or create in the other person a deep sense of relief. Neither act (release or grace) has the implication of condescension toward or condemnation of the other; instead, they suggest that the grantors are in a secure-enough position themselves that they can afford the luxury, as it were, of not holding the other strictly to a prior agreement.

A deeper if more subtle connection between the virtue of gracefulness and the release vs. control conflict is reflected in the metaphorical meaning of *gracefulness*. If we think of the ballet dancer or the gazelle as exhibiting gracefulness, we sense that their beauty of form, composition, movement, and expression involve an ideal relationship *between* release and control. Neither relies exclusively on release, for beauty of form is not merely a matter of "letting loose" with all sorts of physical movements, gyrations, and the like. An indiscriminant flapping of arms and wiggling or shaking of legs will hardly be mistaken for gracefulness. The exercise of control is essential for the physical release—the graceful movement of the gazelle across the fields and hills and valleys.

Something like this physical relationship between release and control can serve as a spiritual ideal as well, and this ideal is especially relevant in the ninth decade of life, when one is likely to be experiencing difficulties in maintaining the physical ideal. Many an eighty-year-old has said of a particular physical movement of theirs, "It wasn't very graceful, was it?" But the awareness that one may be struggling to maintain a certain physical gracefulness may direct one's attention to the possibilities—for oneself and for others—inherent in the capacity for a spiritual gracefulness built on the sense of integrity and virtue of wisdom developed in the previous decade. To see the virtue of gracefulness in this way is to appreciate the fact that the sense of integrity and virtue of wisdom are not ends in themselves but instead, like all the other virtues, provide a springboard for further development and growth.

Psalm 90:10a says, "The days of our life are seventy years, or perhaps eighty, if we are strong." The extra decade may be viewed as involving a combination of the human strength of gracefulness and the grace of God, who grants some a *grace period,* one that one knows is unmerited, but for that very reason one may seek to do one's best to justify the favor.

THE AGELESS SELF

As noted in the preceding chapter, Sharon R. Kaufman (1986) carried out a major research study of the lives of older adults by interviewing sixty persons between seventy and ninety-seven years of age. She presents six cases in her book, three who were in their seventies when they were interviewed, and three in their eighties. All three eighty-year-olds were women. In addition to the six cases, there are brief excerpts from other interviews. Kaufman presents these excerpts in support of her contention that older persons do not speak of being old "as meaningful in itself" but instead "express a sense of self that is ageless—an identity that maintains a continuity despite the physical and social changes that come with old age" (7). Three of the eighty-year-olds in this group make comments that are suggestive of the release vs. control conflict.

Here's how Sara (age eighty-one) responded to the question "What's the hardest thing about growing older?" (10):

> "To tell you the truth, I never noticed it until I had to use the cane. I never really noticed it. I didn't realize I was getting older. But now, I can't hide the symptoms with this blasted stick. You know what hurts most—my vanity.
> . . . I happen to be a little bit vain. On my 80th birthday everybody made

a fuss, and I couldn't imagine why. You see, most of my close friends, my contemporaries, are gone, and I have sort of drifted in with younger people. I like it better. I still feel young in spirit." (10)

Sara feels that her movements are controlled by the "blasted stick" she needs to get around, but she experiences little of this control in her relations with others, where she feels free to be with younger persons. In fact, being with persons her own age gives her a sense of confinement: "I can't stand being with old people, some of them are dead and don't know it. All they talk about is their illnesses, from head to foot. You never ask them how they are because they'll tell you. It's so boring" (10). This declaration is reminiscent of Jesus' response to the man he invited to follow him who said he needed first to go and bury his father: "'Let the dead bury their own dead'" (Luke 9:60a). Having lost her close friends who had been her contemporaries, Sara experiences release from *not* having to associate with persons her own age. She is fortunate that the younger people do not exclude her.

This is how Ethel (age eighty-four) responded to Kaufman's request "I want to know what it feels like to be over 70" (12). Ethel responded, "I'm not over 70. People tell me I look 60 or 65. And I feel like that too. I don't feel over 70" (12). At this point, she showed Kaufman a picture of herself at age twenty-nine. Kaufman asked, "Do you relate to that woman?" Ethel replied, "I feel the same now as I did then, oh yes. The only way I know I'm getting old is to look in the mirror. But I've only *felt* old a few times—when I'm really sick" (12). She added, "You know, people say that all old people do is talk about their memories and the past. Well, I don't do that. Don't say that about me. I think about the future and tomorrow. You can't do anything about the past" (12).

Ethel seems even less controlled by her aging body than does Sara because she does not have the "symptoms" of aging that the cane so visibly reveals. Although she thinks her face may reveal her age, people tell her that she looks twenty or more years younger than her chronological age. But the key element in her response to Kaufman's question that suggests a sense of release is expressed in her claim that she does not think about memories and the past. After all, one can't do anything about the past. Although this statement may be disputed—as we saw in the preceding chapter, one can *reinterpret* the past—she feels that she is not controlled by the past, and because she isn't, she is free to think about tomorrow and the future. This, of course, raises the question of whether the ultimate future is one that she experiences as releasing or controlling, or both, but this is a different issue. She *feels* young, so why should she think about the past as though it were something that is irretrievably lost?

Finally, Gertie (age eighty-nine) was asked by Kaufman about her current health. She responded, "My health is pretty good right now, thank God. I have arthritis in my shoulders. That hurts—it hurts like hell. I get pills for that. For my leg I get a water pill. But that's all I get. So that's not bad for an 89-year-old woman" (12). Kaufman next asked her how it feels to be eighty-nine? Gertie replied, "Well, I'll be honest with you. I might be 89 years old. I feel good. I feel like I could fly the coop. I do. I feel younger, like I'm 45 or 50. I want to doll up, and I like to fuss. Oh, golly, I can break the mirror. I don't know I'm old. I feel like I'm going to live for a long time" (12).

The oldest of the three, Gertie is probably the most resigned to the fact that having some physical liabilities is inevitable. These have the potential to exert a great deal of control over her life. But her internal sense of herself is very different. In an image that speaks directly to the theme of release, she says, "I feel like I could fly the coop." This very feeling undoubtedly gives her an internal sense of freedom and unconfinement. There is also the fact that she still likes to get "dolled up" despite the fact that her face could "break the mirror." She also feels that she is "going to live for a long time" and does not appear to view that prospect with fear and trepidation.

Most of the comments made by these three woman concern their internal sense of being younger than their chonological age would suggest, and this sense of being younger is more important to them than the fact that they may appear younger than they really are. Whatever controls they experience from their environment or diminished physical mobility seem to be countered, and successfully so, by their internal sense of freedom. Due to the nature of the questions Kaufman has asked them, they discuss the release vs. control dynamic largely in terms of their relations with themselves, although Sara does have a few things to say about the control that persons her own age would exert over her if she let them. For further discussion of both dimensions of the conflict, let's consider a couple of Kaufman's more extensive cases.

ALICE: "I HAVE NEVER BEEN SO FREE OF RESPONSIBILITY"

Spiritual Understanding, Discipline, and Service

Kaufman (1986) presents Alice, who was eighty-one-years old when she was interviewed, as a woman whose major life theme is one of searching for spiritual understanding. Alice attributes this search to her mother's example. Her parents were divorced when she was three, and she remembers being worried and upset by her mother's precarious financial situation, caused by insufficient alimony payments from her father. Alice's early childhood years were "a bitter time" and a "tremendous shock" for her mother. A few years after the divorce, her mother married a prominent physician whom they both adored, but due to his professional commitments, he wasn't home very much, and her mother became depressed and lonely (142–43).

Throughout Alice's childhood and youth, her mother "went through life seeking, seeking, seeking" (143). Alice recalls the long hall at home that was lined with books, and how she would come home from school and find her mother on the floor, "books all around her, going through the Bible, looking, looking, looking, and crying her heart out" (143). She would ask her mother what was the matter, and her mother would answer, "I'm hunting for an answer." Her mother made herself physically sick with her longing, but at the end of her life, "she had a very illuminating experience, and the answer came, and it was quite beautiful" (143).

Although Alice resented her mother's preoccupation with religion and philosophy when she was growing up, largely because she felt neglected, later she came to understand her mother's need for spiritual support. In her young adulthood, she, too, experienced "an inner craving for understanding," and experimented with the practices and rituals of a variety of religions over a fifteen-year period until, one evening, she heard an Eastern religious leader give a lecture. She was deeply impressed with his presence and what he had to say. A few weeks later she joined his group, and ever since she has devoted herself to its service and to the acquisition of spiritual knowledge through its teachings (142).

Kaufman identifies discipline as another important theme in Alice's life, especially in her approach to her work. Her mother raised her with a "rigid discipline" (143) that was reinforced by her first job, in which she worked six days a week. Later, the lifestyle required by the religious group to which she belonged was "quiet and disciplined," and through it the discipline that others had imposed on her became an internally felt need, one that was reflected in her search for "a higher level of truth" (144). She now feels that her "disciplined approach" has led her to the answers to the meaning of life that she has received.

Professionally, having realized during college that she would not succeed as an artist, Alice became a fashion designer after graduation. She worked as a fashion designer for several different businesses, struggling to make a living, then started her own business. It was shortly thereafter that she brought religion into her life, and it greatly allayed her fears about not succeeding, enabling her to confront her business problems as they arose and to control her anxiety (145). She never married, so she was totally dependent on herself for support.

At the age of seventy-six, she moved into her own apartment in a beautiful retirement-residence complex. She said to Kaufman, "I love it here. I have never been so free of responsibility" (146). She views her very presence in this environment as the crowning achievement of her life: "Getting in here, where all your care is guaranteed—I'm very grateful and fortunate. It's a luxury. Everything is taken care of" (146). As she looks back on her life's journey, she feels "that all the steps in my life have contributed toward the fact that I have this well-being and security now" (146). As Kaufman notes, until Alice moved into the retirement-residence complex, she had to take care of herself: "Now, for the first time in her life, the responsibility for her survival, and indeed for the quality of her life, is in the hands of others. She views this as a great relief, as security, and as the ultimate sign of having overcome the difficulties of her past" (146).

Kaufman identifies service as a third major theme in Alice's life. For the first several years after she joined the religious group, she wondered if she had made the right choice. She was undecided about her degree of involvement in the group and what form it should take. But then it occurred to her that she could be of service: "I could contribute. I'm not a meditative type, and I'm not the student type. Service was my thing" (147). Her service took the form of the daily administration of the group's temple, which was a center for seminars, lectures, prayer groups, and other activities.

At present, the search for spiritual understanding is no longer a major theme in her life, but service is. Also, because her lifestyle has changed since she entered a new environment and no longer works at the temple, service has taken on a different meaning. In the retirement residence, she categorizes other residents by their service orientation: "She divides the individuals with whom she resides into two groups, those whose lives are empty and meaningless, and those who serve others and have contributed something to this world" (147). She places most of the residents in the first category and says that they "run around, trying to keep busy, filling their time with activities. What are they all rushing for? It's because they have nothing else" (147).

She places herself and a few friends in the second category. One friend had worked hard at her profession as a college teacher in addition to having had full financial responsibility for a number of sick relatives. The other had had a strong religious orientation throughout life and "is disciplined in her point of view," being "consistent in her daily effort to reach spiritual things" and working tirelessly in "trying to gain an inner insight that she longs for" (147–48). Thus, as Kaufman notes, her friends now "are those who have held her determined, no-nonsense attitude toward life and who currently share her disdain for the 'mad house social life' that she feels most other people in this setting maintain" (148). Although it might be questioned whether she and her close friends can, in fact, be of "service" in a setting where "all your care is guaranteed," what most matters to Alice is that the other people are running around, trying to keep busy, and this in itself is evidence to her of the emptiness and meaninglessness of their lives.

Release vs. Control

The most overt sign of Alice's sense of release is the fact that she now lives in an environment where she is not responsible for taking care of herself. She does not seem to feel that she has paid a price for this relief from her earlier tensions of having to make a living for herself. She says nothing about having lost some of her control over her life in exchange for this relief.

Another way in which she experiences release derives from her spiritual life, especially the fact that the search for spiritual understanding is no longer a major concern of her life. Although others might feel that this is negative development, her way of viewing it seems to be that she found what she was looking for when she was desperately in need of answers, but she is at a different place in her life now, due largely to the fact that she no longer has to worry about her basic survival. Her sense of release in this regard is expressed in her appreciation for the fact that she has "this well-being and security now" and feels enormously "grateful and fortunate" (146). She also continues to experience an inner sense of control that takes the form of a disciplined life. She feels that those residents who maintain a "mad-house social life" are, in a sense, out of control, running around trying to keep themselves busy. In her view, her ability to maintain a life of disciplined self-control plays a crucial role in her sense of being free from all that.

The reader may feel that she is basing her judgment of these other residents on rather external criteria, and that one who has a spiritual orientation should not jump to conclusions about these other residents' inner life or their past history (like her friend, many of them may also have been financially responsible for sick relatives), but this does not detract from the fact that release means a great deal to her, and that from the time she arrived at the retirement residence, she has experienced a freedom she had never known before from confinement, duty, work, and cares. Moreover, this relief from daily cares resulted from the fact that she placed her life in the care of others. Sometimes, then, the sense of release derives from accepting one's dependence on others, and this may be the most important lesson we may learn from the case of Alice.

MILLIE: "THEY SAY I LOOK 100 PERCENT BETTER THAN I DID"

Alice's story sheds light on how a person in her eighties may experience the release vs. control conflict in relation to oneself and the residents of a retirement community. But because she was unmarried and did not have siblings, there is nothing in her story about how this conflict may play itself out in relations with family members. Millie's story provides insight into the familial dimension of the release vs. control conflict.

Affective Ties, Acquiescence, and Self-Determination

Millie was eighty years old when Kaufman interviewed her. She had been living in a nursing home for about a year. In Kaufman's view, this was "long enough to recover from the trauma of being institutionalized, to feel comfortable with the routine and personnel of the place, to make some decisions about how she would deal with her new life, and to act on these decisions" (32).

When Kaufman first entered the nursing home where Millie lived and stood in the doorway surveying the large lounge area, Millie called out, "Hello. Who are you? What are you doing here?" (33). She proceeded to chat easily about various things, and Kaufman soon realized that Millie was

> one of the most friendly, outgoing, and lively persons in this large facility. Her eyes shine with enthusiasm for life, and she is quick to laugh. These features make her an attractive-looking woman. Though she looks hardy and robust, she is rather unsteady physically, walks laboriously with a cane,

struggles to sit and stand, and needs help when dressing and bathing. She hardly ever discusses her infirmities, ignores the limitations they place upon her, and is as active as she can be. (33)

Kaufman identifies affective ties as the major theme in Millie's life story. Conversations about the quality and quantity of these affective ties were clearly the most meaningful for Millie during the eight-month period that they talked together. She used the words "attached" and "attachment" repeatedly, and it was obvious that a strong need for affection, of which she is fully aware, dominates her interactions and thinking process. She divides people into two groups, based on the type of emotional commitment others convey to her. There are "family," those whose love and caring she can count on, and there are "strangers," those whose affective attachment to her is unreliable or not very long-lasting.

The qualities in others that are vitally important to her are those that family members are supposed to have, such as loyalty, sincerity and attentiveness. She measures the worth of all relationships in terms of these qualities. She expects everyone who comes into contact with her, regardless of their role, to have these qualities, and is very disappointed when she finds out that this is not the case. She also expects everyone in her environment to have an emotional commitment to her and to think about her.

The persons with whom she interacts most frequently are the nurses, aides, volunteers, and other residents, and she talks about them in terms of whether and how much they care for her. She expects each interaction to be of a loving character: "When an aide hurriedly hands her the breakfast tray and says nothing, Millie feels betrayed. As far as she is concerned, the aide is not treating her as she should, that is, with love, respect, and devotion" (34). When she meets someone new, such as a volunteer or the man who delivers the mail, she speaks of liking this person, and this liking becomes, in a brief period of time, an "attachment." Her expectation of a reciprocal emotional commitment sets her up for frequent disappointment (34). Also, she sees others not in terms of their own character traits but in terms of their affective relationship with her. Thus, when mentioning that her daughter moved to another city, she says, "My daughter left me," and although she mentioned that her son's job change and other factors prompted him to return to the West Coast, she noted that "My son is moving out here to be near me" (35). With the other residents, "she wants to be the best at what she does—gathering affection" (36).

Kaufman suggests that Millie's emphasis on affective ties was related to her childhood experience of being one of ten or twelve children of German-Jewish immigrant parents; she is unsure of the exact number because some of her siblings died in infancy. Although she says that her mother "cherished me" and her adored father "clung to me" (34), her older sister was the favored one in the family—"so beautiful and talented" and "an artist and a singer"—while she was "the domesticated one" who helped her mother with all the housework. Thus, despite the fact that Millie speaks of how her parents had loved her, Kaufman senses a more realistic tone of emotional deprivation: her mother was too beleaguered with household responsibilities to pay much attention to her; her father was out playing cards every night; and her brothers, who were much older than she, were either out working or had moved away from home. She seems, in fact, to have looked outside the family for the affection she craved, and says, "I adored my [school] principal, I'll never forget him"; "I loved my piano teacher and felt so close to her"; and "I was attached to the other children in the neighborhood" and "took care of all of them" (34). One naturally wonders about the extent to which this attachment was reciprocated.

When she was sixteen, she had to quit school and go to work, and a few months later she met the first of her three husbands. They were married when she was seventeen. During the years of their marriage, she blossomed as a mother, homemaker, and business partner to her husband, who had a jewelry business. But fifteen years after they were married, he died, and thus ended a "storybook romance" (38). She married her second husband to relieve her financial struggles. But he was twenty years older than she, and he informed her teenage children that he could not endure their presence in the house because they "cramped his style" (40). After they moved out, Millie discovered that she was pregnant, and her husband "wanted me to do away with the baby" (40). She defied him, and after their daughter was born, he was abusive toward her, and she was unable to get the baby to love her. This marriage ended in divorce after about five years, an experience that filled her with shame (40).

Five years later she married again, and for the twenty-five years that she and her third husband were married, he was frequently hospitalized with various illnesses, and they moved often in search of a better climate for him. During this time, she managed apartment buildings and held numerous clerical and retail jobs. He died when she was seventy. Kaufman notes that her second and third husbands are the only persons she never describes in terms of affective ties (41).

Kaufman identifies acquiescence as a second theme in Millie's life. This theme has two components: other people make decisions for her at critical life junctures, and things happen to her that seem to be out of her hands. She explains the turn of events in her life "with a sense of fate, of external forces playing upon her" (44). Thus, she divorced her second husband because her doctor "ordered" her to, and she had no intention of getting married a third time, but "circumstances led to it" (44). Her brother and sister-in-law liked the man, told her that he would be a good father to her child and provide security, and so she *acquiesced*.

When a doctor told her to move with her husband to a drier climate, and this didn't help him, her daughter suggested they move to the West Coast. Millie commented, "We listened to her and sold everything" (43). Millie arrived and found an apartment, but her daughter "wouldn't let [us] live there," and shortly after they settled into an apartment that was approved by family members, her husband died. At this point, she said, "My son insisted I go to my brother and sister-in-law. They took care of me for awhile. When I came back, the kids made me get out of the house" (45). Then her children "decided" she should move again, first to a retirement residence, then to the institution where she now resides. Kaufman notes, "These moves were not always to her liking, and occasionally she offered some resistance. But she always went along with them" (45).

Kaufman identifies a third theme of self-determination that clearly conflicts with the second theme of acquiescence. When Millie moved to the nursing facility where she currently resides, she realized that she had to learn to cope with this new challenge. At first, she "just wandered around," but in time she came to the conclusion that she "had to really make [her] own way," and although she doesn't know "how [she] managed it, [she] did" (46). From this point on, her story shifts from the passive to the active voice and she "no longer portrays herself as compliant. Instead, she has started to speak of taking her life in her own hands and making decisions about how she will live" (46).

She was effective in getting the staff to reorganize the scheduling of routine procedures to meet her needs. She walks around for at least an hour before a welcome committee meeting saying to various individuals that she wants them to come to the meeting because some important matters will be discussed. She is involved in the history and writing classes offered at the nursing home. And she has taken up knitting. Her knitting fills her time and, more importantly, gives her social status. Kaufman notes, "People constantly praise her work, and she has many requests for custom-made objects. She basks in these compliments, which, I observed, have given her eyes new sparkle and her whole being new energy" (47). Through her knitting, she has found recognition in her community. As she put it, "I've got enough orders to last me the rest of my life. They're keeping me busy. Everyone wants hats" (47–48). We can easily imagine how the prospect of wearing a new hat made especially for oneself would also give the wearer's eyes new sparkle.

Thus, the third theme of self-determination has virtually obliterated the second theme of acquiescence, and, as Kaufman points out, it is "a more optimistic, life-affirming response to her environment than is acquiescence" (48). Millie herself says that she began a "new life" when she moved into the nursing home and sees herself "improving" and "learning" all the time. In addition, "she perceives her own aging as a process of renewal that began when she arrived at the institution" (152). When Kaufman asked her to look in the mirror and describe her image of herself, she responded, "I go by what people tell me. They say I look 100 percent better than I did. I have changed considerably from what I looked like when I first came here, and I see a more pleasant expression in my face, and I'm more inspired about my routine" (152).

Kaufman suspects that her family and physician would say that she was institutionalized because she had suffered a mild stroke and can no longer provide for all her physical needs. In her own view, however, she came to the nursing home because, she said, "I was so lonely" and "I was afraid of going out of my mind" (153). She rarely refers to herself as a "patient," and only does so when she uses her patient status to complain that she has not received the treatment that a woman "in [her] condition" should be expected to receive. Thus, it serves as a "survival tactic, and it is only called into play when needed to gain respect or take control of a situation" (153).

Kaufman concludes her account of Millie's change since coming to the nursing home with some comments on her current relationships with her children. She notes that Millie says that she "is happy living in the Home mainly because it pleases her children that she is there; she takes her cue for her emotional state from them" (154). Thus, when she tells them of her accomplishments in classes, they say, "Wonderful, Mother, I'm so glad to hear it." "I'm so happy that they are thrilled because I'm here," she tells Kaufman (154). She regularly discusses her activities with them by telephone and during their visits, and "their reinforcement of her behavior seems to be crucial to the maintenance of her self-esteem and emotional well-being" (154). When she became depressed or angered by some incident in the Home and broke down crying, she felt, "If I didn't have my children to pull me through, I don't know what I'd do. They're everything to me" (154).

On the other hand, she has said some things to Kaufman that suggest her relationship with her children is not all that she wishes it were. In her view, the two children who live in the same city do not visit often enough. The other two live in another part of the country, but they do not communicate often enough by letter or telephone. She "gets quite distraught if more than a week goes by without a visit and worries about her children's health, jobs, marriages, and children. Her peace of mind is forever being threatened by the perceived lack of attentiveness from them" (155).

Given her primary theme of affective ties, however, it is vitally important to her to believe that her family does in fact live up to her ideals of loyalty, sincerity, and attentiveness, so instead of modifying the theme to conform to their actual behavior, she honors the unspoken contract "by conceiving of her children in the ideal thematic framework she has constructed rather than focusing on their actual shortcomings" (155). We might view this as another survival strategy, one that serves the theme of self-determination over the former, outmoded theme of acquiescence.

Release vs. Control

In Millie's story, the two themes of self-determination and acquiescence are virtually the functional equivalents of the themes of release and control. In fact, we could view Millie's life in the nursing home as one in which, for the first time in her life, many of *Webster's* definitions of the word *release* have become relevant. She is a woman who has been set free from her earlier confinement, has gained relief from pain and cares, has gained relief from emotional tension, and has been let loose, no longer caught or held in position by others. Having experienced her earlier days as ones in which she was largely controlled by others, this change in her life may well be thought of as an "end-of-life transition." It might even warrant the term *conversion*, for she has certainly turned her life around.

Although the most impressive changes are the ways in which her life in the nursing home has blossomed, with compliments about her knitting giving her eyes a new sparkle and her whole being a new energy, the most significant change in the ratio of release vs. control concerns her interpretation of her relationship with her children. Before she entered the nursing home, she felt that she had no choice but to acquiesce to whatever they felt would be best for her or them. Now that she is in the nursing home, she is no longer subject to their control because she no longer lives with any of them. Although we might have thought that going to a nursing home would be the worst fate imaginable, this has not been the case with Millie because she no longer feels that her children hold her fate in their hands.

It is vitally important, however, to Millie's understanding of herself as her children's mother that she feels loved by them. A potential ground for despair is the fact that they do not visit, write, or phone her as often as she considers appropriate in terms of what, for her, constitute ideal affective ties between family members. How to deal with this discrepancy between her ideal and their behavior? She *could* spend much of her waking hours engaging in self-pity because they do not live up to this ideal, but then their behavior would control her mind and emotions. Instead, she conceives of her children "in the ideal thematic framework she has constructed rather than focusing on their actual shortcomings" (155). This way of framing the issue is a form of release, one that involves giving up or surrendering a claim on her children that relieves them of some of their obligations to her. In addition, it relieves her of the unhappiness that she would otherwise feel if she held them to a strict conformity to "the unspoken contract" to which all family members are subject. And this brings us to the virtue of gracefulness.

GRACEFULNESS WHERE AND WHEN LEAST EXPECTED

As we have seen, the word *graceful,* which has to do with "grace or beauty of form, composition, movement, or expression," may be understood in metaphorical terms to relate to everyday interactions between persons, for there can be a certain beauty in the way we relate to one another with simple, everyday thoughtfulness. Retirement communities and nursing homes are a bit like college dormitories: strangers are placed in very close proximity to one another and are expected to make an honest effort to get along. Like college students, the residents of these communities and homes have in common the fact that they belong to the same generation, but there may be little else that would constitute or create a natural bond between them.

In this chapter, we have considered two women who are in the early years of their ninth decade in life, and both are living in settings intended for persons their age. When she entered the retirement-residence complex, Alice felt that virtually all her cares had vanished. For the first time in her life, the responsibility for her survival and the quality of her life was in the hands of others, and she felt that they were carrying out this responsibility as well as anyone could. In contrast, Millie felt extremely lonely and despondent when she entered the nursing home, and, in a very real sense, she felt that her cares were just beginning.

It may be inappropriate to compare the two women in terms of the human strength of gracefulness, but it would seem that Millie, perhaps because she had so far to go, has done more to develop this virtue than Alice has. Alice has an excellent sense for what makes for gracefulness and knows that there is something rather ungraceful in the behavior of the many residents who turn the place into a madhouse, running around, trying to keep busy, filling their time with all sorts of activities. But it also seems that her understanding of grace is more or less limited to a sense of what is right and proper; it does not reflect its more thoughtful and forgiving aspects. It may be that her view of what constitutes "service" is somewhat narrow and does not allow for the possibility that the activities being planned by others may provide a "service," however trivial they may seem to her. After all, her service at the temple was also activities oriented, and someone else may well have judged her own work to have been motivated by a need to keep busy.

Millie, on the other hand, devotes much of her time to engaging in thoughtful acts and expressions of goodwill toward others. She is not motivated by pure or simple altruism. On the contrary, she hopes that the other person will reciprocate her actions in some way and thus help to meet her seemingly insatiable need to feel appreciated for what she does and to be loved for who she is. But her knitting of hats for others has introduced a new dynamic into her relationships with other residents, one that is focused less on her need to be loved for who she is and more on her need to be recognized for the quality of her work.

As the psychoanalyst Heinz Kohut (1985) has noted, one of the signs that a person who displays narcissistic tendencies is experiencing a "transformation" toward a more mature way of relating to others is that she begins to derive genuine pleasure from the fact that her creative work is receiving the approval that she had previously sought for herself (111–15). The narcissistic need is still there, but it has been redirected from the need to be admired—or, as Millie would say, "adored"—for her own sake to being admired for what she creates. Of course, this "transformation" does not need to be so far-reaching that the original desire to be admired for oneself is completely renounced or obliterated. As Kaufman notes, people continually praise Millie's work and pay her the high compliment of asking her to make something for them, and she "basks in these compliments, which, [Kaufman] observed, have given her eyes new sparkle and her whole being new energy. At last she has found a way to be successful and to be recognized in her community" (47). The desire for the admiration of others is still there, but she is prepared to share the limelight with her creative work, even as the recipients of her creative work may also have to share the limelight: "Nice hat you're wearing. It becomes you."

The very fact that knitting has gained for Millie the recognition that she has sought from other residents in the Home establishes an intimate connection between the aesthetic and interpersonal meanings of gracefulness, for the beauty or charm of the objects she knits creates interpersonal occasions of goodwill and favor. The knitted object becomes the basis of a graceful connection between Millie and other members of the community. Also, the seemingly insignificant fact that she made *hats* for others is itself an aspect of the gracefulness of this connection. A hat is less likely to seem an onerous task than an object that requires careful measurement or is more costly to make, and it therefore does not impose on the recipient a reciprocal demand for appreciation and gratitude that may seem equally burdensome. For these recipients, a hat may also have served as a stimulus to memories of persons loved and since lost. In his poem, "The Death of the Hat" (1998, 81–82), Billy Collins notes that his father wore a hat to work every day, and now, "after a life of work," he "wears a hat of earth / and on top of that / a lighter one of cloud and sky—a hat of wind."

RELINQUISHING CONTROL

In this chapter, I have emphasized the importance of maintaining a ratio of release and control that favors release but at the same time recognizes the need for control in the conduct of our lives. Release and control are not necessarily adversaries. Release often has meaning and significance only when it occurs in relationship with control, as when one is granted freedom from a tax, penalty, or obligation, or when something that has been caught or held in position is let loose. Without control, it wouldn't make much sense to talk about release. If a prison has no locks, and inmates are free to come and go as they please, to speak of being released from prison—say, for good behavior or as an act of mercy or clemency—would be rather meaningless.

But the fact that release gets its meaning from its relationship to control does not mean that control is necessarily or invariably a good thing in itself. In fact, we often insist on the necessity of control when there is no need for it, or we emphasize the need for control in our lives because the human or social environment in which we live seems utterly chaotic. Alice felt the need for a disciplined life in part because her early childhood experience was one in which everything seemed so out of control. This very discipline now inhibits her ability to tolerate the community in which she lives because she believes that the others are merely engaging in activities to keep busy. She calls her environment a "mad house of social life" (148).

We saw in the case of Millie that control often plays a prominent role in relations between parents and children. As Millie aged, her children took more and more control over her life, making the decisions for where she was to live. As we have seen, her move into a nursing home provided the stimulus she needed to regain control over her own life.

Another common theme in the lives of persons in their eighties (and often earlier) concerns their own control over their children. This control often takes the form of decisions about how their money and possessions will be distributed after their death. These decisions are typically revealed in advance to their various beneficiaries, often with the intention of exercising control over their behavior. A frequent plot device in British murder mysteries centers around an aging parent's will and the ever-present threat to revise the will based on the behavior of their children. The will exerts enormous power over the children, who, of course, are adults, and it typically causes them to act like preschool children fighting over who gets to play with the snazziest car or wear the dress with all the sequins. While the murder mystery may take this plot device to absurd lengths, typically portraying family members scurrying around the house in search of a will written just before the parent's death and secretly witnessed by a faithful butler or maid, many ordinary families become centers of contention and lasting ill will over this last and ultimate expression of control by an aging parent. Of course, determining how to distribute one's money and possessions in a way that is equitable, fair, and loving is often a difficult task, one somewhat akin to walking through a mine field. But to the extent possible, one would hope that this might be an occasion in which the ratio of release over control is overwhelmingly on the side of the former, and where the virtue of gracefulness is such a commanding presence that the vices of greed, jealousy, and anger go scurrying for cover.

THE GRACEFUL SELF

A poem by William Stafford (1998b) tells about a woman dying of cancer who refused the opportunity her illness afforded to exercise control over others and was therefore exemplary of the graceful self (120–21):

Bess

Ours are the streets where Bess first met her
cancer. She went to work every day past the
secure houses. At her job in the library
she arranged better and better flowers, and when
students asked for books her hand went out
to help. In the last year of her life
she had to keep her friends from knowing
how happy they were. She listened while they
complained about food or work or the weather.
And the great national events danced
their grotesque, fake importance. Always

Pain moved where she moved. She walked
ahead; it came. She hid; it found her.
No one ever served another so truly;
no enemy ever meant so strong a hate.
It was almost as if there was no room

left for her on earth. She straightened its flowers;
she did not weep when she passed its houses;
and when finally she pulled into a tiny corner
and slipped from pain, her hand opened
again, and the streets opened, and she wished all well.

In his reflections on this poem, Stafford (1998a) notes, "In a quiet town of ordinary people and events, and without any fanfare or warning, an absolute event occurs. It is a thing that can happen to anyone, quietly. Its name immediately establishes its power and menace" (98–99). The "anyone" in this case was a dear friend of his wife, a librarian at her school, who had just been diagnosed with cancer. From the beginning, the poem has a somber tone which must, however, "be muted in the lines that follow; for this whole poem will become a holding off of sorrow. Bess will walk our secure streets. In her work she will touch flowers, help children; her hand—that hand with its ultimate task in the last line of the poem—will have a life of its own, will go out to help" (99). At the same time, "Bess will come to see her friends' lives in a new way. Their troubles take on an aspect so trivial that Bess can't bear to let them know what she sees. And the 'world' events also turn into pitiful fictions; the concerns of other people, the important topics of the day—these are abruptly reduced so drastically that Bess can't bear to let others know what they are doing. Part of her work becomes enduring the loneliness of one who knows" (99–100).

As the poem moves to its conclusion, it recapitulates the elements that were established at the beginning: "Bess remembers joy, straightens its flowers, walks ahead past her friends' houses without burdening them with her tragedy. And her hand which had helped is able to open in offering once more. Steady in the face of death and pain, Bess hands a wish to those around her. And her poem, never making much of its music, finally allows itself to remark with a tolling, chiming sound in the last two words, *all well*" (100).

Stafford concludes that "Bess opened her hand for me. In unfolding her story, I let her quality reach out" (102). This was the quality of gracefulness, of grace abounding. Control is noticeably absent, and release is all there is.

Chapter 10

The Tenth Decade:
The Enduring Self

It's nice to know that birthday card companies make cards for persons who are turning ninety. This should give us all a feeling of hope because they wouldn't make them if they were not commercially viable. On the other hand, the cards written for those turning ninety could just as well have been written for those turning eighty, for the basic sentiment is much the same: you have many memories to cherish and you accomplished a lot in your life—your earlier years, that is. This one is typical: "Your ninetieth birthday's a wonderful time to look back on all the changes you've seen in the world and to feel proud as you think of all you've done in your life. May this special birthday be filled with warmth and happiness and even more wonderful moments to cherish." Here is the same litany of memories and a life of activities and accomplishments of the cards received ten years earlier. But this one adds a new wrinkle, the suggestion that this is "a wonderful time to look back on all the changes you've seen in the world."

Most persons turning ninety would not consider looking back on all the changes they've seen in the world as their idea of a "wonderful time." Maybe a few of the advances in medicine and dentistry from which they have profited would be worth thinking about, but such thoughts would almost certainly be shoved to one side by thoughts of what they paid for a night out at the movies when they dating seventy years ago, what they watched on TV back when they were raising kids, or simply how quiet and peaceful it all seemed back then: no honking horns or loud music in department stores, and no tailgating at excessive speeds. Such a retrospective look is likely to cause the receiver of the card to shake his or her venerable head and exclaim, for the umpteenth time, "What's this world coming to?"

I doubt, in any case, that we will get much help from the writers of milestone birthday cards toward identifying the central developmental conflict experienced by persons in their nineties. We *could* adopt Joan Erikson's suggestion in the extended version of *The Life Cycle Completed* (Erikson & Erikson 1997) that the best way to "see and understand the final life cycle stages through late-eighty and ninety-year old eyes" (105) is to take the view that the dynamic conflicts of the earlier stages are now experienced with the ratio of the positive and negative tendencies reversed. I prefer, however, to view the tenth decade of life as no different from the earlier ones, for I believe that it, too, introduces a new dynamic conflict. I propose that the central conflict in the tenth decade involves *desire vs. struggle*.

THE DESIRE VS. STRUGGLE CONFLICT

Webster's defines *desire* as (1) "to wish or long for; crave; covet"; (2) "to ask for; request"; and (3) "to want sexually" (Agnes 2001, 391). It compares the word *desire* with the words *wish, want,* and *crave,* noting that *desire* is generally interchangeable with these other words in the sense that all involve "a longing for," but *desire* conveys an "intensity or ardor" that is not expressed as strongly in the word *wish,* which itself has a certain connotation of "an unrealizable longing"— for example, "she *wished* the summer were already here." The word *want* conveys the sense of "a longing for something lacking or needed," and the word *crave* suggests an "urgent need."

Thus, the idea behind the word *desire* is that we believe the object of our desire is realizable and is no fleeting thing. Nor is it as potentially trivial as a wish might be, as when we say, "I wish it would snow tomorrow so that I won't have to go to school." When I was a college student, I was greatly impressed by the title of J. S. Bach's "Jesu, Joy of Man's Desiring," so much so that when my future wife and I were planning our wedding, I suggested that we ask the soloist to sing it, and she readily agreed. What especially impressed me was the fact that the title contained the word "desiring," which conveyed an *enduring* sentiment, and not a mere wish, or want, or craving.

The desire that exists inside the hearts, minds, and spirits of persons in their nineties is very similar: it is more enduring than a wish, less urgent than a craving, and less a response to something one lacks than to something one has and does not want to lose. This is the desire for life itself. Although individual ninety-year-olds may have very different views and understandings of what is "life" for them, their desire is for life, and not for anything as insignificant as a craving for a particular food or a wish that summer were already here.

This desire, however, comes up against the inevitable struggle that is often experienced long before one reaches ninety but is absolutely unavoidable in the tenth decade of life. *Webster's* offers three definitions of *struggle*: (1) "to contend or fight violently with an opponent"; (2) "to make great efforts or attempts; strive; labor"; and (3) "to make one's way with difficulty (to *struggle* through a thicket)" (Agnes 2001, 1421). The third definition seems tailor-made for persons in their nineties, for many *do* in fact make their way with difficulty, and may even find the illustration of struggling through a thicket an appropriate metaphor. This "thicket" may take the form of a whole congeries of doctor's offices and hospitals, the routines of the social environment of an assisted-living facility, and even, perhaps, the gathering thicket that one may feel inside one's head.

The second definition is also relevant. Persons in their nineties are required to make "great efforts or attempts," learning, for example, how to do the hard way what they previously did with relative ease. For example, there are the six standard activities of daily living that are used as a basis for determining whether a person qualifies for long-term health care benefits: bathing, dressing, eating, continence, transferring, and toileting. There are also the host of changes in one's physical condition that may not fall under any one of these criteria yet make one's daily life a challenge: ringing in one's ears; changes in visual acuity that make it difficult to read a book; inability to climb a flight of stairs because one's back, or knees, or hips, or heart will not cooperate.

Social interaction may also require "great efforts or attempts." One may find it a struggle to react quickly to sudden changes in one's social environment when, for example, the children and grandchildren come to visit or when one is moved from one nursing home to another, or from one room to another room with a different configuration and outside view.

Few ninety-year-olds would easily or readily identify with the following poem by Billy Collins (1999), which portrays that classic fellow whose life we have all, at some point in our lives, *wished* that we ourselves could live (67):

The Life of Riley: A Definitive Biography

He was born one sunny Florida morning
and napped through most of his childhood.
He spent his adult life relaxing in beach chairs,
always a tropical drink in his hand.

He never had a job, a family or a sore throat.
He never mowed a lawn.
Passersby would always stop to remind him
whose life it was he was living.
He died in a hammock weighing a cloud.

If some of us feel we just might live Riley's life when we retire from the world of work, few in their nineties would be able to report to visitors that they have been spending the day relaxing in a beach chair with a tropical drink in their hand, and few visitors would remind them—in case they forgot—that they were living the life of Riley.

The Struggle against an Opponent

The first definition of *struggle* is "to contend or fight violently with an opponent." How is this relevant to those who are in the tenth decade of their lives? The best answer I have heard or read about is the one that Sigmund Freud (1959) proposed in his small book *Beyond the Pleasure Principle,* originally published in 1920 when he was sixty-four years old. Here he presented the controversial idea that we have not one but two basic instincts or drives. One is the drive to maintain and sustain our life; the other is the drive to end or terminate our life. These two drives contend with one another. They are similar to St. Paul's declaration that the law of his members is at war with the law of his mind (Rom. 7:23) except that, in Freud's understanding, the two drives are at war *within* the law of our minds and this creates a war *within* our members as well.

The idea that we have an inherent instinct for keeping ourselves alive seems indisputable. But the idea that we have an instinct for terminating our life was one that even Freud's closest colleagues found difficult to accept. In fact, he had questions about the idea himself, so he presented it with a great deal of tentativeness, even saying at one point in the book that it would be perfectly alright with him if the reader felt he was merely playing devil's advocate (103). The idea had come to him, however, when he was thinking about the fact that some of our instincts obey the pressure for novelty and unprecedented experience while others obey the pressure to repeat what we have already experienced time and time again. Some of this repetition may be pleasurable, as when a child begs for the retelling of a story exactly as it was told before, but some of this repetition seems to have a different purpose, as it brings no sense of pleasure—or, as Sharon Kaufman (1986) says of Millie, no sparkle in the eyes, no energizing of one's whole being (47). It seems, rather, to favor inertia, a tendency to remain in the same fixed condition without change or movement.

Freud reasoned that this second form of repetition is a sort of living death and that it may be the outward expression of a deeper instinct for not living at all, of falling into a deep sleep from which one does not awaken. Thus, we seem to have a silent death drive that seeks to reduce living matter to an inorganic condition and wants to end the existence of the organism in its own way—not by something done *to* it, such as homicide, a fatal accident, a virus, food poisoning, and so forth, but by some internal process that overcomes the instinct for life and effects a permanent state of inertia, or death.

As indicated, when Freud wrote the book, he wasn't entirely convinced that it was a sound idea. But by 1924, four years after the book was published, he employed the two-basic-drives idea in an article (Freud 1963) and did so quite casually, as though there wasn't anything controversial about it at all. He never wavered from the idea after that (Gay 1988, 402). His certainty may have been due to his own physical struggles. He began experiencing a painful swelling on his palate in 1917 due to a longstanding addiction to cigar smoking, and by early 1923 a cancerous growth had developed on his palate and jaw (Gay 1988, 420–21). The book about the two drives was published in 1920, midway between the painful swelling and the cancerous growth six years later. The growth was surgically removed, but it returned at various times in subsequent years, and by 1939 several cancerous lesions in his jaw were causing what he called "paralyzing pain," and his ulcerated cancer wound gave off such a disagreeable smell that his dog would cringe from him and could not be lured into his presence (640–49).

In September of that year, he reminded his doctor of his earlier agreement that he would not leave his patient in the lurch when his time had come, then said to him, "Now it is nothing but torture and makes no sense" (651). His doctor said that he had not forgotten. Freud thanked him and asked him to talk it over with Freud's daughter, Anna, and if she thought it was right, then he was to "make an end of it." His daughter wanted to postpone it, but the doctor insisted that to keep her father going was pointless, and she submitted to the inevitable. That evening, he injected Freud with three centigrams of morphine—the normal dose was two centigrams—and he sank into a peaceful sleep. The next day the doctor repeated the injection, and Freud lapsed into a coma and died the following morning (651).

Why would Freud's struggle with cancer convince him that the idea we have a silent death drive within ourselves was really true? The answer is relatively simple: A cancer is a group of cells (usually derived from a single cell) that has lost its normal control mechanisms and therefore grows in an unregulated manner. These cells can develop from any tissue in the body and can spread from their initial site throughout the body. Cancerous cells develop from healthy cells in a complex process, called transformation, that may occur spontaneously or be brought on by a cancer-causing agent or carcinogen. Carcinogens include many chemicals, tobacco, viruses, radiation, and sunlight. But not all cells are equally susceptible to carcinogens. A genetic flaw in a cell may make it more susceptible (Beers 2003, 1031).

When Freud first experienced swelling in his palate in 1917, he tried to ignore it because he was certain that it was caused by his addiction to tobacco, and he didn't want to give up smoking. In fact, the first time he experienced the swelling, it had receded immediately after he lit up a cigar. But by 1923, when the growth had become too large and too persistent to be ignored, he decided he could face a cigarless future and consulted a doctor (Gay 1988, 419). Thus, his cancer was originally triggered by a carcinogen that was attacking the cells of his body, but it may not have taken a malignant course if he had not also had a warring in his mind, a conflict between his desire to smoke and his awareness that smoking could cause a malignant cancer. It would seem, therefore, that a repetitive act that was pleasurable was serving the interests of the silent death drive, as though they were actually working together.

In any event, the ultimate cause of death was a form of *growth* within the body that was no longer *regulated.* We normally think of growth as conducive to life, but cancer is a type of growth that destroys life. Thus, we can see how Freud's awareness that he was in danger of developing a malignant cancer together with his awareness that he was reluctant to change his lifestyle in the face of this danger would lead him to propose that we have within ourselves a silent death drive. Our minds are trying to reconcile two different laws, one devoted to life and the other equally devoted to death.[1]

Whether we have a drive toward death or not, the very fact that we use phrases like "rest in peace" and sing hymns at funerals which declare that the struggle is over and the strife is done, and that our loved one has entered a peaceful sleep, suggests that we do not view inertia as an unmitigated evil. There are times and situations where we think it is best to allow a loved one to enter a deep and lasting sleep and not be forced to awaken again. And even though we tend to think of death as an external force—an enemy we name Death who may even have his own residence (we say a person is "at death's door")—death is actually the conclusion of an internal process in which one's vital organs cease to function.

If these things are true, it then seems appropriate to view the struggle that occurs in one's nineties (if not earlier) as one in which the conflict between desire vs. struggle is more internal than external. Environmental factors certainly play a role in this struggle, but the nineties are a decade in which one's struggles have mainly to do with what is going on *inside* one's body and mind. And this brings us to the human strength of endurance.

THE VIRTUE OF ENDURANCE

Webster's defines *endurance* as (1) "the power of enduring—specifically, the ability to last, continue, or remain"; (2) "the ability to stand pain, distress, fatigue"; and (3) "duration." It defines *endure* as (1) "to hold up under (pain, fatigue, etc.); stand; bear; undergo"; and (2) "to put up with; tolerate." It defines *enduring* as (1) "to continue in existence; last; remain"; and (2) "to bear pain, and so forth, without flinching; hold out" (Agnes 2001, 470).

The very fact that a person has lived into the tenth decade of life suggests that he or she has a proven capacity to continue in existence, the ability to last and remain. Many factors are responsible for why some persons live into their nineties and others do not, and the majority of these factors are outside one's own con-

---

1. The relationship between cancer and the death drive is discussed at greater length in two books by David Bakan, *The Duality of Human Existence* (1966, 160–81) and *Disease, Pain, and Sacrifice* (1968, chap. 1).

trol or ability to influence. But those who *do* make it to ninety often marvel at the fact that they are still around while so many of their contemporaries are not. For some it's a blessing; for others, a curse; and for most it's a *mixed* blessing—good in some ways, not good in others—or they say that it *would* have been a blessing if only their beloved companion were here to share the nineties with them.

But simple duration is not what makes endurance a virtue. What makes it a virtue is how one expresses or exhibits the *power* of enduring, especially in the ability to stand pain, distress, and fatigue, and the *strength* to put up with or tolerate what is happening and what is being done to oneself. The apostle Paul has some very positive things to say about endurance in this regard. In his letter to "God's beloved in Rome" (Rom. 1:7) he said that "we also boast in our sufferings, knowing that suffering produces endurance, and endurance produces character, and character produces hope" (Rom. 5:3–4). In his letter to "the church of God that is in Corinth" (1 Cor. 1:2), he noted that love "bears all things, believes all things, hopes all things, endures all things" (1 Cor. 13:7).

In both cases, *endurance* has an association with hope, the virtue that Erikson assigns to the first stage of life. In fact, Erikson (1964a) makes a connection between endurance and hope when he points out that hope is verified by a critical acquisition in infancy, namely, "the secure apperception of an 'object'" (116). He notes that psychoanalysts think of this as the first "love-object," and the infant's experience of the caretaking person as a *coherent being,* while genetic psychologists "mean by this the ability to perceive the *enduring quality of the thing world*" (116–17). Hope, then, is based on the sense that the external world—or some object within it—has endurance, that it has the very power of enduring: the ability to last, continue, or remain; the ability to stand pain, distress, fatigue; and the ability to put up with and tolerate the stresses that come its way, some of which are caused by the very one whose hope depends on its endurance.

This way of thinking about the connection between the virtues of endurance and hope enables us to see that the ninety-year-old person's endurance is not based on personal fortitude alone but also depends on the strengths that come from some form or expression of mutuality between this person and an "object" in the external world. And this brings us back to desire, the positive tendency of this decade of life.

Desire differs from mood (like happy or sad), attitude (like friendliness or unfriendliness), or temperament (like optimism or pessimism) because a person may express or exhibit a mood, attitude, or temperament without expecting any reciprocal response from anyone or anything in the world. Not so desire, for desire is inherently relational. *Webster's* says that the word *desire* is derived from the Latin word *desiderate,* which means "to await from the stars" (Agnes 2001, 391). *What* is awaited is not specified, but *that* one expects an act or response from the stars is an essential feature of desire. If there is no response, one has desired in vain.

The dictionary definitions of *desire* bear this out. *Desire* means to long for, to ask for, and there is an "intensity or ardor" about it. *Desire* says, "I really long for *this*" or "I beg you to give *this* to me." It may even add, "I cannot live without *this*" or "without *this,* life has no meaning or purpose."

LIBIDO IN THE NINETIES

Why suggest that desire is especially relevant to persons who are in the tenth decade of their lives? Let's recall that *Webster's* offers three definitions for the word *desire:* (1) "to wish or long for; crave, covet"; (2) "to ask for; request"; and (3) "to want sexually" (Agnes 2001, 391). Up to this point, I have emphasized the first definition. Although the second definition is rather formal, as when we are told that Mr. and Mrs. Jones *desire* our presence at the wedding of their daughter and Mr. Smith, it *does* raise the interesting question of why, if we long for something, we are so reluctant simply to ask for it? Young men who are obviously in love sometimes need to be prompted by young women to ask for their hand in marriage. Because this chapter is concerned with persons in their nineties, it may seem wise to ignore the definition about sex altogether. But, strange as it may seem, this definition is the most important of all.

When we think of sexually active adults, ninety-year-olds do not come immediately to mind. The very incongruity of the thought has led to the creation of a whole genre of jokes on the topic. Here's a typical one: A guy goes into a bar that he had frequented daily for the last sixty years. It was his ninetieth birthday, so the bartender and his friends decided to surprise him. They wheeled in a big birthday cake and out popped a beautiful young woman who said, "Hi, I can give you some super sex!" And the old man said, 'Well, I guess I'll take the soup" (Tapper and Press 2000, 139).

Here's another: A ninety-year-old man went to his doctor and said, "Doctor, my wife, who is eighteen, is expecting a baby. I'm going to be a father!" The doctor said, "Let me tell you a story. A man went hunting, but instead of his gun, he picked up an umbrella by mistake. And when a bear suddenly charged at him, he pointed his umbrella at the bear, shot at it, and killed it on the spot." "Impossible," said the man. "Somebody else must have shot that bear." "Exactly my point," replied the doctor (Becker et al. 2003, 167).[2]

But these jokes actually make *my* point: When we think of sex, we tend to think about genital sex. In fact, Erikson (1950) emphasizes genital sex in his discussion of the intimacy vs. isolation conflict (230–31). So the fact that genital sex is a laughing matter where ninety-year-old persons are concerned leaves us with two alternatives: forget about the third definition of *desire* altogether, or

2. The biblical story of the conception of Isaac tells of Abraham's and Sarah's incredulity when informed that they will be the parents of a new baby at their age. The news causes Abraham to fall on his face in laughter: "'Can a child be born to a man who is a hundred years old? Can Sarah, who is ninety years old, bear a child?'" (Gen. 17:17). I discuss this story in *A Time to Laugh* (Capps 2005, 76–84).

think about sexuality in a different way. The second alternative appeals to me, and writings by Freud and Erikson explain why.

The point of Freud's book *Beyond the Pleasure Principle* (1959), was that there is another "principle" or "law" within the organism—the silent death drive—that conflicts with "the pleasure principle," an idea he had developed years earlier. The pleasure principle was his term for the primitive instinct in the newborn that seeks gratification of the immediate desire for pleasure and the avoidance of pain. In due course, this principle rapidly comes into conflict with "the reality principle," with the fact that the world is not centered around the child and its needs. There is a real world out there that also makes demands, and one needs to adapt one's view of the world to accommodate it. In effect, the child needs to acknowledge the "reality principle" (Rennison 2001, 88–89).

The conflict between the pleasure principle and the reality principle was the primary emphasis of Freud's writings until, as we have seen, he began to develop the idea that there is also an internal struggle between two primitive instincts, the pleasure principle (the concern to satisfy one's needs) and the death instinct (an escape from all stimulation, including positive ones, into a state of total inertia).

Freud used the term *libido* to convey the idea that the pleasure principle is directed toward individuals and objects in the outside world. *Libido* is based on the Latin word *libet*, which means *it pleases*, hence, *pleasure.* Over the years, the term *libido* has lost much of its original meaning. A popular view is that it applies only to genital sexual acts and that it implies an uncontrollable sexual drive. In fact, the word *libidinous* is now defined as "full of or characterized by lust; lewd; lascivious" (Agnes 2001, 826).

In its original meaning, however, *libido* referred to psychic energy generally and more specifically "to a basic form of psychic energy comprising the positive, loving instincts and manifested variously at different stages of personality development" (Agnes 2001, 826). In a sense, then, the two internal "principles" or "laws"—the one oriented toward pleasure, the other toward death—are two very different ways of dealing with pain. The pleasure principle, through the psychic energy of *libido,* seeks to escape pain by actively seeking the satisfaction of one's needs by other persons. The death drive seeks to escape pain by ending life itself. The question that arises with particular existential force in one's nineties (though it obviously arises before this for many persons) is whether the first path is sufficiently effective or worthwhile that one should continue on it or whether one should shift to the other path. An important consideration in one's nineties is that one does not expect to be around much longer anyway.

But I would like to focus our attention on *libido* itself, and on the fact that it takes different forms at different stages of development. What forms might it take in the tenth decade of one's life? Since *libido* is virtually a synonym for the word *desire,* this question will enable us to explore more deeply what constitutes desire in the life of a ninety-year-old person.

I do not believe that persons in their nineties enter "a second childhood," but I *do* think that the ninety-year-old person's *libidinal energies* are very similar to those of infants. Having become a grandparent, I have become aware again of the simple pleasure that an infant experiences from seeing a familiar, smiling face. A baby may experience pleasure through manipulation of her own body parts, but because her body is also the locus of painful experiences, there is a greater tendency to seek pleasure from the external world. And although objects—rattles that make sounds, toys that make movements—offer pleasure, the most pleasure derives from human others and from what they do in direct interaction with the infant.

As we saw in chapter 1, Erikson (1964a) suggests that the interchange of smiles between infant and mother is the first step in the development of the virtue of hope, but this initial step needs to be followed up with food "both pleasurable to ingest and easy to digest" (116). So one pleasure begets another, and another, and before long, the infant has forgotten that before this encounter she was experiencing discomfort or pain.

How does this relate to an adult in the tenth decade of life? Basically, it invites the inference that the ninety-year-old's *libido* assumes a form or expression that is similar to that of an infant or small child. It may, in fact, exemplify the *metanoia* that Jesus envisions in his declaration, "Truly, I tell you, unless you change and become like children, you will never enter the kingdom of heaven" (Matt. 18:3; Erikson 1981, 348).

An illustration in support of this inference is provided by Lawrence J. Friedman (1999) in his biography of Erikson. Friedman begins the biography with an episode that occurred when Erikson was on the verge of his ninety-first birthday. In June of 1993, Friedman was determined to bring Erikson a special birthday gift, namely, information to establish the identity of his father. He had been in Copenhagen with Erikson's Danish relatives, exploring historic family records, documents, and memories, and had returned to the United States with a detailed family tree extending from the eighteenth century, a photograph of Erikson's mother as a young woman, and information on two potential fathers—both named Erik; both photographers.

Erikson sat passively in his wheelchair in the study of his home in Cambridge. He glanced at the material Friedman had gathered. The detailed family tree was of little interest, and he barely looked at the information about the identities of the two prospective fathers. Watching him, Friedman realized that Erikson's "lifelong quest to discover the identity of his father would remain unfulfilled" (19). So, too, would his own desire to be the one who was instrumental in bringing this quest to a satisfying conclusion. But "all was not lost," for Erikson picked up the photograph of his young mother and gazed at her for many minutes. Finally, he remarked, "What a beauty." Friedman notes, "Although he was very frail and nearly immobile, his eyes had come alive. A smile crossed his face. Erikson was enjoying himself amid the flow of memories of his Danish mother. He glanced at the small Danish flag on the mantel above his fireplace and back again at the photograph" (19). Then, after several minutes, he was ready for a nap. Friedman concludes, "Even in late old age, as mind and body gave out, there could be joy, buoyancy, discovery, and even a measure of playfulness" (19).

What was happening within Erikson himself as he gazed at the photograph? Friedman's conclusion suggests that Erikson's own *libido* was activated by the photograph, a photograph of the woman who may well have activated the *libido* of the (presumably) male photographer many years earlier, a young man who may have been Erik's biological father. At this age, the discovery of the identity of his father through the historical materials that Friedman had assembled may well have seemed too taxing. Or perhaps for a man who was about to turn ninety-one, it was no longer useful information because the question of his own identity had been settled through the very life that he had lived. But the desire that he had known as an infant was alive and well even as his mind and body had begun to give out. And what could be a more appropriate conclusion to this experience of the activation of his libido than a nap, the typical response of the infant when his needs have been met and his body and mind are at peace with one another.

DESIRE: THE ENGINE OF LIFE

One of the most well-known sayings in Ecclesiastes, one of the major books of wisdom in the Bible, is the admonition to "Remember your creator in the days of your youth" (12:1a). When I was a teenager, this admonition was often the basis for sermons to us kids at youth camp. The rest of the passage (1–7) was never cited, probably because it was felt to be irrelevant to teenagers, too despairing, or both. Here it is in full, and presented, appropriately, I believe, in poetic form:

> Remember your creator in the days of your youth,
> before the days of trouble come, and the years draw near
> when you will say, "I have no pleasure in them";
> before the sun and the light and the moon and the stars
> are darkened and the clouds return with the rain;
>
> in the day when the guards of the house tremble,
> and the strong men are bent, and the women
> who grind cease working because they are few,
> and those who look through the windows see dimly;
>
> when the doors on the street are shut,
> and the sound of the grinding is low,
> and one rises up at the sound of a bird,
> and all the daughters of song are brought low;
>
> when one is afraid of heights, and terrors are in the road;
> the almond tree blossoms, the grasshopper drags itself along,
> and desire fails; because all must go to their eternal home,
> and the mourners will go about the streets;
>
> before the silver cord is snapped, and the golden bowl is broken,
> and the pitcher is broken at the fountain, and the wheel
> broken at the cistern, and the dust returns to the earth
> as it was, and the breath returns to God who gave it.

In *Words of Delight*, Leland Ryken (1992) suggests that this passage is a highly metaphorical depiction of old age. The image "the sun and the light and the moon and the stars are darkened" refers to weak eyesight; "clouds [that] return after the rain" is an allusion to tears from eyestrain; "the keepers of the house that tremble" are shaking hands and arms; "the strong men that are bent" are stooping shoulders; and the loss of teeth is figuratively described as "grinders cease because they are few." Weak eyes are pictured in the figure of "the windows are dimmed"; weak hearing is evoked by "the doors on the street that are shut"; the "almond tree [that] blossoms" relates to white hair;[3] and the allusion to "the grasshopper [that] drags itself along" refers to the loss of sprightliness in walking (326–28).

Even if Ryken were mistaken about certain specific images and their metaphorical meanings, the poet is obviously thinking about advanced age. He admonishes his reader to "remember your creator in the days of your youth, before the days of trouble come, and the years draw near when you will say, 'I have no pleasure in them.'" This lament—"I have no pleasure in them"—is directly relevant to the internal conflict that Freud (1959) discusses in *Beyond the Pleasure Principle*.

Another indication of the poem's relevance to the desire vs. struggle conflict in the tenth decade of life is its suggestion that in old age *desire fails*. No pleasure, no desire—it's time to anticipate or even arrange for one's death. No wonder, then, that the mourners appear on the streets and that there is evidence—in the snapping of the silver cord; the breaking of the golden bowl, the pitcher, and the wheel at the cistern—that one's world appears to be disintegrating all around oneself. It's as though the mind, which may itself be disintegrating, no longer perceives the object world as having the quality of endurance. This poem, then, emphasizes the preeminence of struggle over desire. In fact, it suggests that the time will come when desire fails, when one sees no reason to endure merely for the sake of endurance.

However, a poem by Stanley Kunitz (2000), who was at least ninety years old when he wrote it, challenges the idea that desire might fail. Instead, desire is never extinguished for good, for it is always on the alert for the revivifying touch of another (266). The first line is from his poem "As Flowers Are" (92), written in his fifties.

Touch Me

Summer is late, my heart.
Words plucked out of the air
some forty years ago
when I was wild with love
and torn almost in two
scatter like leaves this night

---

3. White hair seems the one good thing about aging! Proverbs 20:29 concurs: "The glory of youths is their strength / but the beauty of the aged is their gray hair."

of whistling wind and rain.
It is my heart that's late,
it is my song that's flown.
Outdoors all afternoon
under a gunmetal sky
staking my garden down,
I kneeled to the crickets trilling
underfoot as if about
to burst from their crusty shells;
and like a child again
marveled to hear so clear
and brave a music pour
from such a small machine.
What makes the engine go?
Desire, desire, desire.
The longing for the dance
stirs in the buried life.
One season only,
          and it's done.
So let the battered old willow
thrash against the windowpanes
and the house timbers creak.
Darling, do you remember
the man you married? Touch me,
remind me who I am.

Roger Housden wrote about this poem in his article "One Life, One Season," in the July/August 2003 issue of *AARP.* Noting that the crickets are trilling their mating song, he writes, "It is late summer for Kunitz, too, and he is keenly aware that his last days are all too near. But does that mean he has nothing to do? Far from it. The marvelous thing in this poem is that Kunitz realizes his season lasts for the duration of his lifetime. The desire, the engine of his life, will continue until his dying breath. Knowing this, he is not afraid" (37). Thus, we have in this poem the testimony of a man in his nineties that desire need not fail. This does not mean, of course, that the poet in Ecclesiastes is wrong about desire, for surely there are those for whom desire eventually fails. But if Ecclesiastes can invoke the grasshopper that drags itself along in support of its view, Kunitz has just as much right to invoke the cricket in support of his. So let the battered, old willow thrash against the windowpanes and the house timbers creak. Listen, instead, to the purring of the engine.

WHEN DESIRE MEETS DESIRE

Stanley Kunitz died in 2006 at the age of one hundred. In the spring of 2003, he experienced a health crisis during which it was evident that he was dying. He had been in a nursing home for three days following a hospitalization. As his condition worsened, he was released so that he could be more comfortable at home.

For the next three days he rested, mostly in silence though responsive to those around him. On the third day, he began to emerge, and within a week he was eating three meals a day. He referred (Kunitz and Lentine 2005) to this three-day period as the time "when I was in the other world" (118). That summer he wrote, "The garden instructs us in a principle of life and death and renewal. In its rhythms, it offers the closest analogue to the concept of resurrection that is available to us. I feel I experienced a kind of resurrection and I'm absolutely grateful for having emerged and yet I have no delusions. I've not been promised anything but a period of survival" (120).

The following spring, his wife, Elise, died. They had been married for forty-seven years. That summer, a friend, Genine Lentine, asked him about his "resurrection" experience the year before. In response, he said,

> I feel I've gone through a whole transformation. It's like moving into another element, really. In general it's a sense of being in control of your world, and going where you want to go. It's a strange feeling because you have absolute control of your reality and you can make things happen instead of being a prisoner. You're in command of your life and of your spirit, and of your love and everything else. . . . There seems to be a transformation going on in which I have a sense of a new life that I'm possessing. That I am not at all lost. I feel I have found myself, my strength. And I feel in possession of my destiny, not a victim of it. (131–32)

He reflected on the fact that during his health crisis he had a sense of being lost, uncertain of what was happening, in which there appeared to be a split, as if his consciousness was operating on another level from his body. He had felt a need to reconcile the two because "one wants above all to have a sense of identity" (133). And yet "behind the sense of who you are—that something is happening and you're aware of what is happening—there is a sense of another state, a state of being that is both yours and not yours" (133).

Lentine asked him whether experience of a kind of awareness outside his body opens up any possibility for him about what happens when one dies? He replied that the two experiences are impossible to separate, "and that's why it's always associated with images of being lost," and that the state of awareness "gradually dissolves as one dies" (133). Lentine noticed his use of the word "gradually" and said, "So you think it's even still around for a period after your physical body has died?" He replied, "Yes. There's no reason to think that the passage of the body from the state of being happens instantaneously. I think it's a gradually dissolving image" (133). He added, "My experience with the loss of another, a companion, is that there is a moment when the awareness of the world moves out of the body" (134)

Did he feel that this was the case with his wife, Elise, when she died a few months earlier? He said, "Yes, I could determine that *moment,*" and in response to Lentine's further queries, he noted that he had a sense that there had been a state of passage and then it was over, that it occurred before the cells of her body ceased to function, and that it was a progressive thing that "had been going on all that last night" (135).

Could he feel her awareness after her medical death? If so, how did it manifest itself? He said he did and that it manifested itself through her hands, which he had been holding in his. Does he feel her presence now? "Yes. But there's no proof. It's a function of your body as much as it is of the other's" (136).

Lentine asked him if he ever dreams that she is with him, adding that when she has dreams of persons who have died, in some dreams "they're just characters in the dream and they're like anyone else, and I don't necessarily think they're there. In other dreams, there's a very palpable sense of a presence" (136). He said he has had the same experience:

> There's a presence and there's an image attached to that presence and it's different from any other experience. It is so much a part of one's own being and yet there is a definite sense of another being. A presence that is as real as anything else, but it's not a physical image, and yet it's definitely there. . . . In the dream state, she is always grabbing my hand and it's so real. It's so much a feeling of togetherness. It's really unlike any other experience. (136)

Their conversation ended on this note.

In *Dreaming and Storytelling*, Bert O. States (1993) suggests that dreams follow a logic similar to our daily life. In daily life, there is a continual tension or reciprocity between motive ("Today I must go to the hardware store") and contingency ("Suddenly, who walks up to me but John!"). Dream narratives are much the same (158). In Kunitz's dreams of Elise, motive and contingency are inseparable. There is something profoundly motivated about these experiences of her presence—they reflect a mutual desire—yet there is also a contingency about them because, however much two persons may desire the presence of the other, they must often rely on some contingency over which they themselves have no control to enable this meeting to happen. Some call this contingency "fate," others call it "providence."

THE DESIRED COUNTRY

The very idea that desire meets desire across the chasm of death—and does this most reliably in the experience of a dream—brings us back to John Bunyan's (1957) *The Pilgrim's Progress* (mentioned in the introduction). The original title page reads, "The pilgrim's progress from this world to that which is to come delivered under the similitude of a dream wherein is discovered the manner of his setting out, his dangerous journey, and safe arrival at the desired country, by John Bunyan." Beneath the title, there is a quotation from Hos. 12:10: "I have used similitudes." Modern translations substitute the word "parables" for "similitudes."

Whereas the author of Ecclesiastes associated the failure of desire with the necessity of going to one's "eternal home," Bunyan suggests that the "eternal home" is the very object of desire. As the dream nears its conclusion, Christian and his companion Hopeful are also nearing the end of their journey. They pass through Enchanted Ground and enter the country of Beulah, where "they heard continually the singing of birds, and saw everyday the flowers appear in the earth, and heard the voice of the turtle in the land" (149). In the country of Beulah, the sun shines night and day because it is beyond the Valley of the Shadow of Death and also out of the reach of Giant Despair. Doubting Castle is so distant that they are unable to see it at all.

In this land, the Shining Ones commonly walk because it borders on heaven. So they meet some of the Shining Ones and are also afforded a perfect view of the Celestial City, their ultimate destination. It is so beautiful that Christian "fell sick with desire," and Hopeful "also had a fit or two of the same disease" (149). So they lay there for awhile, crying out because of their pangs, "If you see my beloved, tell him that I am sick of love" (149). But after awhile, they feel a little strengthened and better able to bear their sickness, so they continue on. Their final test is the river, and as they cross it, Christian begins to sink, overwhelmed by the sorrows of death, and he begins to lose his senses and to experience "horror of mind and heart-fears that he should die in that river" (151).

So Hopeful has "much ado to keep his brother's head above water" (152). He tries to comfort his companion by telling him that he is able to see the gate and the men who are standing by to receive them, but Christian replies that they are there to receive his friend Hopeful. But Hopeful persists, telling Christian to be of good cheer, for "Jesus Christ maketh thee whole" (152). With that, Christian breaks out with a loud voice and says that he has seen Jesus and that Jesus tells him, "When thou passest through the waters, I will be with thee; and through the rivers, they shall not overflow thee" (152). Just then, he discovers that he is on solid ground, and the rest of the river is shallow. Then they see the two Shining Men on the bank of the river on the other side who are waiting for them. They are ministering spirits, sent to attend to those who are the heirs of salvation.

Bunyan's parable is about desire, desire to be in the company of the One who has been the very object of his long and arduous journey. However difficult Christian's struggles have been, they are outlasted by his desire.

THE LORD'S COUNTENANCE

Desire vs. struggle is the central conflict in the ninth decade of life, but both have their origins in the very earliest period of life. In the section of his *Toys and Reasons* titled "Infancy and the Numinous: The Light, the Face, and the Name," Erikson notes, "The human being which at the beginning wants, in addition to the fulfillment of oral and sensory needs, to be gazed upon by the primal parent and to respond to the gaze, to look up to the parental countenance and to be responded to, continues to look up, and to look for somebody to look up to, and that is somebody who will, in the very act of returning his glance, lift him up" (1977, 91).

He notes that "the religious element in any collective vision responds to this first stage," and cites as an example an illustration in the *Visconti Hours* where the painter, Barbello, depicts Mary's death and "God in heaven is shown holding in His arms her spirit in the form of a swaddled baby," and "returning the gaze of Mary's soul" (91). Desire meets desire.[4]

It seems appropriate that Erikson concluded his discussion of the first stage of life—in the book that he wrote in his seventies—with a reference to the portrayal of the mother's own spirit in the form of a swaddled baby held in the arms of God, who gazes on her as she gazes on him. For myself, this reference recalls the benediction that, as a boy, I wanted and needed to hear the minister declare at the close of a service, "The Lord bless thee, and keep thee. The Lord make his face shine upon thee, and be gracious unto thee. The Lord lift up his countenance upon thee and give thee peace." The minister no longer uses the word *countenance* but says, "The Lord look upon you with favor." I beg the reader to indulge my need to cite *Webster's* once more and to point out that whereas the word *face* is the basic, direct word for the front of the head, *countenance* refers to the face *as it reflects one's emotions or feelings* (Agnes 2001, 507). Thus, as Erikson points out, "In religion, vision becomes Revelation" (1977, 91): the revelation on the face of the Desired One that our desire is not merely reciprocated but was itself inspired by the desire of the Other.

THE ENDURING SELF

In response to a questionnaire on the subject of religious belief circulated in 1904 by James Bissett Pratt of Williams College, William James responded to the question, "Do you believe in personal immortality?": "Never keenly; but more strongly as I grow older." To the follow-up question, "If so, why?" he answered, "Because I am just getting fit to live" (Brown 1973, 125). James was sixty-two years old when he responded to this questionnaire, and therefore in what I propose to be the generativity vs. stagnation decade of his life. He lived six more years, dying at age sixty-eight.

In this chapter, we have been focusing on the endurance of the ninety-year-old in the face of external and internal struggles. However, in noting Stanley Kunitz's reflections on his experience of "a kind of resurrection" and John Bunyan's parable about the "eternal home" being the very object of one's desire, we have touched on the question of the endurance of the self after the body has succumbed to

4. Erikson misidentifies the painter as Barbello. He was Belbello da Pavia. *Books of Hours,* popular in the later Middle Ages and the Renaissance, owe their name to the Hours (or Little Office) of the Virgin Mary, which consisted of a sequence of eight short services to be recited in private at intervals during the day. *Visconti Hours,* one of the first major Italian ones, was begun around 1388–1395 for Giangaleazzo Visconti, Duke of Milan from 1378–1402, and completed for his second son, Filippo Maria Visconti, Duke of Milan from 1412–1447. Belbello contributed to the *Visconti Hours* in the second period (Backhouse 2004; De Hamel 1997; and Walther and Wolff 2001).

death. In effect, this question picks up on the word "continue" in the primary definitions of endurance and enduring. For some, this is not a question because the answer has been settled once and for all by means of our Lord's victory over death. For others, like William James, it remains a question because he is aware of the extent to which his own desires affect the answer.

What is certain, however, is that one of the selves that makes up our composite Self is the enduring self, and that this is the self among our various selves that envisions our continuation beyond the parameters of our earthly life. It seems appropriate, then, to assign this self to the tenth decade of life, the decade which few of us expect to complete, but also to see this self as the one that justifies the idea that life is a cyclical affair. As we saw in chapter 1, Erikson defined hope as "the enduring belief in the attainability of fervent wishes, in spite of the dark urges and rages which mark the beginning of existence" (1964a, 118). This definition suggests that the enduring self was there all along, quietly doing its work behind the scenes. This is the self who guided the pen of fifty-year-old John Bunyan as he wrote the words he attributed to Jesus, "When thou passest through the waters, I will be with you; and through the rivers, they shall not overflow you," and the self who guided the pen of sixty-two-year old William James as he responded to Pratt's questionnaire, "Because I am just getting fit to live."

Epilogue: The 100 Club

There are contemporary birthday cards for persons turning one hundred. One says simply, "May your birthday be filled with happiness and the warmth of family and friends. Have a wonderful day." Short and to the point. Here's another: "Hope your 100th birthday is a combination of all your favorite things—things that make you smile, things that make you sigh with contentment, things that fill your heart with special memories—and anything else that makes you feel good and happy and loved." Maybe I'm wrong, but there seems to be an unstated assumption here that you are pretty much alone in the world, so you are basically down to what the song in *The Sound of Music* refers to as "a few of my favorite things."

If so, the picture this card conjures up in my mind is the rather pathetic guy played by Steve Martin in "The Jerk" who has suffered a huge financial catastrophe. On leaving his palatial home for the last time, he declares that he doesn't need much of anything as he pauses to collect his ashtray, his paddle game, and his remote control. He then decides he may need a few matches and a lamp, and as he leaves the house, he picks up a chair and finally a magazine. When I mentioned this card to a friend of mine, he said it brought to mind the medicine bottles that he places beside his bed when he is suffering from the flu. He said that they didn't exactly make him "feel good and happy and loved," but they at least have a few medicinal benefits. The picture he portrayed caused me to think that the card may have been written for a relative of mine from an earlier generation who didn't quite make it to one hundred, but if he had, he would have assumed that the birthday card was referring to his highly cherished whiskey bottle.

I mentioned in the introduction that I would briefly consider those who have lived to see their hundredth birthday, and that I would use the term "The 100 Club" that my denominational magazine uses to identify this group. I've been keeping tabs for the past eighteen months and am able to report that it has 354 members; 307 of these are women and 47 are men, an 87 to 13 percent ratio. The two oldest women are 111 years old, and the oldest man is 107. Of the 23 members who are 106 or older, 21 are women. Thus, if longevity is a good thing in itself—and many of us tend to believe that it is—one would be wise to arrange to be born a girl, not a boy. Of course, because more church members are women than men, we would expect the women to outnumber the men. But this does not account for the wide margin between the two.

These statistics run counter to what the Bible tells us about the longevity of men and women. According to Genesis, men lived a lot longer than women. Methuselah (Adam's great-great-great-great grandson and Noah's grandfather) was 969 when he died; Jared lived to 962; and Noah made it to 950, despite a tendency to abuse alcohol (Gen. 9:20–24). The first ten patriarchs (from Adam to Noah) lived an average of 858 years while the next ten lived an average of 317 years, a rather dramatic reduction in life expectancy that has caused a few biblical literalists to think that maybe the flood had something to do with it.

When Nathan Carlin and I were doing research for an article (Capps and Carlin 2008) on the fact that women tend to live six to seven years longer than men (at least in countries where there is equal access to medical care) we asked a well-known expert in the field, Thomas R. Cole, author of *The Journey of Life: A Cultural History of Aging in America* (1992) and coeditor of *The Oxford Book of Aging* (Cole & Winkler 1994) why women live longer than men do. He told us that there is a lot of speculation but that he favors the view that women are biologically hardier because they must carry and give birth to children and then assume the primary responsibility for their care in the first years of their lives (Cole 2005).

If this is so, we figured that women probably lived longer than men, on average, during the time that these biblical genealogies were being written, and it is therefore reasonable to assume that the vastly exaggerated ages of the men were due to men's envy of women's greater longevity. We could hear these fellows muttering to themselves (as men occasionally do today), "Hey, we're the *stronger* sex, so why does the *weaker* sex outlive us? It doesn't make sense." We could even imagine that over the centuries men have expressed their sense of outrage that God would design things this way by leaving the churchgoing to women.

But we didn't want our article to give even a hint of bias, much less complaint, so we ended it on a positive note. We suggested that if men are envious of women's greater longevity, there is a bad side and a good side to envy: the bad side seeks to tear the envied person down while the good side seeks to emulate the envied person. So we suggested that fathers should attempt to become "good-enough mothers." Donald W. Winnicott, the psychoanalyst who coined the phrase, noted that the "good-enough mother" is not necessarily the infant's own mother. Instead, "she" may be anyone "who makes active adaptation to the infant's needs" (1991, 10). On the other hand, "the infant's own mother is more likely to be good enough than some other person, since this active adaptation demands an easy and unresented preoccupation with the one infant; in fact, success in infant care depends on the fact of devotion, not on cleverness or intellectual enlightenment" (10).

There are reasons to be skeptical that fathers would be candidates for "good-enough mothering," for they are likely to be a bit resentful that the baby becomes the object of mommy's devotion, devotion they were used to having showered on them, and they are likely to think that "cleverness or intellectual enlightenment" are more effective methods of infant care than simple "devotion." Thus, their active adaptations to the infant's needs may fall rather short of the "good-enough mother" ideal and nullify any of the potential life-prolonging effects (for themselves) of infant care.

On the other hand, if the desire to emulate the genuine article is there—plus the added stimulus that it *could* add years to one's life—the development of a large cohort of motherized fathers is not out of the question. And, in any case, this is certainly a better approach to the problem of women's greater longevity than, say, seeking to reduce the gap through a *decrease* in women's life expectancy, or adopting an antilongevity philosophy based on godless hedonism: "Eat, drink, and be merry, for tomorrow we die."

Of course, the fact that males will never carry and give birth to babies means that the longevity gap will never fully close, and this being the case, I would advise men to view this difference in life expectancy with the characteristically good humor that they have cultivated in response to other disappointments in life. To illustrate and facilitate this strategy, I would like to end this epilogue (as we ended the article) with a relevant joke and a couple of relevant poems. First, the joke (Becker et al. 2003, 227):

> This old guy goes to the doctor for a checkup.

> **Doctor:** You're in great shape for a sixty-year-old.

> **Guy:** Who says I'm sixty years old?

> **Doctor:** You're not sixty? How old are you?

> **Guy:** I turn eighty next month.

> **Doctor:** Gosh, eighty! Do you mind if I ask you at what age your father died?

> **Guy:** Who says my father's dead?

Doctor: He's not dead?

Guy: Nope, he'll be 104 this year.

Doctor: With such a good family history your grandfather must have been pretty old when he died.

Guy: Who says my grandfather's dead?

Doctor: He's not dead?!

Guy: Nope, he'll be 129 this year, and he's getting married next week.

Doctor: Amazing! But why at his age would he want to get married?

Guy: Who says he wants to?[1]

The following poem was written by Billy Collins (2005, 59) when he was in his sixties. No doubt he was struggling with the generativity vs. stagnation conflict and having a bit of trouble with the virtue of care:

The Order of the Day

A morning after a week of rain
and the sun shot down through the branches
into the tall, bare windows.

The brindled cat rolled over on his back,
and I could hear you in the kitchen
grinding coffee beans into a powder.

Everything seemed especially vivid
because I knew we were all going to die,
first the cat, then you, then me,

then somewhat later the liquefied sun
was the order I was envisioning.
But then again, you never really know.

The cat had a fiercely healthy look,
his coat so bristling and electric
I wondered what you had been feeding him

---

1. Evidence that the birth of a child when the mother is relatively old may increase female longevity (Muller et al. 2002) prompted us (Capps and Carlin 2007) to wonder if our biblical male ancestors believed that fathering a descendent son later than earlier would mean that they would live longer? We calculated the years between the patriarch's age when his descendent son was born and his age at death and found no support for this or any other theory that we could think of that would suggest a relationship between fathering a descendent son and personal longevity. A more exactly comparable test of Muller et al.'s findings would be the patriarch's age when he fathered his *last* child, but Genesis does not provide this information. It typically asserts that other children were born after the descendent son's birth, but the birth dates of later children relative to the father's age are not provided.

and what you had been feeding me
as I turned a corner
and beheld you out there on the sunny deck

lost in exercise, running in place,
knees lifted high, skin glistening—
and that toothy, immortal-looking smile of yours.

So, let's raise our collective hats to the members of the 100 Club, for they give form and substance to our dreams of immortality and, more importantly, to our desire for "a better country, that is, a heavenly one" (Heb. 11:16). And while we're at it, we might as well raise our glasses to Methuselah, who, as the following poem by an anonymous poet contended many decades ago (Felleman 1936), made optimal use of the present world and suffered not a whit for doing so (482):

Methuselah

Methuselah ate what he found on his plate,
and never, as people do now,
did he note the amount of the calory count;
he ate it because it was chow.
He wasn't disturbed as at dinner he sat,
devouring a roast or a pie,
to think it was lacking in granular fat
or a couple of vitamins shy.
He cheerfully chewed each species of food,
unmindful of troubles or fears
lest his health might be hurt
by some fancy dessert;
and he lived over nine hundred years.

References

Agnes, Michael, ed. 2001. *Webster's New World College Dictionary.* Foster City, CA: IDG Books Worldwide.

American Psychiatric Association. 1994. *The Diagnostic and Statistical Manual of Mental Disorders (DSM-IV).* Washington, DC: American Psychiatric Association.

Augustine. 1960. *The Confessions of St. Augustine.* Trans. John K. Ryan. Garden City, NY: Image Books. Originally written around 397–400.

Backhouse, Janet. 2004. *Illumination from the Book of Hours.* London: British Library.

Bakan, David. 1966. *The Duality of Human Existence.* Chicago: Rand McNally & Co.

———. 1968. *Disease, Pain, and Sacrifice.* Chicago: University of Chicago Press.

Becker, Brian, et al. 2003. *A Prairie Home Companion Pretty Good Joke Book.* 3rd ed. Minneapolis: Highbridge Co.

Beers, Mark H., ed. 2003. *The Merck Manual of Medical Information,* 2nd home ed. New York: Simon & Schuster, Inc.

Bergman, Ingmar. 1960. *Four Screenplays.* New York: Simon & Schuster.

Brown, L. B., ed. 1973. *Psychology and Religion: Selected Readings.* Baltimore: Penguin Books.

Bunyan, John. 1957. *The Pilgrim's Progress.* New York: Washington Square Press. Originally printed in 1678.

Capps, Donald. 1993. *The Depleted Self: Sin in a Narcissistic Age.* Minneapolis: Fortress Press.

———. 1995. *The Child's Song: The Religious Abuse of Children.* Louisville, KY: Westminster John Knox Press.

———. 2000. *Deadly Sins and Saving Virtues.* Eugene, OR: Wipf & Stock Publishers. Originally published in 1987.

———. 2001. *Agents of Hope.* Eugene, OR: Wipf & Stock Publishers. Originally published in 1995.

———. 2005. *A Time to Laugh: The Religion of Humor.* New York: Continuum.

Capps, Donald, and Nathan Carlin. 2008. "Methuselah and Company: A Case of Male Envy of Female Longevity." *Pastoral Psychology* (forthcoming).

Cole, Thomas R. 1992. *The Journey of Life: A Cultural History of Aging in America.* Cambridge: Cambridge University Press.

———. 2005. Personal communication to Nathan Carlin, coauthor of Capps and Carlin (2008).

Cole, Thomas R., and Mary G. Winkler. 1994. *The Oxford Book of Aging.* New York: Oxford University Press.

Collins, Billy. 1995. *The Art of Drowning.* Pittsburgh, PA: University of Pittsburgh Press.

———. 1998. *Picnic, Lightning.* Pittsburgh, PA: University of Pittsburgh Press.

———. 1999. *Questions About Angels.* Pittsburgh, PA: University of Pittsburgh Press.

———. 2002. *Nine Horses.* New York: Random House.

———. 2005. *The Trouble With Poetry and Other Poems.* New York: Random House.

Day, Dorothy. 1952. *The Long Loneliness: The Autobiography of Dorothy Day.* San Francisco: Harper & Row.

De Hamel, Christopher. 1997. *A History of Illuminated Manuscripts.* 2nd ed. London: Phaidon Press Ltd.

Dodd, C. H. 1933. The Mind of Paul: A Psychological Approach. *Bulletin of the John Rylands Library* 17: 91–105.

Dormandy, Thomes. 2000. *Old Masters: Great Artists in Old Age.* London: Hambledon and London.

Dunn, Stephen. 1994. *New and Selected Poems 1974–1994.* New York: W. W. Norton & Co.

———. 2000. *Different Hours: Poems.* New York: W. W. Norton & Co.

Erikson, Erik H. 1950. *Childhood and Society.* New York: W. W. Norton & Co.

———. 1956. The Problem of Ego Identity. *Journal of the American Psychoanalytic Association* 4:56–121. Subsequently published as chapter 3 of *Identity and the Life Cycle,* (1959), 101–64.

———. 1958. *Young Man Luther: A Study in Psychoanalysis and History.* New York: W. W. Norton & Co.

———. 1959. *Identity and the Life Cycle.* New York: International Universities Press. Republished by W. W. Norton & Company (1980).

———. 1963. *Childhood and Society.* 2nd rev. ed. New York: W. W. Norton & Co.

———. 1964a. "Human Strength and the Cycle of Generations." In *Insight and Responsibility,* 109–57. New York: W. W. Norton & Co.

———. 1964b. The Golden Rule in the Light of New Insight. In *Insight and Responsibility,* 217–43. New York: W. W. Norton & Co.

———. 1968. *Identity: Youth and Crisis.* New York: W. W. Norton & Co.

———. 1974. *Dimensions of a New Identity.* New York: W. W. Norton & Co.

———. 1975a. "Identity Crisis" in Autobiographic Perspective. In *Life History and the Historical Moment,* 17–47. New York: W. W. Norton & Co.

———. 1975b. "Once More the Inner Space." In *Life History and the Historical Movement,* 225–47. New York: W. W. Norton & Co.

———. 1977. *Toys and Reasons: Stages in the Ritualization of Experience.* New York: W. W. Norton & Co.

————. 1978. Reflections on Dr. Borg's Life Cycle. In *Adulthood*, ed. Erik H. Erikson, 1–31. New York: W. W. Norton & Company.

————. 1981. "The Galilean Sayings and the Sense of 'I'". *The Yale Review* 70: 321–62.

————. 1982. *The Life Cycle Completed*. New York: W. W. Norton & Co.

————.1987a. Environment and Virtues. In *A Way of Looking at Things: Selected Papers from 1930 to 1980*, ed. Stephen Schlein, 503–21. New York: W. W. Norton & Co. Originally published in 1972.

————.1987b. On Protest and Affirmation. In *A Way of Looking at Things: Selected Papers from 1930 to 1980*, ed. Stephen Schlein, 699–705. New York: W. W. Norton & Co. Originally published in 1972.

————.1987c. *On the Protest of Women*, ed. Stephen Schlein, 660–69. New York: W. W. Norton & Co. Originally published in 1965.

————.1987d. Plans for the Returning Veteran with Symptoms of Instability. In *A Way of Looking at Things: Selected Papers from 1930 to 1980*, ed. Stephen Schlein, 613–17. New York: W. W. Norton & Co. Originally published in 1945.

————. 1987e. Statement to the Committee on Privilege and Tenure of the University of California Concerning the California Loyalty Oath. In *A Way of Looking at Things: Selected Papers from 1930 to 1980*, ed. Stephen Schlein, 618–20. New York: W. W. Norton & Co. Originally published in *Psychiatry* 14 (1951): 243–45.

————. 1987f. The Human Life Cycle. In *A Way of Looking at Things: Selected Papers from 1930 to 1980*, ed. Stephen Schlein, 595–610. New York: W. W. Norton & Co. Originally published in 1968.

————. 1987g. Words for Paul Tillich. In *A Way of Looking at Things: Selected Papers from 1930 to 1980*, ed. Stephen Schlein, 726–28. New York: W. W. Norton & Co. Originally published in the *Harvard Divinity Bulletin* 30 (1966): 13–15.

Erikson, Erik H., and Joan M. Erikson. 1997. *The Life Cycle Completed: Extended Version*. New York: W. W. Norton & Co.

Erikson, Erik H., Joan M. Erikson, and Helen O. Kivnick. 1986. *Vital Involvement in Old Age*. New York: W. W. Norton & Co.

Erikson, Joan M. 1988. *Wisdom and the Senses: The Way of Creativity*. New York: W. W. Norton & Co.

Felleman, Hazel. 1936. *The Best Loved Poems of the American People*. Garden City, NY: Doubleday & Co.

Fennel, Jan. 2005. *The Seven Ages of Man's Best Friend*. New York: Collins.

Ferm, Robert. 1959. *The Psychology of Christian Conversion*. Westwood, NJ: Fleming Revell.

Fowler, Gene. 2004. *Caring Through the Funeral: A Pastor's Guide*. St. Louis: Chalice Press.

Freud, Sigmund. 1939. *Moses and Monotheism*. Trans. Katherine Jones. New York: Vintage Books.

————. 1959. *Beyond the Pleasure Principle: A Study of the Death Instinct in Human Behavior*. Trans. James Strachey. New York: Bantam Books.

————. 1963. The Economic Problem of Masochism. In *General Psychological Theory: Papers on Metapsychology*, ed. Philip Rieff, 190–201. New York: Collier Books.

————. 1966. *Introductory Lectures on Psycho-Analysis*. Trans. and ed. James Strachey. New York: W. W. Norton & Co. Originally published in 1917.

Friedman, Lawrence J. 1999. *Identity's Architect: A Biography of Erik H. Erikson*. New York: Scribner.

Fromm, Erich. 1962. *Beyond the Chains of Illusion: My Encounter with Marx and Freud*. New York: Simon & Schuster.

Frost, Robert. 1975. *The Poetry of Robert Frost*. Ed. Edward Connery Latham. New York: Holt, Rinehart & Winston.

Furman, Ben, and Tapani Ahola. 1992. *Solution Talk: Hosting Therapeutic Conversations*. New York: W. W. Norton & Co.

Gay, Peter. 1988. *Freud: A Life for Our Time.* New York: W. W. Norton & Co.

Gilligan, Carol. 1982. *In a Different Voice: Psychological Theory and Women's Development.* Cambridge, MA: Harvard University Press.

Hall, G. Stanley. 1904. *Adolescence: Its Psychology and Its Relations to Physiology, Anthropology, Sociology, Sex, Crime, Religion, and Education.* New York: D. Appleton.

Harper, Michael S. and Anthony Walton, eds. 1994. *Every Shut Eye Ain't Asleep: An Anthology of Poetry by African Americans Since 1945.* Boston: Little, Brown & Co.

Hawthorne, Nathaniel. 1946. The Great Stone Face. In *Hawthorne's Short Stories,* ed. Newton Arvin, 291–311. New York: Vintage Books.

Housden, Roger. 2003. One Life, One Season. *AARP,* July/August.

Hubley Studios. 1975. *Everybody Rides the Carousel.* Santa Monica, CA: Pyramid Media.

Indick, William. 2004. *Psychology for Screenwriters.* Studio City, CA: Michael Wiese Productions.

James, William. 1907. The Energies of Man. *The Philosophical Review* 16:1–20.

———. 1922. *On Vital Reserves.* New York: Henry Holt.

———. 1982. *The Varieties of Religious Experience.* New York: Penguin Books. Originally published in 1902.

———. 1987. *William James: Writings 1902–1910.* New York: Library of America.

———. 1992. *William James: Writings 1878–1899.* New York: Library of America.

Kahn, Michael. 2002. *Basic Freud: Psychoanalytic Thought for the Twenty-First Century.* New York: Basic Books.

Kaufman, Sharon R. 1986. *The Ageless Self: Sources of Meaning in Late Life.* Madison: University of Wisconsin Press.

Kohut, Heinz. 1985. Forms and Transformations of Narcissism. In *Self Psychology and the Humanities: Reflections on a New Psychoanalytic Approach,* ed. Charles B. Strozier, 97–123. New York: W. W. Norton & Co.

Kunitz, Stanley. 2000. *The Collected Poems.* New York: W. W. Norton & Co.

Kunitz, Stanley, and Genine Lentine. 2005. *The Wild Braid: A Poet Reflects on a Century in the Garden.* New York: W. W. Norton & Co.

Levinson, Daniel J. 1978. *The Seasons of a Man's Life.* New York: Alfred A. Knopf.

———. 1996. *The Seasons of a Woman's Life.* New York: Alfred A. Knopf.

Lewis, Michael. 1992. *Shame: The Exposed Self.* New York: Free Press.

Lynd, Helen Merrell. 1958. *On Shame and the Search for Identity.* New York: Harcourt, Brace.

Marling, Karal Ann. 2006. *Designs on the Heart: The Homemade Art of Grandma Moses.* Cambridge, MA: Harvard University Press.

Miller, Arthur. 1976. *Death of a Salesman.* New York: Penguin Books. Originally published in 1949.

Miller, Patrick D. 1993. "Things Too Wonderful: Prayers of Women in the Old Testament." In *Biblische Theologie und gesellschaftlicher Wandel,* ed. Georg Braulik, Walter Gross, and Sean McEvenne, 237–51. Freiburg: Herder.

Moorman, Margaret. 1992. *My Sister's Keeper.* W. W. Norton.

———. 1996. *Waiting to Forget: A Mother Opens the Door to Her Secret Past.* New York: W. W. Norton.

Muller, Hans-Georg, Jeng-Min Chiou, James R. Carey, and Jane-Long Wang. 2002. Fertility and Life Span: Late Children Enhance Female Longevity. *Journal of Gerontology* 57A: B202–B206.

Pickhardt, Carl E. 2005. *The Everything Parent's Guide to the Strong-Willed Child.* Avon, MA: Adams Media.

Pollack, William S. 2000. *Real Boys' Voices.* New York: Penguin Books.

Rennison, Nick. 2001. *Freud and Psychoanalysis.* Harpenden, Great Britain: Pocket Essentials.

Ricoeur, Paul. 1978. Listening to the Parables of Jesus. In *The Philosophy of Paul Ricoeur*, ed. Charles E. Reagan and David Stewart, 239–45. Boston: Beacon Press.

Ryken, Leland. 1992. *Words of Delight: A Literary Introduction to the Bible*. Grand Rapids: Baker Book House.

Scot, Barbara J. 1995. *Prairie Reunion*. Iowa City, IA: University of Iowa Press.

Scroggs, James R. and William G. T. Douglas. 1977. Issues in the Psychology of Religious Conversion. In *Current Perspectives in the Psychology of Religion*, ed. H. Newton Malony, 254–65. Grand Rapids: Wm. B. Eerdmans Publishing Co.

Shakespeare, William. 2000. *As You Like It*. New York: Penguin Books.

Spock, Benjamin. 1946. *The Common Sense Book of Baby and Child Care*. New York: Duell, Sloan & Pearce.

Stafford, William. 1982. *A Glass Face in the Rain: New Poems*. New York: Harper & Row.

———. 1987. *An Oregon Message: Poems*. New York: Harper & Row.

———. 1996. *Even in Quiet Places*. Lewiston, ID: Confluence Press.

———. 1998a. *Crossing Unmarked Snow: Further Views on the Writer's Vocation*. Ed. Paul Merchant and Vincent Wixon. Ann Arbor: University of Michigan Press.

———. 1998b. *The Way It Is: New & Selected Poems*. Saint Paul, MN: Graywolf Press.

States, Bert O. 1993. *Dreaming and Storytelling*. Ithaca, NY: Cornell University Press.

Tapper, Albert, and Peter Press. 2000. *A Guy Goes Into a Bar: A Compendium of Bar Jokes*. New York: MJF Books.

Tillich, Paul. 1952. *The Courage to Be*. New Haven, CT: Yale University Press.

———. 1957. *Dynamics of Faith*. New York: Harper & Row.

Walther, Ingo F., and Norbert Wolff. 2001. *The World's Most Famous Illuminated Manuscripts*. Koln: Taschen Books.

White, Robert W. 1963. "Sense of Interpersonal Competence." In *The Study of Lives: Essays on Personality in Honor of Henry A. Murray*, ed. Robert W. White, 72–93. New York: Atherton Press.

Winnicott, Donald W. 1991. *Playing and Reality*. London: Tavistock/Routledge.

Index

Abraham, and conception of Isaac, 200
acquiescence, as life theme, 184–86
Adam, 212
adolescence, xviii, 3–4
affective ties, as life theme, 183–84
ageless self, the, and eighty-year-olds,
    177–79
Ahola, Tapani, 159
artists, in old age, 168–69
autonomy
    definitions of, 24
    as relational, 24
    as self-governance, 24
autonomy vs. shame and doubt conflict
    in Erikson's life-cycle model, xviii,
        xxiii–xxiv
    in Erikson's writings, 24–29
    in second decade of life, 29–30
Bach, J. S., 194

Bakan, David, 198
basic trust vs. basic mistrust. *See* trust vs.
    mistrust conflict
beatings, in childhood, 15–16
Bergman, Ingmar, *Wild Strawberries,* xxv
Blos, Peter, 53
Blume, Judy, 38
Borg, Dr. Isak, xxv
Bunyan, John, *The Pilgrim's Progress,*
    xii–xiii, 207–10
Burlingham, Dorothy, 53–54

Calment, Jeanne, 172
cancer
    and death drive, 197
    and relinquishing control, 190–91
care
    definitions of, 128–29
    in Erikson's schedule of virtues, xxi